Urban Music Governance

Urban Music Studies

Series editors:
Alenka Barber-Kersovan, Lisa Gaupp, Volker Kirchberg, and Robin Kuchar
Print ISSN: 2752-4442 | **Online ISSN:** 2752-4450

Urban Music Studies aims at an inter- and trans-disciplinary exchange between researchers working on the relationship between the music and the city. The series covers a broad range of topics and musical practices, current as well as historical. With its cross cultural point of departure and the focus on countries and geographical regions that are normally excluded from the scientific discourse (such as the Global South), this series will bring fresh perspectives on the role of music in the accelerated urbanisation processes.

The theoretical model of Urban Music Studies is based on the assumptions that: there is a vital exchange between the music and the city; music is a part of the intrinsic logic of cities; music contributes to the image design of a city; music is an important part of the economy of cities and urban regeneration; music can become an issue of urban politics and policies; music is an essential component of the cultural heritage of cities; and music is a pivotal part of urban culture and the creative industries.

In this series:

Sonic Signatures: Music, Migration and the City at Night, edited by Derek Pardue, Ailbhe Kenny, and Katie Young (2023)
Popular Music in Leeds: Histories, Heritage, People and Places, edited by Brett Lashua, Karl Spracklen, Kitty Ross and Paul Thompson (2023)
Urban Music Governance: What Busking Can Teach Us about Data, Policy and Our Cities, by Jess Reia (2025)

Urban Music Governance

What Busking Can Teach Us about Data, Policy and Our Cities

Jess Reia

Bristol, UK / Chicago, USA

First published in the UK in 2025 by
Intellect, The Mill, Parnall Road, Fishponds, Bristol, BS16 3JG, UK

First published in the USA in 2025 by
Intellect, The University of Chicago Press, 1427 E. 60th Street,
Chicago, IL 60637, USA

© Jess Reia

The electronic version of this work is licensed under the Creative Commons Attribution Non Commercial ShareAlike (CC BY-NC-SA) Licence. To view a copy of the licence, visit https://creativecommons.org/licenses/by-nc-sa/4.0/deed.en.
Some rights reserved. Without limiting the rights under copyright reserved above, any part of this book may be reproduced, stored in or introduced into a retrieval system, or transmitted, in any form or by any means (electronic, mechanical, photocopying, recording or otherwise).

No part of this book may be used or reproduced in any manner for the purpose of training artificial intelligence technologies or systems without written permission from the publisher.

A catalogue record for this book is available from the British Library.

Copy editor: MPS Limited
Cover designer: Tanya Montefusco
Cover image: ©OpenStreetMap. http://openstreetmap.org/copyright.
Production manager: Sophia Munyengeterwa
Typesetter: MPS Limited

Hardback Print ISBN 978-1-83595-086-9
Paperback ISBN 978-1-83595-089-0
ePDF ISBN 978-1-83595-088-3
ePUB ISBN 978-1-83595-087-6

To find out about all our publications, please visit our website. There you can subscribe to our e-newsletter, browse or download our current catalogue and buy any titles that are in print.

www.intellectbooks.com

This is a peer-reviewed publication.

This book is dedicated to all the street performers, activists, researchers and citizens fighting for our cities. These pages speak to those contesting skewed power dynamics, to the outsiders, to the lawbreakers and to all the radical policymakers. I will always respect your endurance.

It is also dedicated to those who believe in hope as a survival mechanism. To those who try to build a better world for us all. Our cities are mostly made of buildings, laws and infrastructure; however, dreams, loopholes and some disobedience turn them into places that lure us across continents and oceans, in our hopes for a good life.

I also dedicate this book to my parents, who taught me to always ask the hard questions, no matter how unattainable the answers. It also goes out to Pedro, who held my hand in the dark, and to my friends, who never allowed me to give up. And, lastly, to my two cities: Rio (with its intensity) and Montreal (with its yearning).

Contents

List of Figures and Tables	ix
Foreword	xi
Will Straw	
Acknowledgments	xvii
Note on Translations	xxi
Introduction: What Does Street Performance Teach Us about Cities?	1
PART I: NUMBERS AND NORMS	13
1. More than Numbers: Counting, Categorizing and Describing Buskers across Time	15
2. Regulation: Engaging with (Dis)order in Everyday Life	30
PART II: ABOVE GROUND AND BEYOND REGULATION	57
3. Legitimation: The Blurred Boundaries between Policy and Control	59
4. Disputes: Busking as Public Service and Lawmaking	94
PART III: GOING UNDERGROUND, BEING UNDERSTOOD	125
5. Disobedience: Lawbreakers and Talented Stars	127
Afterword: Pandemic, Digitalization and Evidence-Based Policy	159
References	163
Index	181

Figures

3.1:	The city of Montreal, QC, Canada.	60
3.2:	Festival de Théâtre de Rue de Lachine, August 14, 2015.	70
3.3:	Ville-Marie borough in Montreal, QC, Canada.	74
3.4:	Busker performing from a van in the Plateau Mont-Royal, Montreal, September 26, 2015.	78
3.5:	Busker performing at Place Jacques-Cartier, Old Port, Montreal, July 28, 2015.	85
4.1:	The city of Rio de Janeiro, RJ, Brazil.	95
4.2:	Musicians performing at Boulevard Olímpico during the 2016 Summer Olympics in Rio de Janeiro, Brazil.	107
4.3:	Opening ceremony of the Second Carioca Festival of Public Art, Praça Seca, April 18, 2015.	118
4.4:	Grande Cia Brasileira de Mysterios e Novidades performs at Praça Seca during the Second Carioca Festival of Public Art, April 18, 2015.	118
4.5:	Artists sitting in front of the municipal legislative chamber in Rio during the third Carioca Festival of Public Art, November 10, 2016.	121
4.6:	CHAP performance during the Third Carioca Festival of Public Art, November 10, 2016.	122
4.7:	Kosmo Coletivo Urbano performs during the Third Carioca Festival of Public Art, November 11, 2016.	122
5.1:	Palco Carioca, Rio de Janeiro, 2022.	134
5.2:	Lyre sign in the Montreal subway system indicating buskers can play there upon reservation, 2022.	139
5.3:	Jocelyn plays at the Place des Arts station with her "Étoile du Métro 2015" banner, Montreal, November 2015.	144

5.4:	Auditions to become one of the Les Étoiles du Métro, Berri-UQÀM station, Montreal, November 3, 2015.	144
5.5:	The band Eclectic Django performs at the Festival Nuit Blanche, Montreal, February 26, 2016.	145
5.6:	Wagner José e seu Bando performing in Praça Seca, May 23, 2015.	152

Tables

3.1:	Regulatory framework for buskers in Montreal, 2022.	80
3.2:	Categories evaluated by the evaluation committee during auditions.	83
3.3:	Number of permits issued by the Ville-Marie borough, per category, 2015–16.	86
4.1:	Selected legislation and draft bills related to busking activities in the city of Rio de Janeiro.	100
4.2:	Comparison between Article 1 of Law 5.429/2012 and draft bill 1.267/2015.	108

Foreword

Will Straw

This fine new book is many things. It is, I can say without hesitation, the best study to date of street musicians in Montreal, the city in which I live and work, though it is many other things as well. It is written by someone who immersed themselves in the cultures of street performance in both Montreal and Rio de Janeiro and won the trust and cooperation of that culture's most important and exemplary participants. Dr. Reia's book is strengthened as well, by the author's fluency in English, French and Portuguese, without which the nuances and diversity of the cases studied might not have been so effectively captured.

Street art and street performance are disciplinary orphans, studied with equal interest by scholars of media, urban life, performance and contemporary art. Reia's book, in its range of historical and theoretical references, exemplifies the interdisciplinarity that is necessary for any adequate account of these phenomena. Reia examines clusters of street performances in two very different cities, looking at street music in Montreal and the more theatrical street performance practices of Rio de Janeiro. Necessarily, though, Reia moves from circumscribed examples to examine the broader status of the street in an era of global gentrification. This is an era in which, under the influence of circulating global doctrines, cities of all kinds point to their street art as proof that they have become creative, tolerant and tourist-friendly. Street art finds itself the object of official recognition, even as rampant speculation in the real estate markets of major cities has led to new regimes of regulation intended to constrain the informalities and sensorial economies of urban space. Much of the richness of Reia's book lies in its capacity to conduct analysis at several levels, digging deep into the lives of those engaged in street performance even as it sets these lives against the background of urban transformation.

As the Australian historian Andrew May shows in his study of Melbourne street life, the street performer has long been romanticized as a nostalgic figure (May 2017: 107–08). In the twentieth century, the street performer evoked the world of the traveling medieval troubadour, or the nineteenth-century street of rag pickers, hawkers and street performers remembered in the work of Walter Benjamin and others. In the twenty-first century, this romanticization persists, given new energies by the backlash against modernist, rationalist city planning and the consequent embrace of notions of the informal street and the aesthetically inexhaustible city. In this embrace, it is difficult to separate the much-loved signs of festive informality (so valorized by progressive urban thinkers such as Jane Jacobs) from the symptoms of growing economic inequality and expanding economic precarity. The street vendors of *L'Itinéraire*, the magazine produced and sold by members of Montreal's homeless population, are an uncomfortable reminder of the city's inadequate social assistance programs, but their disturbing presence is diminished by the ways in which they recall a cherished and vanishing tradition of newspaper sellers on city streets.

Writing about the preference of New York-based artists for old industrial buildings, American sociologist Sharon Zukin has suggested that forms of commerce acquire romantic appeal (to progressives, in particular) only when they are perceived as obsolete (Zukin 1982: 59). In this respect, the visible street performer becomes legible less as a symptom of present-day itinerance and reduced opportunity than as evidence of a city's tolerance and continuities with its past.

The nostalgic appeal of the street performer is particularly strong in Montreal, which embraces its traditions of street music and performance as evidence of a "European" character extending far back into the past. Even as it became a global entertainment conglomerate, Quebec's *Cirque du soleil* glorified its roots in the lives of traveling street performers from Europe and Quebec itself.

As Reia's analysis shows, however, street musicians are in many respects a quintessentially late-modern phenomenon. They are subject to the rationalization and commodification of urban space, whose constraints they must learn to navigate. Their own professional "informality" is limited by policing and municipal administration, then turned into a resource for place-making and other ideologies of the "ludic city." In a world where polls regularly identify the "happiest" cities in the world and where cities incorporate this status within their branding campaigns, street art of all kinds is marketed as a sign of the joyful, lightly managed exuberance which marks the attractive city. In Montreal, where the ongoing erosion of club-based live music limits the opportunities for musicians to be remunerated for their labor, pianos are installed on street corners so that musicians may contribute, without being paid to an atmosphere of spontaneous festivity.

In their recent call for an "urbanism beyond the city," Vyjayanthi Rao and Erica Robles-Anderson (2022: 325) suggest that "[u]rbanism is a play of small forces moving through agencies, pleasures, surprising connections, and ambiguities." Set against the transformative power of immigration and gentrification, street performance may well seem like one of these "small forces," but this does not diminish its complexity. Reia is particularly effective in tracing the multiple forms

FOREWORD

of discourse and governance that gather around street performance and endow it with a bureaucratic solidity—the "[p]aperwork, regulations, laws, reports, charts, spreadsheets, stamps and all sorts of documents [that] are a crucial part of urban governance." Much of the originality of this book stems from the ways in which, even as it captures the performative dimensions of street art, it is concerned, from its title onward, with the ways in which busking and street theatre pose the challenges of measurement, classification and regulation. Street performers may embrace these challenges as necessary to their survival, even as, in Reia's words, they remain committed to "informally occupying the gaps, scratching surfaces, contesting rules and existing beyond official numbers."

Like the best qualitative social research, Reia's book moves back from the moment of street performance into the negotiations and preliminary labor that make it possible. The deep ethnography at the heart of this book reveals the variety of tests and rituals to which the street performer is subject in both cities studied. These might include auditions, the acquisition of identity cards and permits and registration on waiting lists for attractive performance spaces. Like recipients of social assistance, street performers become experts in the navigation of multiple sites of authority and governance—an invisible activity that may take up much of their daily schedules. Alongside these skills, performers acquire an understanding of public spaces and their various characteristics. They become experts in judging the extent to which certain spaces attract "consumers" willing to pay money, in evaluating their own vulnerability to sexual harassment and police surveillance, and in gauging the proximity of performance spaces to washrooms or other amenities.

The urban intelligence of the street performer is tactical intelligence. It is shaped, in part, by the street performer's sense of where they are located within social and cultural hierarchies. Typically, street performers are seen to exist, simultaneously, at the "respectable" upper end of itinerance and poverty but at the lower, unrecognized level of the professional performative arts. One of the great surprises, for me, in reading Reia's account of the lives of street musicians in Montreal, came from learning how much these performers were engaged in multiple contexts and sites of music-making. Street performance was not the sole domain to which life circumstances or personal pathologies had relegated them. Rather, much of the time, it was one dimension of a varied musical career that unfolded across a variety of places and forms of collaboration.

For those, like me, who study popular music, the study of street performance invites us to rethink our ideas of improvisation and commercialism. The street performer improvises, but not (or not merely) within the romanticized interplay between musicians to which theories of improvisation have been so attentive. The improvisation of the street musician unfolds in relation to a shifting configuration of people, attention, climates and moods. Street performance requires that, in the very act of performance, one be attentive to threats of all kinds, lapses of listener interest and recognition of the moment at which remuneration might be most effectively elicited before a crowd disperses. The complexity of this attentiveness requires, of the performer, tactical choices that go far beyond the simple alternatives of pandering to an audience's tastes and remaining true to one's artistic vision. The urban smartness on which these choices rest must accommodate, as well, urban prohibitions on the direct solicitation of money or the linguistic complexities of a city like Montreal.

Reia's study of street performance in Montreal and Rio de Janeiro is not a comparative study in the conventional sense of a work engaged in the back-and-forth inventorying of differences and similarities between cases. There are, to be sure, commonalities in the histories of Rio de Janeiro and Montreal. Each, for instance, has functioned in its national imaginary as a festive city of nocturnal pleasures and relaxed authority (even if both these features have found themselves under threat in recent years). More concretely, both have lived through periods in which the hosting of global mega-events has led to the enactment of significant social and material violence against the spaces and practices of the poor. Between the building of the site for Montreal's international exposition, Expo '67 and the construction of the complex in which the 1976 Olympics were held in that city, working-class neighborhoods were destroyed, traditions of popular entertainment disrupted and the "sanitization" of the city, to render it palatable for visitors, eradicated many vestiges of street-level commerce and popular expression. As Reia notes, the Montreal Metro, the site of much of the musical activity Reia analyses, is one legacy of these events. The conflicts over Rio's 2016 Summer Olympics were followed closely by Montrealers who remembered the false promises and brutal acts of dispossession that marked their own moment as Olympic host, 40 years earlier.

In 2018, the University of Toronto, Canada's largest post-secondary institution (as measured by the number of full-time students), a announced a major new initiative, a "School of Cities," designed to unify the various strands of urban research transpiring across the human, social and natural sciences (University of Toronto 2018). This followed the announcement of other, similar initiatives, like the Andrew W. Mellon Foundation's "Architecture, Urbanism, and the Humanities" program, which provides support for interdisciplinary city-focused research at universities in four continents (Andrew W. Mellon Foundation 2018). These initiatives respond to ongoing recognition of the extent to which cities constitute the key arena of social change and conflict in the world, but they involve something else as well.

In the analysis of culture, the interdisciplinarity heralded in these initiatives involves recognition of the ways in which the social and political dimensions of music, theatre and the visual arts have become "urbanized." If the politics of music, for example, once organized themselves in relation to time and history—such that the key questions were those of a fidelity or resistance vis-à-vis musical tradition—music's politics are increasingly conceived in relation to space. More and more, the most interesting currents in music, performance and the visual arts pose the question of their right to occupy space and their role in assembling the public and communities.

To think of the urban arts in these terms is not simply to relocate them, from what in English is called the "humanities," concerned with meaning and expression, to those social sciences preoccupied with questions of policy and social organization. As Reia's important study shows, such divisions no longer make sense amidst the "urbanization" of cultural forms. For the arts of the street (as for contemporary culture more broadly), the occupation of space and the struggle for a right to the city have become central to the very meaning and value of artistic expression.

REFERENCES

Andrew W. Mellon Foundation. (2018). Architecture, urbanism, and the humanities. https://mellon.org/initiatives/architecture-urbanism-and-humanities/. Accessed May 5, 2018.

May, A.J. (2017). *Melbourne street life*. First published 1998. North Melbourne: Australian Scholarly Publishing.

University of Toronto. (2018). U of T's new school of cities to bring wide-ranging experts together to address urban challenges, University of Toronto website. https://www.utoronto.ca/news/u-t-s-new-school-cities-bring-wide-ranging-experts-together-address-urban-challenges. Accessed July 23, 2023.

Vyjayanthi, R., & Robles-Anderson, E. (2022). Urbanism beyond the city: Variations on a theme. *Public Culture, 34*(3), 319–25.

Zukin, S. (1982). *Loft living: Culture and capital in urban change*. Baltimore and London: The Johns Hopkins University Press.

Acknowledgments

The work presented here reflects the labor of many people and the support of multiple institutions. I am grateful for everyone who offered me their time, ideas, expertise and kindness during the years in which this research project was developed. Thank you for answering all of my questions. Some names will not appear here for different reasons—such as a request for anonymity—but they know who they are, and I sincerely appreciate their help and support.

This book exists, first and foremost, because of all the street performers working in our cities tirelessly, every day, below and above ground, in broad daylight or after dark. They brighten up our days, they highlight power dynamics and they share with us perspectives on a common city. I want to thank all the people who participated in this research project in Montreal, Canada, especially the artists, musicians, scholars, public servants in the local government and the street music association representatives who helped me with fieldwork—*merci beaucoup*! I also thank all the artists, city councilors and scholars in Rio de Janeiro, Brazil, who helped this work see the light of day—*muito obrigade*!

It would also never have happened without the endless support of Will Straw, my mentor and dear friend. Thank you for believing in me at all times. Thank you for the life lessons, the laughter and the companionship. I always look up to your generosity, and I hope to carry your way of looking at (and being amazed by) the world with me.

This book would not have seen the light of day without the constant support of Pedro Augusto, who stayed by my side along the way, holding my hand and helping me to become a better person. In the face of adversities, sharing a small apartment with me in Botafogo or spending 23 months physically separated by a pandemic, we made it through. Thank you for joining me on this journey, on either side of the continent, and for being such an inspiration. Next, profound thanks to my beautiful friends and my queer community in Rio. Guto Franco, for being my friend, and for teaching me about overcoming a troubled upbringing and the importance of laughing our despair away. Bruna Castanheira: Thank you for the hours I spent in your company and for everything I learned from you, especially about being brave and embracing change. I am stronger because of you all.

A huge thanks to my beautiful friends who made Montreal feel like home. Gabi Kielich, who has been by my side for years, offering nothing less than kindness, wisdom and laughs; you amaze me. Ana Brandusescu: Thank you for always being there for me, for sharing your beautiful way to see life, and for helping me to learn that homes and families can be whatever (and wherever) we want them to be. Also, Sandra Evoughlian, for your help, and for teaching me how to show up for myself despite the chaos outside. And Cynthia Liu, for the constant encouragement and generosity. When I felt lost at sea, you all were there for me. All my dear friends who have been part of my life in Canada (Dov, Jonathan van Geuns, Filipa Pajević, Maria Teresa Soldani and many others), I appreciate you.

Thank you so much to the School of Communication at the Federal University of Rio de Janeiro (UFRJ), for offering me critical, public and free education for more than six years. For allowing me to grow and to be part of such a strong community. Special thanks to my supervisor, Micael Herschmann, for the support during my MA and PhD. I greatly appreciate the attention and knowledge shared with me by faculty and students in our department, as well as all the help from the staff at UFRJ. I am also grateful for the time I spent teaching and doing research at the State University of Rio de Janeiro (UERJ), working with Cintia Sanmartin Fernandes, and learning about equality and endurance. Both UFRJ and UERJ are magnificent examples of the resilience and the power of public education in Brazil, and I am honored to be a tiny part of their history.

I would also like to thank McGill University and its vibrant community. All the faculty, staff and students who helped me, personally and professionally, and who welcomed me with open arms. A special thanks to the McGill Institute for the Study of Canada, the Centre for Interdisciplinary Research on Montreal (CIRM) and the Department of Art History and Communication Studies. Thank you to the Center for Technology and Society at FGV Law School (CTS-FGV), where I worked for almost nine years and made friends for a lifetime.

A shoutout to my new academic home, the School of Data Science at the University of Virginia (UVA), for the support offered by the institution and my dear colleagues (especially Siri Russell) while I was writing this book. Also need to mention the kindness, accountability and support offered by my writing peers— Amanda, kt and Sophia—and by my Brazilian Virginian friend Fernanda Rosa.

I must thank the Fundação Carlos Chagas Filho de Amparo à Pesquisa do Estado do Rio de Janeiro (FAPERJ) for funding my fellowship as a Graduate Research Trainee at McGill University (2015–16). I also want to thank the Mellon Foundation for funding my fellowship as a Postdoctoral Researcher (2019–21) at McGill University and for providing me with the opportunity to return to Montreal and to write this book, and the 2020–21 BMO Postdoctoral Fellowship at CIRM that allowed me to deepen my connections with the city and local government.

I also owe a special debt of gratitude to my students at FGV, UFRJ, UERJ, McGill University and UVA: Thanks for asking the hard questions and for allowing me to learn and to teach with you. The feedback I got at conferences, from reviewers and the academic community is also much appreciated, and it is reflected throughout this book.

Finally, I am grateful for all the scholars who studied this before me, and the ones who are starting to look at these issues right now. Thank you to those who are engaged in building a more inclusive, open and collaborative academia. I hope to help with these efforts, and I genuinely wish this work will contribute to so many voices and the constant fight for the right to the city.

June 30, 2023
Montreal, QC

Note on Translations

This book was written across three languages: Brazilian Portuguese, Quebec French and US English. Translating content is fascinating and tricky at times. I did my best to preserve the ideas and experiences shared with me while shortening excerpts from interviews to fit the format of this book. And because language is powerful and constantly shapeshifting to reflect our advancements in diversity and equity, I chose to use inclusive language as much as possible.

Introduction:
What Does Street Performance
Teach Us about Cities?

The street is a component of life in the cities; the street has soul! In Benares or in Amsterdam, in London or Buenos Aires, under every differing sky, in every sundry clime, it is the street that is the refuge of the poor. The wretches do not feel completely deprived of the help of the gods, as long as, before their eyes, one street opens into another. The street acclaims the mediocre, the luckless, the paupers of art. [...] The street continues, killing nouns, transforming the meaning of words, imposing on the dictionaries the terms it invents, creating the jargon that will become the standard legacy of the lexicons of tomorrow.

João do Rio, *The Enchanted Soul of the Streets* (1908)

Montreal's inhospitable and long winters stretch from October to April, with temperatures below −30°C on the harshest days. On a typically snowy and freezing morning in 2015, I left my home to interview a street musician. I met her in one of the only environments where it would be humanly possible to hold a performance in late November: underground. She was performing at the Metro station Place-des-Arts, right before lunchtime, and we had agreed to meet up for coffee after her presentation. As one of the *"étoiles du metro"* ("Metro Stars")—a program designed by the public transport agency to support and promote the talented buskers of the region—she could perform at a premium spot, featuring a banner with her name, Jocelyn, for up to an hour.

Jocelyn had cultivated a passion for music from childhood. The daughter of a piano teacher, she enjoyed playing the instrument and singing at church. After spending many years working as a nurse and, later, as a teacher, she decided to give music another chance. In her words: "I went (to play) in the metro a few times, and I was busking with some friends outside the metro in a farmers' market. I loved it!

So, I said: 'When I retire, that's what I'm going to do'" (Jocelyn 2015). By the time of our interview, Jocelyn had been performing in the streets and metro stations in Montreal for about eight years. An anglophone originally from Winnipeg, the musician celebrates Montreal's busker culture and has been featured in local newspapers. For her, the opportunity to play underground with a spot reserved in advance really makes a difference, and she always prefers to play in public spaces (an "intimate experience") rather than in music venues. To perform as an "*étoile du métro*," she had to pass an audition and pay annual fees; decades before her, other musicians had to fight for the right to play in the metro—a right acquired through persistence and regulation. Her background is far from being the norm, but it adds to the mosaic of experiences and storytelling surrounding buskers.[1] These experiences merge with issues of infrastructure, urban governance, policymaking and a myriad of motivations behind every artist playing in our cities' ephemeral stages.

Wandering artists have existed around the world for centuries. Jocelyn's stringed instrument, the hurdy-gurdy, has been around for more than a thousand years. During its long history, this instrument "has experienced wide swings in its social status and desirability" and it "played a role [...] associated with troubadours and was used by traveling musicians" (Green 2016: 16–17). At times associated with poverty and beggars, and eventually, with upper-class amateurs, the hurdy-gurdy is a relevant part of the history of street performance. In interviews with buskers, in the literature, in online forums and in many other circumstances, I found references to busking as an old, "ancestral" practice, rooted in the Middle Ages. From minstrels and *jongleurs* in sixteenth-century France to organ grinders and brass bands in Victorian London, street performance has been intertwined with urban life and the variety of conflicts that mark that life. It has also been subject to attempts to quantify, control and police it. As Sally Harrison-Pepper (1990) famously put it, the history of the music performed in public spaces is usually found within the laws prohibiting it—as well as in newspapers' op-eds on the inconvenience they cause, and police department archives. Official numbers about busking barely exist, limiting our understanding of the activity. At the same time, stigmatization and criminalization are also characteristics intrinsic to the history of busking. Artists struggle with arbitrary law enforcement, the lack of cultural policies that understand and support their craft, and a constant battle between regulation and legitimation.

A few days after my interview with Jocelyn, a contrasting situation was making the headlines in Rio de Janeiro, Brazil. On December 15, 2015, two musicians were assaulted by four private security officers in the subway system (Gomes 2015). Still holding their instruments, the artists were violently taken from the train, under protests from passengers. A passenger recorded the aggression with a smartphone, and the association of metro artists ("*Coletivo AME—Artistas Metroviários*") shared it on their Facebook page, highlighting that this is a recurrent issue. Only a month before, three artists were assaulted under similar circumstances while performing in the metro. In 2013, a music teacher was assaulted while playing on a train in the South Zone (Bessa 2013). Countless complaints, statements and pieces of evidence exist about the truculent intervention of private security guards and police officers against buskers in Rio de Janeiro, both below and above ground. These confrontations usually reveal power imbalances and historical inequalities, such as racism, classism and gender—aggravated by local politics and corruption. These artists learned that organizing as a category, trying to count how many street performers there are and actively participating in policymaking to seek regulation or better cultural policies are crucial mechanisms for surviving as a street performer in Brazil. Buskers in other cities worldwide face similar issues when it comes to using the urban infrastructure as their ephemeral stages.

Above ground, street performers in Rio had to help shape (and approve) a law to protect them from arbitrary law enforcement and repressive interference from the police forces. After years of debate and organization around a movement that presented street performance as a form of public art—and, thus, a public service to the city and its citizens—the *Forum Carioca de Arte Pública* ("Carioca Public Art Forum") finally convinced the mayor to pass the bill into the law 5.429/2012. That law became known as the Street Performer's Law in Rio de Janeiro. Years after the law had come into force, while I was doing my fieldwork, I heard from many artists that it was still necessary to carry a printed version of the law in their pockets or to have it at hand on their phones, in case a police officer asked them to move along. Even after a regulatory framework was created to protect and legitimize the activity in the entire city territory, the precarity of these buskers' situation is just another proof of the distances, gaps and skewed power dynamics that exist between institutions, people and spaces. In 2014, the buskers organized an informal "census" of all street performers in town to present to the city government, in the hopes that those (unofficial) numbers could convince the mayor that there were many artists working in public spaces—and that they matter.

From London to Paris, Montreal to Rio de Janeiro, the urge to govern, quantify and regulate informal activities like street performance points to power relations and the contested character of public spaces. Artists have been using urban infrastructure, such as subways and sidewalks, for almost as long as these infrastructures existed. The act of designing frameworks to enforce how busking should be performed has a significant impact on the right to the city, especially in the context of neoliberal approaches to city planning (Gordilho Souza 2018; Maricato 2015; Rolnik 2019), in its reimagination for a global market (Sánchez 2010). And whenever we encounter a busker performing in a public space, it is hard to imagine how such ubiquitous activity can challenge local governments.

An aspect rarely covered when discussing busking is the lack of official numbers that facilitate an understanding of how this activity exists in urban territories. There is no such thing as a demographic report on these informal workers. This gap in knowledge has two dimensions. On the one hand, being overlooked as an activity keeps these artists invisible in datasets (or not properly portrayed) for city governments—which can result in a lack of cultural policies directed toward them, no proper funding for their activities, and the perpetuation of their precarity as informal laborers. On the other hand, official numbers do not necessarily tell all the stories—or tell them inaccurately—and, if we look at other categories of informal workers (such as street vendors), attempts to count them can also result in more surveillance, control and restrictive laws that negatively impact the work of buskers.

Just by occupying a street corner to play, buskers subvert the pursuit of controlled public spaces by holding fluid shows, exploiting the loopholes and using everyday fleeting opportunities to make a living or question the limits of (institutionalized) art. It's challenging to govern such activities: they happen for short periods, transform the space and then vanish. The complex ecosystem of laws, numbers, paperwork, departments, data, policies, people and infrastructure behind the right to perform (or not perform) on a street corner amazed me. As an often overlooked and misunderstood practice, street performance is a rich object of study, given the fact that it questions, via its existence, established notions of public (dis)order. As I will attempt to show, these artists contextualize and repurpose urban spaces, consciously or not.

The two stories shared so far—those of Jocelyn and the metro musicians in Rio—give us a glimpse of some of the main questions addressed in this book. They also relate to common problems in many cities on different continents. In the book, the focus is on people informally occupying the gaps, scratching surfaces (Ahmed 2017), contesting rules and existing beyond official numbers. They are part of a process older than they are that will probably go on despite adversities. When questioned about her future perspectives as a busker, Jocelyn said to me: "I'll just keep going until I fade away (laughs)." In 2017, right after the election of a far-right candidate as mayor in Rio de Janeiro, artists involved in the Public Art Forum told me: "We can see the storm approaching; it's scary, but we will survive. We always do." This book is a way of listening to these voices, putting them in perspectives both local and global and critically rethinking the role of busking in contemporary society.

Why do street performance and urban music governance matter?

In many cities across the world, buskers navigate several statuses, from lawbreakers to policymakers—and their experiences in performing in ephemeral urban stages are valuable, controversial and worth recounting. Urban music governance is essential to understand contemporary cities and the artists who choose the streets as their stages. The notion of street performance is embedded in a multitude of attitudes, feelings and memories and involves social groups of multiple kinds. There is no single definition of busking, nor of street performance. Even artists who occupy streets may describe themselves differently, from one to another: from those who see the street as a space of rehearsal to activists who see the street as an essential platform for their existence as artists. The practice of street performance consistently challenges the binaries of amateur/professional, legal/illegal, activist/sell-out, official/unofficial and donation-dependent/publicly-funded. Performers' personal and professional backgrounds are varied and allow us to glance at the diversity of languages, origins, motivations and careers that shape contemporary street performance.

The work presented in this book is an effort to understand why street performance and urban music governance matter to cities and people. By trying to control such informal activities taking place in their public spaces, often without evidence and numbers, municipal governments shed light on who has (and does not have) the right to inhabit specific parts of the city and under which circumstances. These are matters of access and exclusion, and they pose the question of whose voices are heard in such processes. Other historical issues permeate these artists' daily activities, such as those involving legal status, gender identity and expression, race and ethnicity, class and (the lack of) cultural or economic public policies properly designed for them. In urban spaces, the attempts to control something that cannot be easily monitored, quantified or put into categories, boxes or tables can backfire—or take civil servants frequently back to the drawing board.

By addressing the role of busking in our cities, I discuss rights (to use public spaces, to the city, to silence, to the night), cultural policies (what kind of activity can or will be funded, how, by whom), the invisible stories in data collection (about people, activities and spaces), legal frameworks and presumptions about the conceptions of togetherness and sociability. This book is guided by questions that try to identify what street performance—specifically street music—is in the twenty-first century and how, as an informal activity in public spaces, it is a useful tool to critically analyze our urban territories. Issues of gender, immigration, class, race and ethnicity are intertwined in the narrative, and so are inquiries about our obsession with control, comparison and measurements. The work presented here aims to offer a transnational comparative perspective that establishes a dialogue between global cities (Montreal and Rio), acknowledges their similarities and disparities and provides a much-needed in-depth study of street performance in the Global South. It contributes to the ongoing Latin American reflections on critical urban epistemologies (Bieletto-Bueno 2020) that bring together public spaces, sounds and the social implications of policy frameworks.

Methodological notes: Local challenges, transnational perspectives

In Copacabana, Rio de Janeiro, the local government usually closes Atlântica Avenue, a famous postcard location, to traffic to allow pedestrians, cyclists and skaters to enjoy the space. On an afternoon in 2012, while I was putting together my application for a PhD program, I was surprised by the number of street vendors on the beach's sidewalks—visibly more than the previous weeks. I had worked with street vendors in the context of studying piracy and contrafaction in São Paulo a couple of years before, and the ways in which informal labor is so omnipresent and resilient in Brazil highlight many urban planning issues and our historical inequalities. That day, right before dusk, numerous street performers were cheering the crowds. I stayed there until late, willing to learn more about busking in a city like Rio. In 2013, I was admitted to a PhD program at the Federal University of Rio de Janeiro to dedicate the next few years of my life to understanding the role played by the regulation of public spaces and street performance. In 2015, I was awarded a fellowship to do part of my PhD at McGill University in Montreal.

As I write this book, years later, I realize how Rio and Montreal are such intrinsic parts of myself. In the process of understanding these places, they became home(s). These cities kept me company in good and bad times while I wandered through their streets, parks, undergrounds and shores. They brought me beautiful people, many opportunities, endless love, hard work, lots of trouble and lessons to be learned. Montreal kept me afloat during a global pandemic, while most street activity and social life came to a halt. Comparing such different cities was rarely easy: South and North, bustling seaside and river island, so warm and so cold. Why compare them? Does it even make sense?

Yes, it does. I am comparing modes of existence (and resistance) in these cities. I am also comparing historical processes, power dynamics, local challenges and rights. The action of governing such ephemeral activities, in such diverse contexts, reinforces a notion that our cities are being challenged continuously to readapt. The street, as the Brazilian journalist João do Rio wrote in 1908, transforms the meaning of words and, therefore, reality. People were surprised to listen to me talking more about similarities than divergences in the ways these cities were adapting to the resilience of "illegal" actors. Rio and Montreal, separated by more than 8200 kilometers, share more critical concerns than it first appears.

In the introduction to the book *Urban Enigmas: Montreal, Toronto, and the Problem of Comparing Cities*, Johanne Sloan (2007) argues that "disciplines have their own logic of comparison," and that "each act of comparison, no matter how casual, can be understood as a contribution to the identity of a city." Here, I compare a phenomenon (street performances) embedded in cities: Rio and Montreal are not mere backgrounds; the way these cities are constituted and administered shapes the entire urban experience of busking.

Cities are always being compared; through rankings, lists or awards like the most liveable, most happy, the coolest and the smarter city. We compare cities when we want to move, to visit, to love or hate them. Given the relevance of cities as an essential part of so many people's everyday lives, it is not hard to comprehend how we continuously create (often loose) criteria to compare our urban environments. As Alan Blum puts it,

> the need and desire to compare cities, to search for likenesses and differences among and between them, is part of an interest in the question of how places manage to retain an aura of individuality in the face of overriding impressions of their substitutability in certain external respects.
>
> (2007: 16)

The efforts made throughout this book are more toward understanding transnational patterns than they are about homogenizing cities.

Under multiple names, the object I analyze—street performance, busking, wandering musicians—inhabits the margins of history and urban space (Bieletto-Bueno 2019; Campbell 1981; Genest 2001; Gétreau 1998; Harrison-Pepper 1990). This object exists informally, above and below ground, in the cracks of our system, out in the daylight or in the shadows after dark. Its presence in public spaces is fleeting, but it leaves behind traces and patterns. Following these clues in such big cities was not easy. I had to be creative and persistent in tracking down ephemeral performances and their temporary stages in the city. I also had to search for records, numbers, data and evidence of busking.

Paperwork, regulations, laws, reports, charts, spreadsheets, stamps and all sorts of documents are a crucial part of urban governance, and thus they are a fundamental part of the work presented here. I spent many days attempting to understand different bureaucratic elements in three languages and learning to navigate their complexity. Despite the dead ends I encountered, this is an attempt at capturing the ever-changing governance mechanisms of ephemeral performances.

This book talks about urban music governance and street performance broadly, but the scope of my fieldwork was limited to two different practices, street music and street theatre, for specific reasons. The first is the importance of their continued occupation of public spaces over the centuries. The second has to do with their fascinating particularities: street theatre requires the creation of boundaries between reality and performance; music has to deal with the configuration of boundaries between audience and artist, often without an actual stage (and not to mention the battles involving noise complaints). Here, my main focus is on street musicians, with context and policies led by street theatre groups.

One of this book's core contributions is its account of fieldwork carried out between 2013 and 2018 in Canada and Brazil and monitoring the policy and regulatory landscape in the following years. Over five years of fieldwork, I mapped a diverse range of stakeholders who, in a variety of ways, had an influence on busking practices in Rio and Montreal. I learned a lot about the intricacies of municipal cultural policy and (official and unofficial) data collection efforts.

Fieldwork was based on three approaches to deal with the randomness of the object. First, I utilized participant observation in festivals, performances, auditions and meetings—this allowed me to know more about processes, institutions and key people to be interviewed. Then, I conducted in-depth qualitative semi-structured interviews with civil servants, artists, sponsors, associations and city councilors. The interviews provided insights into complicated administrative structures, lawmaking and the daily experience of being a busker. Some names are pseudonyms to protect people's privacy at their request. Others said I could use their names, including buskers and public figures, city councilors and spokespersons. Another relevant approach was the use of images, such as photos that I took during participant observation and archival images collected throughout the research project. For the work presented here, visuality is a non-descriptive method of understanding the object; the use of pictures taken by me during my research aligns with Anna L. Tsing's (2015: viii) words in "*Mushroom at the End of the World*": "I use images to present the spirit of my argument rather than the scenes I discuss."

This work is anchored in a critical analysis of urban public spaces that takes into account historical inequalities such as structural racism (Kwon and Nguyen 2023; Santos 1998), gender perspectives beyond the binary and inclusive of the transgender community (Myrdahl 2023) for "queering public space" (Catterall and Azzouz 2021; Bain and Podmore 2023) and disability justice in urban planning (Stafford et al. 2022). The thoughts present here are also rooted in more than six decades of thinking about traditional notions of the "right to the city" (Lefebvre 2001; Harvey 2014; Mitchell 2003), and contemporary Latin American perspectives that build upon the notion of the right to the city (Maricato 1985; Tavolari 2016), neoliberal cities (Gordilho Souza 2018), the financialization of cities (Rolnik 2019), "market urbanism" (Schiavo and Gelfuso 2018) and the city as a commodity (Maricato 2015). Raquel Rolnik, one of the most influential urban planners in Brazil, affirms that metropolises in Brazil are "marked by concentration of wealth and power" (Rolnik 2022: 24), posing many challenges to think about what a city for everyone would look like. Urban areas in Brazil and Canada are also the product of colonialism by different European countries and brutal years of enslavement of African populations, brought to the Americas to do forced labor (Santos 2012), and the use of unceded indigenous territories.

My book then offers possible ways of comparing cities and studying practices that are mostly informal and erratic, spread across public spaces. It presents the path I have chosen and crafted; it might be useful to other wanderer researchers who are (or will be) chasing invisible stages, unofficial numbers, power dynamics and hopeful endurance in urban spaces around the world. Going back to Blum (2007: 47), he affirms that "the places to which we have been and the places that we want to be become parts of our biography, an intimate archive of telling or passing moments." Perhaps my journey with street performance is not over yet, but the main lesson I take with me from the years spent with this research is how these artists survive in a world that is falling apart.

Structure

This book is organized into five chapters and a afterword. The first chapter, "More than numbers: Counting, categorizing and describing buskers across time," explores the urge to quantify, count and categorize activities taking place in public spaces, and how these processes relate to busking being entangled with city life. This chapter draws from several sources and archives in an attempt to retrace the somewhat fragmented emergence and development of street performance. A closer look offers us the opportunity to understand buskers navigating stigma and contested realms of public spaces in different periods and to explore the lack of data on their existence throughout the centuries. Given the multifaceted aspects and ever-changing nature of what being a busker means, the chapter is also an attempt to draw a classification system for buskers that challenges binaries that have been constructed over time within systems of regulation and histories of practice—such as beggars/artists, amateurs/professionals and legal/illegal.

The second chapter, "Regulation: Engaging with (dis)order in everyday life," presents a brief discussion around the multiple understandings of regulatory frameworks, urban public spaces and why I see them as a spectrum (from totally private to fully public). After addressing the dynamic reality of public spaces, a problematization of the idea of order (and, therefore, disorder) is introduced, followed by the questioning of surveillance, policing and controlling these spaces. When it comes to public spaces, narratives of messiness and smartness compete to impact urban governance and, consequently, the activities taking place in these shared spaces—and that is the case for street performance. Consolidated approaches and concepts, such as the "right to the city" (Harvey 2014; Lefebvre 2001; Maricato 1985; Tavolari 2016) and "illegalism" (Foucault 1997; Telles 2009, 2010; Telles and Hirata 2007, 2010), are incorporated into this chapter to situate commonly marginalized practices, like busking, into a broader ecosystem and skewed power relations. A brief summary of influential works on street performance's regulation, legitimation and institutionalization is also presented, focusing on three countries: England, France and the United States.

Following these historical, classificatory and political perspectives, the third chapter, "Legitimation: The blurred boundaries between policy and control," analyzes the intricate process of urban music governance in the city of Montreal. It covers crucial historical moments and changes in legislation, cultural policy and urban infrastructure in the Canadian city known for its festivals, universities and vibrant cultural life. Montreal's administrative structure is fragmented in boroughs and has a daunting municipal regulatory framework. From a policy perspective, it is the combination of administrative intricacy with boundless creativity and a harsh winter that makes this city such an exciting case. Buskers fought (and keep fighting) for their rights to perform in public spaces, sometimes under strict regulation, and they offer us relevant lessons to be learned.

After looking at Montreal, the book turns its focus to Rio de Janeiro in its fourth chapter, "Disputes: Busking as public service and law-making." It covers how buskers had to become policymakers to guarantee their right to use public spaces. Having its roots in the street theatre and prominent figures of a bohemian downtown neighborhood, the movement of so-called "public artists" face arbitrary law enforcement, design public policies and redesign funding for the city's wandering creators. Rio, the "marvellous city," is known for its effervescent nightlife, bustling music scenes and brutal inequalities. Rio de Janeiro is a good case study because it shows us the tangled relationship between people, institutions and precarity. It also points out the fragility of specific regulations. Complex, intense and charming, this city can teach us about persistence and legality limits on many levels.

The final chapter, "Disobedience: Lawbreakers and talented stars," covers the relationship between busking and public transit, centered primarily on street musicians. Starting with the literature that tried to understand the intricacies of playing underground in global cities, we will then dive into tales of civil disobedience and multi-stakeholder mobilization led by buskers in subway systems in both Rio de Janeiro and Montreal—noticing how different the outcomes can be depending on the context, policy framework and (lack of) public data. By turning challenges into opportunities, these artists turn the personal into political action, and here they share the joys and issues of bringing their art to the public spaces, above and below ground, in our cities.

From the moment I started my fieldwork to the drafting of this manuscript, many years have passed, and a lot has changed in the world. The global COVID-19 pandemic had an everlasting impact on cultural events, night-time economies, sociability and busking. Even if the pandemic is not the central topic of this book, its effects on the object being studied need to be addressed. I decided to write a short afterword to provide updates on busking during—and following the (hopefully) worst waves of Covid. The afterword also covers a few lingering issues, and it is named "Pandemic, digitalization, and evidence-based policy." More than an attempt to predict whatever comes next, this last section offers clues, gaps, cracks and potentialities. Such a complex topic deserves all the attention it can get.

NOTE

1. Here, busking and street performance are used interchangeably, as well as busker and street performer.

PART I

NUMBERS AND NORMS

1

More than Numbers: Counting, Categorizing and Describing Buskers across Time

"OBJECTIVITY" arouses the passions as few other words can. Its presence is evidently required for basic justice, honest government, and true knowledge. But an excess of it crushes individual subjects, demeans minority cultures, devalues artistic creativity, and discredits genuine democratic political participation. Notwithstanding such criticism, its resonance is overwhelmingly positive.

Theodore Porter, Trust in Numbers (2020)

In 2014, street performers in Rio de Janeiro started an informal census of the artists performing in the streets of the city, mostly musicians and street theatre groups—but also clowns, mimes, comedians and dancers. They came up with over 750 names of individuals or groups in a couple of weeks. Later, they claimed to have over 4000 artists mapped. It is a significant number, even for such a large metropolis. The initiative was not led by the government; instead, it was proposed by one of the most influential street theatre groups in Rio, Tá na Rua, founded in the 1980s by Amir Haddad and occupying, for many years, a historic building at Rua Mem de Sá, near the iconic *Arcos da Lapa*.

This attempt to count and register all street performers in the city comes from, on the one hand, a desire to make busking visible in the eyes of the government, specifically, and society, at large; on the other hand, there is power in numbers and data (Bouk et al. 2022) that allows the artists to bargain for public funding, comprehensive public policies and legitimacy as a valuable cultural practice to the city. Even if the data collection on busking was conducted by non-state actors and the methodology was never disclosed publicly, they did it within the context of a publicly funded festival, with the intention of making these numbers perceived as official by the local government.

In their efforts to count such a fleeting activity—it rarely has a fixed spot or a pre-established schedule—the artists shed light on questions that are central to this book. As Bouk, Ackermann and boyd (2022: 2) affirm when discussing powerful numbers, society relies on official numbers and public data as trustful sources for decision-making, "given with authority and always there for the taking." But we often forget that official numbers are crafted and they are political. The lack of data, combined with the difficult task of categorizing what is busking or who is a busker, offers us the opportunity to inquire about the role that counting marginal cultural practices plays in contemporary society. Also, to understand the meaning of this data invisibility today, it is crucial to look at descriptions of busking across time.

This chapter is divided into three parts. The first part presents the challenges in transforming busker into data and the pitfalls that should be avoided in the face of the growing datafication of everything. The following part portrays an attempt at categorizing what busking means, drawing from historical accounts and fieldwork. Lastly, a deep dive into archives shows us that definitions, names and categories change over time. It also highlights the qualitative nature of researching urban informal cultural practices and the need to rely on small data.

Counting buskers and the issues surrounding data invisibility

The role of data changed significantly over the last two centuries, specifically

> [o]ver the past 150 years, ideas have shifted drastically as to what counts as data, which data are reliable and who owns them. Once regarded as stable objects whose significance was determined by a handful of professional interpreters, data are now reusable goods.
>
> (Leonelli 2019: 317)

Increasingly, data become commodities, which are used not only to inform policy and governance but also to help us make sense of the world around us. Some cultural practices are easier to count, such as the number of movie theatres or parks in a city. It is possible to count the number of licenses for bars and restaurants, the total number of public libraries in a territory and how many people have registered their food carts in the last year. However, there are spaces and activities that fall in the cracks of these official ways to measure city life (Reia 2022). Certain do-it-yourself (DIY) spaces, "irregular" street vendors, garage sales and buskers are a few examples that add layers of complexity when governing urban life.

Recent initiatives to uncover the number of cultural sectors combine different methods to estimate the relevance of night-time economies in cities worldwide

(VibeLab 2023) and propose indicators. The music industry also struggles with the lack or inconsistency of numbers, as well as the role of statistics (Osborne and Laing 2021). From the "magic numbers" of media piracy (Karaganis 2011) to non-replicable estimations of the value of creativity, it is hard to escape the ever-present weight of data in cultural policies. Data is increasingly the corner-stone for the scientific—and economic—understanding of the world around us.

The emphasis on economic value with numbers as the sole evidence can be harmful to informal urban cultural labor. "The government believes in numbers; we need to show them we exist—and that we are numerous." This was the over-arching argument behind buskers' informal census efforts, and also a belief rooted in the struggle for visibility of many groups in cities, such as night shifters, street vendors, queer and racialized artists and DIY venue owners (Reia 2021). Becoming visible to the local authorities might be a first step toward better working conditions, awareness of challenges and financial support.

Counting and measuring things is important in designing evidence-based policymaking. However, how we count, when we count and who we count has implications way beyond numbers. From privacy and data protection concerns to accuracy or transparency, counting people and their activities must be a critical, multifaceted approach within broader social frameworks. Even in Science, Technology, Engineering and Mathematics (STEM) disciplines and in settings we usually associate with high scientific accuracy (such as laboratories), there are nuances and errors when counting people and things (Martin and Lynch 2009). Uncounted populations abound, often the result of negligence, politics, neoliberalism or a combination of all the above. In literature, interesting work on global health equity shed light on the politics behind the uncounted populations (Davis 2020), and more recent reflections on gender identity being considered (or not) in the national census became a battlefield in different countries (Guyan 2022; Reia 2022a). Ethically and responsibly counting fluid identities, informal activities and marginalized communities are part of our path toward meaningful data justice.

In the quest to understand how datasets might not be an accurate representation of reality, there is a need to acknowledge datasets are prone to statistical errors, missing links and invisibilization of entire communities. If we ask the wrong questions, can we really hold a grasp of the complexities around us? Official numbers are fundamental to democracy (Bouk 2022) and to decision-making. However, while insights on stories not being told matter, visibility might not always be desirable, safe or possible. Visibility in datasets must always be aligned with principles of ethics (Wylie 2020), justice (Taylor 2017), responsibility and digital rights (Digital Freedom Fund 2020).

When dealing with marginalized communities—and busking as an informal and oftentimes criminalized activity fits into this category—it is essential to think beyond mere data collection as a visibility tool. We must consider the broader social impacts and trends in policymaking. Street musicians make use of public spaces that are increasingly under surveillance. The rapid advancements of data-centric systems (such as artificial intelligence, machine learning and large language models) and their many promises to long-existing problems make them appealing to local governments (Brandusescu and Reia 2022). The deployment of controversial technologies in public spaces, especially facial recognition systems, raises several questions about the right to the city, discrimination and over-policing of spaces.

Streets, squares, subways, music festivals—these spaces are becoming a testbed for irresponsible artificial intelligence-based surveillance. The use of surveillance technologies has also been shown to increase racial (Browne 2015) and gender (Scheuerman et al. 2021) discrimination because they often incorporate biased datasets and disregard historical inequalities. Various campaigns around the world have been asking for a total ban on facial recognition systems. While the technology is being rolled back in certain cities in the Global North, the market is unsurprisingly booming in the Global South in an attempt to tackle safety and crime issues. It is not hard to imagine how an already criminalized and stigmatized activity such as busking could be harmed by these data-centric systems that have artificial eyes everywhere. City governments must consider the challenges and consequences of real-time data collection for those often uncounted, barely visible or existing in the gray areas of society.

Finding the balance between official numbers, community-based data collection and non-harmful technologies is a starting point. The buskers in Rio are not alone in their attempt to measure—and officialize, in a certain way—their activities. The Busking Project,[1] based in the United Kingdom, has mapped over 10,000 buskers from around the world on their platform; you can search for buskers by keywords or genre (clown, juggler, musician, statue, circus, storyteller, etc.) and sort them alphabetically or by popularity. You can like the content, tip the artists, hire them and access their social media pages. The Busking Project's platform also allows the user to search for artists on a world map by country and city, with data from all continents (except the Antarctic). Another project that maps and relies on data to showcase buskers worldwide is the Street Music Map,[2] created in 2014 on Instagram and later unfolding into projects on other platforms.

When I interviewed Amir Haddad, in 2014, he said there were no concrete plans for the data they have been collecting about the street performers. They delivered the findings in a comprehensive report to the Municipal Department of Culture, the city councilors and the mayor. One of the goals would be to design policies from buskers for buskers, organizing their collective efforts as the negotiations advanced. Another ambitious project the artists had in mind was the intention to institutionalize street performance, framed by them as public art, via the establishment of a specific department dedicated to busking within the formal organization of the Municipal Department of Culture (Haddad 2014)—or as a foundation dedicated to advancing street performance in the city. According to Haddad, this bureaucratic infrastructure would

> think about how these groups present themselves, how they survive, in which regions they work, how they perform, study their ways to strengthen them—without the sole intention of taking these artists to the market because we are not talent scouts.
> (Haddad 2014: n.pag.)

This translation of cultural practice into numbers, and later into policy and governance is more common for street performance throughout history than one could initially imagine. In the face of non-existing official numbers, scholars, journalists, advocates and policymakers must seek information where it is available, be it small or big data to define the boundaries of the activity. The following section is an exploratory attempt to reflect the complex and fluid categories encompassed by contemporary busking.

Categorizing the boundaries of street musicians' identity

Being a musician and performing in the streets does not necessarily make one a busker. As contradictory as it may sound at first, the years of fieldwork with various artists shows the complexity of trying to frame busking within rigid categories. Street music is not a homogeneous activity: it contemplates fluid, ever-changing practices. While conducting fieldwork, two main questions were frequently asked: "What is busking?" and "Who is a busker these days?" These questions are rooted in the confusion surrounding practices as varied as at stop lights, one-person bands, living statues, entire music bands, theatre companies, clowns or balloon artists being occasionally considered as street performers or buskers. An attempt to classify or create a typology for these activities, as flawed as it may be, could help us to understand some of the underlying aspects of contemporary street performance—leading to reflections on how these are counted and quantified by local governments.

There is an explosion of "type creation" on numerous fronts, from algorithms to policymaking (Sadre-Orafai 2020: 194), despite their controversial origins in Anthropology, in an attempt to "make sense of difference" through a practice of typification. Sadre-Orafai (2020: 195) affirms "Typologies are abstract systems of classification and comparison that render the complexities and nuances of everyday life [...] discrete and comparable through the modelling and use of types." These typologies can help us to sort things out, with a defined purpose; they are not a flawless representation of the world. Here, trying to define and create a system of classification for busking is rooted in an effort to point out similarities while highlighting differences.

For example, a differentiation that emerged among the subjects being interviewed was related to the authenticity of certain practices. For some artists, "street musicians" are those who have the street as their main stage, centering their performance on interactions with public spaces and passers-by. However, these artists also perform in private events, concert halls, bars and restaurants—an additional source of income and visibility for their art. Other artists are only using the street temporarily to rehearse—or are on the lookout for better opportunities—and are neither considered buskers by their peers nor consider themselves buskers.

Another differentiation worth making is the one between "street music" and "music in the street." The first one refers mostly to the consistent practice of being a street musician; the latter encompasses the existence of a myriad of musical practices taking place in public spaces, from free festivals and private or state-sponsored concerts to traditional musical territories connected to music genres and communities, such as *rodas de samba* in Rio (Herschmann and Fernandes 2014). In the cities studied, these practices and spaces intertwine, creating a complex cultural network that brings together varied experiences (Reia et al. 2018).

With this complex scenario in mind, the following proposed classification of different types of buskers was established, with street musicians as the main object of classification, based on research findings from fieldwork. It encompasses a spectrum of classification with three categories: (1) self-definition, i.e., artists who claim to be buskers and play in public spaces often; (2) artists who are framed as buskers by laws, rules and associations, both via imposed rules (such as regulation in the metro that designates specific spots for musicians to perform), or when artists demand to be recognized as buskers (via municipal laws or grants for cultural production, for example) and (3) the transitory busker status, often an artist who is just using public spaces as a temporary venue—for rehearsal, while in-between jobs, or for a specific project. An artist can be in more than one category simultaneously or throughout a period.

Some internal differences among the busking community must also be discussed. There is a plethora of notions of belonging for artists who define themselves as street performers, artists who are externally framed as buskers and those who see busking as a transitory condition. Their backgrounds usually differ, making for a heterogeneous practice, and one busker's trajectory is rarely similar to the others; there are various paths one takes to find themselves performing in the street. Being an artist who is using the streets to present their work to mutable audiences also invokes constant negotiations—not only with the government and institutions but also with the built space, the city rules, other artists, passers-by, street vendors and the artists' own physical and emotional limitations.

There are many variables involved in performing on the streets—such as timed performances, pre-reserved spots, noise regulation, zoning and special events—that musicians (more than any other form of busking) need to understand and abide to. A busker might be playing legally one day and illegally the next one; or be within the permitted rules at a certain time and not an hour later. All these nuances require the artist to know rules, policies, categories and even how certain authorities operate in each urban space.

The formality or informality of the artist who performs on the streets can also be questioned since many of them have steady jobs in other areas, which often guarantee the payment of bills (with a formal job) and life as an artist on the streets.

Even the boundaries of their labor and income are blurred. A common topic among buskers is the various levels of professionalization within their communities. Many try to present themselves as professional musicians, delineating the category of the professional artist who chooses the street as a venue and separating them from those who play as an equivalent of panhandling ("talentless," "amateurs" and "beggars"; Gétreau 1998).

The importance given to the existence and continuity of street performance also varies among artists, most of whom believe that performing in the city can create a more festive and joyful daily life by transforming people's monotonous commute, at least for a few moments. However, not all artists have this optimistic view of the practice. During fieldwork, some buskers shared with me how they perceive and use the street in a pragmatic way, to either earn money to pay bills or to rehearse and test the audience's reception to new compositions.

The buskers' engagement in activism or mobilizations to legitimize or regulate their activities, or even to resist police brutality, is not homogeneous either. Only a few groups and individuals participate more actively in policymaking or lawmaking by attending forums, working voluntarily in associations, participating in public hearings, proposing projects and providing inputs to laws. The involvement of street performers in such tactics and strategies has guaranteed, to different extents, the persistence of street performance in contemporary cities, as we will see in the following chapters. By navigating restrictions and relying oftentimes on civil disobedience, buskers keep going. The specific role played by musicians in subways in the Americas, from New York (Tanenbaum 1995) and Montreal (Wees 2017; Chatterjee 2022) to Santiago (Bieletto-Bueno 2020) and Rio de Janeiro (Reia 2019), exemplifies the importance of their fight for the right to perform.

These fights for the right to perform in the city have roots centuries ago, visible through archives and qualitative small data. Next, a historical account is presented that ties together the discussion about descriptions, categories and the boundaries of busking across time.

Tales from another time: Describing a journey through busking in archives

On June 5, 2013, several street performers gathered together in Rio de Janeiro's downtown, at Cinelândia, to celebrate the anniversary of a municipal law commonly known as the Street Performer's Law. Between the majestic Municipal Theatre and the Municipal Chamber of Rio de Janeiro, right next to the National Library and other cultural landmarks in Rio, Cinelândia is a public square whose official name is Praça Floriano Peixoto. It was home to famous street cinemas in the twentieth century, from where its nickname ("cinema land") derived. Despite the decay of movie theatres in the area over time, the square remained a central meeting point for nightlife, protests and street performances.

A street theatre group shared a short clip on social media inviting artists and citizens to get together for a cortege honoring the law and the people behind it at Cinelândia. Performers of all kinds arrived with fanfare, costumes and colorful props. The Municipal Police Band played in front of the Municipal Chamber as part of the festivities. A clown was handing plastic flowers as a souvenir of the day's celebrations, on which hung a small piece of paper stating: "Souvenir of the 1st year of the law 5.429/2012—Long live the street performer." Announcements were made and the city councilor who helped the law to come into force, Reimont, attended the party. Soon, various simultaneous performances started across Cinelândia.

The celebration involved talks, performances, gift distribution and even a cake—with candles—was served to the audience as part of the anniversary. The artists kept repeating a few catchphrases, such as "this is the law that works for us" and "street performance is an ancestral practice." The idea of "ancestrality" ("*ancestralidade,*" in Brazilian Portuguese), based on the idea that contemporary street performers descend from the medieval jugglers, was ingrained in some groups in Rio. By claiming a perennial presence in urban public spaces across the centuries, the artists were seeking validation of their right to be there.

Indeed, street performers have been using urban infrastructures for centuries, exposing, with their activities, cultural and political aspects of urban life in different historical moments. The idea of an "ancestrality" of busking, widely adopted among groups of artists in Rio de Janeiro, was ever-present. However, even if buskers have been around for centuries, why is it so difficult to find consistent, reliable data and information about them? What does one have to look at to learn more about these practices?

Digitized public archives and libraries are a good starting point. Given the French tradition of jugglers since medieval times, and the efforts the country has put into digitizing and publicizing part of its history, Gallica—the digital library of the *Bibliothèque Nationale de France*—became a source of information to understand the connections between contemporary and ancient buskers in the West, as well as western views of busking in non-western countries. A significant part of these works written in the nineteenth century turned to the analysis of the history of street performers and the urban life of French cities throughout the Middle Ages until the period that comprises their publications. Information about the artists, their behavior and how they used the cities for their presentations are detailed in these reports.

However, some works introduce us to the French point of view on the various forms of public art and entertainment on other continents. For example, Daniel Arnauld's illustrated work *Fakirs et jongleurs* (1889), published in Paris, presents a western, colonial perspective on jugglers and fakirs in India, dervishes in Anatolia and entertainers in Fiji. Often, these documents reflect the point of view of explorations and colonization efforts, featuring skewed power dynamics and prejudices that are intrinsic to colonialism around the world. As Ann Laura Stoler (2009) puts it, "colonial administrations were prolific producers of social categories," and the knowledge produced about street performers contained in such archives must be analyzed from a critical perspective of Eurocentrism (Quijano 2000; Gandarilla Salgado et al. 2021).

Here, the focus is on French-speaking authors writing about buskers in French cities. An example is the Parisian book *Les spectacles populaires et les artistes des rues* written by Victor Fournel in 1863. The work addresses many practices carried out in public spaces—primarily at popular fairs—such as quack doctors, comedians, jugglers, minstrels, troubadours and dancers. Fournel (1863) describes the activities and social relationships of popular jugglers, troubadours and minstrels, claiming that the jugglers (and their various denominations) occupied prominent places in the daily life of courts, at family parties and entertaining people in public squares during the Middle Ages. Nonetheless, there were also jugglers who performed "with the people, following them in the streets" (Fournel 1863: 117)—an interesting, less studied category of public entertainers.

The "ancestrality" of street performers is reflected by accounts of their presence in a variety of documents and historical texts. They appear in Latin documents as "joculator" and were found mainly throughout the twelfth and thirteenth centuries. Performances involved more than music and declamations, including tricks, jokes, animals and other forms of entertainment—a "complete comedian" capable of making people laugh or cry, but which did not have the same recognition as minstrels and troubadours (Fournel 1863: 120). The hierarchies and differentiation among performers existed in earlier centuries and persist today. Even with all these talents, jugglers "were considered far below the troubadour and the minstrel: while glories, money and consideration rained down on the latter, the juggler often remained poor and despised" (Fournel 1863: 120–21). The lack of recognition also reflects how troubadours and minstrels were closer to the nobility, living with and being financed by wealthy families, while the jugglers were normally nomads, demeaning their art and themselves to earn a living.

It is hard to understand the intricacies of denominations, typologies and divergences in relation to the names and activities practiced over time, especially due to the ever-changing practices, behaviors and social acceptance of certain performances. In the twelfth and thirteenth centuries, it was common to have poets and musicians of higher income classes being called jongleurs, but it is from the fourteenth century on that the term falls into disregard and becomes associated with a despicable way of life (Barbot 1899; Fournel 1863).

Different musical activities took place in French public spaces in the period portrayed. The *"ménestrellerie"* encompassed many different activities, and the artists are described over the years with various names, of similar meanings, which can cause confusion when trying to understand the many existing categories (Fournel 1863: 118). This variety makes it more difficult to count and understand the organization and relevance of busking throughout history. For example, there was the "trouvère," which designated the poet; the minstrels (*"menestreux, menestriers"*) were singers and musicians who recited the compositions of the trouvères accompanied by musical instruments. Usually, the minstrel was the head of a *"menestrandie,"* a troupe made up of singers, storytellers, musicians and pranksters, who worked together to enhance their talents and profits.

The historical accounts of busking also include insights into musical instruments used at the time. Fournel (1863: 141–46) divides them into three categories. First, string instruments, such as harp, lyre, lute, guitar and citole, among others, many of which are versions that do not exactly correspond to the instruments that currently exist, as they have changed over time or even disappeared. There was a differentiation between some types of instruments and the social class of those who played them. Second, there were also brass instruments, such as trumpet, trombone, organ and flute, which were mainly used in the military, and reserved for jugglers who accompanied the armed forces (although there are records of more ordinary uses of these instruments). There were also portable organs, but they were too cumbersome to be widely used (Fournel 1863: 144–45). Finally, there were percussion instruments, such as bells, cymbals, triangles, castanets, drums and tambourines. Some instruments could be embellished and adorned with materials, such as gold when they belonged to aristocratic minstrels. However, most of the time, the jugglers of the streets and the nomadic artists used common versions of these instruments.

Escudier (1875: 199–205) mentions the *"marquis de la Vessie,"* known in Paris and elsewhere: an itinerant musician who played an instrument partially made of a bladder, with an intestine string and a wooden stick. There are other improvised instruments, clowns who play songs from glasses and flower vases, or even primitive xylophones. In addition to these practices, there is also the "one man orchestra" (*"l'homme orchestre"*), also known as one-man band—an activity that is still quite popular in several cities (see, e.g. Tanenbaum 1995). These one-person orchestras present themselves playing more than one musical instrument simultaneously.

The professions of juggler, minstrel and other denominations were mostly performed by men, although there are some records of women working with their husbands, collecting donations from the audience. Fournel mentions these women who helped in the presentations, including the existence of a reference to women exercising these professions (*"jongleresses"* and *"ménestrelles"*) in a regulation of 1321, but reaffirms the exceptional character of these practices (Fournel 1863: 139). Given the historical invisibility of women in data (Criado Perez 2019) and in archives, this information can be used as is but requires more studies and accounts to understand the extent of women's participation in busking throughout the centuries.

Records available in digital archives also tell us about the jugglers' mise-en-scène and their relationship with urban life in French cities. Jugglers created real open-air shows, often with chairs available for the public to sit in if someone wanted to pay for this convenience. Beyond skills to play instruments, declamation and singing, buskers should have other exceptional talents to amuse minds and eyes; the exemplary juggler was at the same time a poet, musician, singer, joker, animal trainer, mime, doctor, sorcerer, messenger of love, moreover, a skilled worker and "craftsman of all kinds" (Fournel 1863: 150).

However, historical documents point more to the reputation of being skilled than to the dignity and moral consideration of these artists. At some point, the jugglers had to extend their repertoires, a process in which few remained "faithful to the purity of their art" (Fournel 1863: 148–49) to serve the general public, changing the reputation and acceptance of these artists by society. It was common for minstrels gathered in a troupe to have jugglers to complement the shows, traveling all over France. Fournel (1863: 159) mentions a stamp in a tenth-century bible depicting one of these troupes at work, suggesting that this type of arrangement had been common for several centuries. But in general, these professionals were described as "vagrants and miserable" unless some aristocratic lord took them to live in his palaces.

Another interesting historical account of street performers is the book entitled "*Les saltimbanques*" written by Gaston Escudier and published in 1875 in Paris. In addition to the text with Escudier's impressions and experiences on the streets of the city, the book features 500 illustrations by P. de Crauzat, providing visual representations that help in the understanding of busking in nineteenth-century France. Given the scarcity of materials and numbers available that address and portray street performers, these illustrations help to see urban life in the Parisian streets through the eyes and worldview of the authors. The practices described are varied, encompassing acrobats, tricks, quackery, wild animals, occult arts, dance, music, theatre, circus and the shows of horrors and "aberrations."

An additional aspect of busking that is often overlooked relates to the income and financial sustainability of the activity. Hard to quantify and normally consisting of off-the-books transactions, the amount of money street performers make is rarely known. Escudier (1875) argues that a "*chanteur de chansonnettes*," a busker who took off his hat, picked up his guitar and started playing in front of cafes and other establishments earned twelve to fifteen francs a day, and on Sundays, depending on the spot chosen by them, it was possible to earn twice as much.

Jacques Attali (2009) makes references to the musicians of this period based on the argument that it took centuries for music to enter the exchange of goods and be commodified. Throughout the Middle Ages, the jongleur (from the Latin *joculare*, "to entertain") remained on the margins of society, whose lifestyle was seen as unworthy of respectability and led to their condemnation by the church: "[h]is itinerant lifestyle made him a highly unrespectable figure, akin to the vagabond or the highwayman" (Attali 2009: 14).

Music consumers were from all social classes: from peasants during fairs and popular festivals to the banquets of the nobility. The content of the songs, at the time, did not change much from one environment to another. In this period, songs were rarely written (apart from religious music) and jongleurs played them from memory. If a song became popular, texts were based on them. In general, jongleurs ended up causing "a permanent circulation between popular music and court music" (Attali 2009: 14). The music and songs composed by these artists—as they are an important way of transmitting and circulating information in precapitalist society—were either appropriated by governments or used satirically (and, of course, censored):

> [T]he jongleurs could be utilized for purposes of political propaganda. [...] In
> wartime, jongleurs were often hired to compose songs against the enemy. Conversely,
> independent jongleurs composed songs about current events and satirical songs,

and kings would forbid them to sing about certain delicate subjects, under threat of imprisonment.

(Attali 2009: 14–15)

Until the fourteenth century, the music was the same at court, market and village, with two exceptions: very abstract and erudite texts by the troubadours were not sung in villages; moreover, the courts were financially able to hire multi-artist jongleur orchestras. Apart from these two cases, according to Attali, music was not elitist, nor did it monopolize creativity. However, from the fourteenth century onwards, the context changed considerably:

> On the one hand, church music became secularized and autonomous from the chant; [...] On the other hand, the techniques of written and polyphonic music spread from court to court and distanced the courts from the people [...]. Musicians became professionals [...], producers of spectacles exclusively reserved for a minority.
>
> (Attali 2009: 15)

In three centuries (from the fourteenth to the sixteenth centuries) the courts had banned jongleurs, "the voice of the people," and they only listened to music played by artists hired for this purpose. A change in vocabulary confirms this transformation, with the musician being referred to as a minstrel ("ménestrel" or "ménestrier") from the Latin "ministerialis" (employee). These musicians were no longer nomads and were formally linked to the courts or residing in cities. Musicians began, at some point, to organize themselves into corporations, similar to the guilds of artisans and merchants, with a patron saint (St. Julien of Minstrels), banquets, municipal laws and retirement and disability funds. They had a monopoly on ceremonies and weddings, leaving out jongleurs—normally unprofessional and independent. In addition to the moral and socioeconomic decay of jongleurs triggered by these changes, little by little, a subtle separation between popular music and court music took shape, although it never fully materialized (Attali 2009). As the capitalist system was not established suddenly and immediately after the feudal system, court musicians continued to use popular repertoire and jongleurs did not disappear. The latter ended up suffering from their decadence and becoming predominantly traveling musicians in the villages, often amateurs who played musical instruments or even beggars.

Over the centuries, musicians gradually became legitimized by instruments of economic and political power and recognized as artists by a portion of society. However, those who do not fit into a mold are relegated to forms of itinerant work, subject to moral judgment as inferior practitioners. In her work with New York subway musicians, Susie J. Tanenbaum (1995: 32–33) states that she heard from some musicians, during interviews, references to the ancestry of what they did, but that there is no consensus between them on the subject. In fact, itinerant musicians have existed for centuries, in different countries, in the most varied forms, and have been changing over the years—being shaped, mainly, by the regulation and institutionalization of their practices. Throughout the history of street performers, the regulation of the activity has played an important role in these processes of institutionalization and legitimation since they control who can carry out certain activities, and in what way, according to interests and control mechanisms present in each period.

These historical accounts are centered in the Global North and western societies, which does not mean that itinerant artists were nonexistent in the Global South and non-western countries. Stories and narratives about street musicians, errant artists or fairs featuring entertainment in public spaces abound (see, e.g. Breyley 2016; Stevens 2016; Wong 2016). However, the stigmatization of busking, combined with the fact that many public archives and libraries are not digitized or publicly available, or the existence of language barriers, make finding sources and data about buskers quite challenging. Descriptions and stories written by scholars, journalists, essayists and artists themselves show us a glimpse of these musical activities and help us to expand our knowledge of informal urban cultural labor.

Street musicians are part of Latin American history, even if often overlooked. Natalia Bieletto-Bueno (2019, 2020) offers a much-needed perspective on busking in Latin American cities, pointing out the importance of bringing Latin American voices to the international debate and decolonizing urban epistemologies (Bieletto-Bueno 2020). By uncovering and making visible the history of street musicians in cities that are often left out of the scholarship because of their geography, language or status in global rankings, it is possible to expand our understanding of contemporary urban challenges. Here, Brazil and Rio de Janeiro become significant examples for the rest of the world.

In Brazil, João do Rio wrote about city life in the streets of Rio in the early twentieth century. A classic in Brazilian Portuguese literature, the book "The Enchanted Soul of the Streets" ("*A alma encantadora das ruas*") was published in a bilingual (Portuguese and English) edition in 2010. João do Rio was a writer and journalist born in 1880 and deceased in 1921 whose full name was João Paulo Emílio Cristóvão dos Santos Coelho Barreto. He wrote influential chronicles about Rio de Janeiro, describing everyday life and communities in that bustling city undergoing an intense period of transition. Originally published in 1908, *The Enchanted Soul of the Streets* is a collection of chronicles about people in the streets of the city at the time. With perspectives of a flaneur—an urban wanderer—João do Rio wrote about groups of people and activities on the margins of society, many of them working informally in the streets, and addresses issues of labor conditions, traditions and culture.

One of the chronicles written by João do Rio in the volume is named "Street musicians."[3] It portrays street music in the early twentieth century, during the wider adoption of gramophones and pianos in bars, restaurants, hotels and shops that led to a decrease in the presence of buskers in the streets. Slowly, they were returning to public life:

> For a few months now a German band, equipped with music stands and instruments that badly need tuning, has been tormenting the city's squares; and the other day I caught a glimpse of a creature that I thought was as dead as the dodo—the man with seven instruments! And there he was, bedecked with instruments, strolling around, rosy-faced and smiling as though he had just earned himself a good day's living. All the musicians have returned.
>
> (do Rio 2010: 193)

João do Rio (2010: 195) also says that "[m]usic is a vital part of this city; it could not live without its street musicians," being an inspiration for "any bohemian who desires a happy existence." He goes on to mention two blind Portuguese buskers who have been playing in the streets for over two decades, and the fact that these itinerant musicians made money and traveled around the country. Another story is about an Italian musician and other local busker "celebrities" in Rio de Janeiro intertwined with stories about musicians playing in bars or benefiting from a pitiful appearance—so by-passers would put more money in their hats.

In the twentieth century, the reports and accounts of buskers playing in underground infrastructure, such as the subway, emerged as these infrastructures were built and became a place of transit—thus, a place of audience. These spaces also become places of regulation (Caiafa 2013; Wees 2017), as well as socio-territorial order and control of behaviors (Bieletto-Bueno 2020), often more intensively than above ground, nonetheless entangled with notions of public order that will be explored in the next chapter.

NOTES

1. See: https://busk.co/buskers. Accessed June 9, 2024.
2. The project is curated by Daniel Bacchieri since 2014. More information here: https://www.instagram.com/streetmusicmap/. Accessed June 9, 2024.
3. Here I use the translation by Mark Carlyon, published in the bilingual edition of "The Enchanted Soul of the Streets" (2010) by Editora Cidade Viva, River of January Series.

2

Regulation:
Engaging with (Dis)order in Everyday Life

If laws show the most dignified and elevated face of rules [...], then regulations are rules with sleeves rolled up, the ones that get things done on the ground. Laws are rules with a telescope, far-seeing and aiming for the stars; regulations are rules with a microscope, myopic and focused on detail. Ideally, laws are relatively few and seldom altered; regulations are many and constant in need of updating. [...] The average citizen rarely collides with a law; we bark our shins against regulations almost every day.

Lorraine Daston, *Rules* (2022: n.pag.)

Like the discriminatory designs we are exploring in digital worlds, hostile architecture can range from the more obvious to the more insidious—like the oddly shaped and artistic-looking bench that makes it uncomfortable but not impossible to sit for very long. Whatever the form, hostile architecture reminds us that public space is a permanent battleground for those who wish to reinforce or challenge hierarchies.

Ruha Benjamin, *Race after Technology* (2019: n.pag.)

When we cross paths with buskers in our daily commute through the city, it is hard to imagine how many layers of bureaucracy they had to face to be there—or the number of norms governing the occupation of a single square or street corner. Mariana Valverde wrote in *Laws of the Street* (2009) that the order and peace perceived in a street corner in Toronto "are the products not only of global economic forces and nation-wide cultural trends but also—to an extent that cannot be quantified but is definitely non-trivial—by the force of local law" (Valverde

2009: 179). Valverde writes about the importance of incorporating legal structures and tools in our comprehension of urban life. Moroni and Chiodelli (2014: 1) build upon Valverde's work, describing how "policing city life through municipal regulations" known as "municipal ordinances" has been increasing recently. By increasing "control of public space, the regulation of access and behaviour can hugely condition the way in which people live in their cities and enjoy them." In this controlled setting of norms, it is easier to restrict activities or even the presence of urban "undesirables" (Belina 2011; Froment-Meurice and Fleury 2016).

Laws are extremely relevant to understanding busking throughout history (Harrison-Pepper 1990). The lack of data about this activity in archives, libraries, museums, open data portals and official numbers leaves researchers and policymakers struggling to find information. Police records, legislation, urban governance mechanisms and news articles are often seen as reliable sources when it comes to street performance—probably because they are the few formal records that exist. Paul Simpson, academic and street musician, affirms that because buskers are on the margins of society in so many ways, the history of these artists ends up being sparsely recorded:

> Being in the most part in the lower classes of society such musicians were not necessarily in a position to write their own history or even have their say on what was written about them. [...] Much of the existing written history of street music takes the form of letters written by those complaining about the nuisance street music posed for them, and in the records of the debates that took place in the development of street music legislation.
>
> (Simpson 2015: 2–3)

The interactions between law enforcement and informal labor, especially in Latin America, crack open skewed power dynamics around what is considered legal (Telles and Hirata 2010) and highlight the long road to the right to the city. Similar to the persecution faced by street vendors (Rabossi 2011; Francisco 2014), buskers also deal with arbitrary policing of spaces where they perform. The increasing policing of urban areas (Herbert 1997), the militarization of police forces (Graham 2011) and the pursuit of public order (Keller 2010; Reia 2018) shape the often-hostile environment that informal workers have to navigate—and fight against. Even when there are regulations and permit systems in place, buskers still need to negotiate the legality of their presence in the street. According to Wagner José (2017), one of the street musicians in Rio, "everyone has to 'carry the law' [...] You must always have it with you, in your case, phone or pocket." Street musicians complained about the lack of preparation of the Municipal Guard to deal with artists and people occupying public spaces, stating that between the approval of a law and law enforcement, there is a huge gap that leaves room for biased assumptions on the side of the police.

Street performance is part of a complex ecosystem formed by a multiplicity of actors, urban infrastructures and expectations about how a city should present itself simultaneously to its residents and the world. By looking at regulation as urban governance, I am also shedding light on various layers of control of communicative processes between people, the built environment and cultural life. The perspective adopted here is that street performance is a communicative practice that helps to connect people to each other and to the urban environment through their occupations in the city. The constructed urban space is also communicative (Dickinson and Aiello 2016: 1295) and is exacerbated when occupied by busking, mediating the relationships that occur in it during and after the presentations. For Ferrara (2008: 43, translation added), "while built environment, the city is a mean, while image and plan, the city is media, while mediation, the city is urbanity." Buskers demonstrate a shared rhetoric that shapes both their perspectives and their role in contesting the public order. Therefore, this type of artistic intervention, which can be considered a form of activism (Fernandes and Herschmann 2014), resumes a conception of public space as a communicational platform for human exchanges. The street, as a metaphor for public space, is above all a common place where the public is constituted as a group and the city as a stage (Chaudoir 2004).

In the introduction to the book *Urban Communication Regulation* (2018: x–xi), Harvey Jassem and Susan D. Drucker offer an understanding of regulation as "resource allocation and conflict resolution. [...] Sometimes governments regulate who can say what to whom through what channels and under which conditions." These regulatory processes shape freedom of expression, access, actions and voices. Regulations are grounded in the idea of conflict resolution but end up creating consequences beyond the written norms.

It is crucial to keep in mind that street performance regulation is multifaceted, assuming mainly three (non-exclusive) roles. First, it serves to legitimize activities by recognizing their existence and creating a legal framework associated with them. Second, it is a mechanism of protection, given that it allows busking to happen and establishes the conditions for its legal, acceptable existence. Third, regulation can also produce exclusion and exacerbate inequalities, especially if its norms and frameworks are too strict, and if it does not take into account all the complexities of an activity.

As with the concept of street performance, there is no single, simple definition of "public space," nor does it necessarily exist in opposition to "private space" (see, e.g. Lefebvre 1991; Carr et al. 1993; Sennett 2002; Jacobs 2011). People often have to deal with different types of spaces and their nuances, from the personal space of the body to impersonal spaces in the city: the transition between spaces in the urban environment begins in the private space of the self (of the individual's mind), moving on to the personal space of each person, the intimate space of the home, the interpersonal spaces (such as schools and work environments), then arriving at the impersonal spaces of the streets (Madanipour 2003). In addition, this work draws from analyses on how streets (Fyfe 1998), avenues, sidewalks (Duneier 1999; Loukaitou et al. 2009) and squares (Low 2000; Low and Smith 2006) can be contested (Amster 2004, Ellickson 1996), occupied and re-signi-fied, since their uses and purposes vary over the years and according to who uses a certain space, with different purposes. Fraya Frehse's (2016: 134) analysis of inequality in Brazilian public spaces played a key role in thinking about how the dynamics of coexistence between passers-by and non-passers-by in public spaces define the types of access and reproduce inequalities.

Here, public space is understood and used as a spectrum of urban spaces with various degrees of openness. Public space is not opposed to private space but encompasses different degrees of access, availability and promotion of encoun-ters. It is based, in principle, on the idea of spatiality that can be accessed freely and free of charge, and it is transformed as the barriers of access increase, such as paying a fee or using physical elements like fences, gates and hostile architecture (Benjamin 2019; Petty 2016). However, it is important to emphasize that even when these spaces can be publicly accessed, it does not mean that people will have equitable access, as class, income, gender identity and expression, race and ethnicity, influence the way in which public spaces are accessed. The privatization of public spaces takes many forms, from visible features to subtle forces (such as policing and lighting), and the nuances of "urban illegalisms" (Telles 2009) require an acknowledgment of the porous ambiguity of legality in public spaces. Another relevant approach to public spaces is to frame them as liminal:

> Buskers performing in spaces where ownership is uncontested, such as shopping malls, find themselves subject to summary ejection. It is only in public spaces where they can, within the limits of the law, perform freely. And it is more useful to define those spaces as liminal, rather than the people who move within them. In the street we are all liminal, we are all in transit; and so, the liminality of individuals or groups in the street is not a useful differentiation from others. It is more helpful to consider the street itself as liminal—as a space in which normally socially disparate groups not only may but must interact—and then to look at what those different groups do with the street.
>
> (Bywater 2007: 103)

When looking at the street as a liminal space, one can think of performances in public spaces as marginal, understanding "marginal" as something that contests the ownership of the liminal street—and this is what street musicians do. In more formal performances, the space in which they take place is often already an indicator of their legitimacy—these artists usually have to adapt to the space given to them (with the exception of the circus, which carries its own space). The "liminal artists" find themselves in a different position: they need to create the performance space, before or during the presentation, at the same time that they are influenced by the space in which they act (Bywater 2007: 107–08).

Street music can also be interpreted as an imposed sound that catalyzes conflicts. It is difficult to contain sound, even more so in certain environments such as subways and squares. The annoyance of music (Trotta 2020) can cause a negative perception of street music by residents, leading to the demand for more incisive regulation to decrease the street music nuisance. At the same time, there are urban design strategies to prevent buskers from occupying certain spaces, such as the tunnel connecting the Champs-de-Mars metro station, on the orange line, in Montreal. In it, there are signs that say "loitering" (*"flânage"*) is prohibited, and speakers play instrumental ambient music throughout the day. To play in the tunnel, the musician would have to compete with the sound coming from the official sound system, which is practically unfeasible.

It is not uncommon to see people walking past buskers wearing headphones or covering their ears while grimacing at the sound coming from the instruments and amplifiers. When carrying out participant observation with subway musicians, for example, it was easy to notice that a large number of people navigate the public transit system with their headphones on and eyes glued to their phones. As Simone Pereira de Sá (2011: 6–7) affirms, the specificity of mobile media allows passengers to use music to regulate their moods, affections and sensibilities while walking around the city (Pereira de Sá 2011: 6–7). Raphaël Nowak and Andy Bennett (2014: 11), when analyzing sound environments, show us how space usually implies music being imposed on listeners (such as in stores or shopping malls) or being used to block sounds that one does not want to hear (on iPods or phones), raising "the question of collective forms of listening (music being imposed) and personal forms of listening (music being chosen). [...] Yet, the choice over music within a sound environment does not overrule all variables of the sound environment."

In the regulatory framework of the city, another aspect to take into account when studying busking is the urban night, a contested realm of the city that offers many possibilities to understand the social and cultural dynamics of life after dark. Conflicts emerging from disputes over silence, zoning, occupation of public spaces and Bohemian districts are usually translated into regulation and, in many cases, controversial law enforcement. According to Will Straw (2017: 222):

> The night is a period of time, but it is a "territory" as well, with its own populations, rituals, and forms of citizenship. Across the practices of the night, that territory may be occupied or traversed, regulated or made free.

As an emerging transdisciplinary field, Night Studies (Celis and González 2020; Gwiazdzinski et al. 2020; Gwiazdzinski and Straw 2015; Kyba et al. 2020; Straw 2020) offers us a lens to think about busking at night.

Noise complaints and regulation play a big role in night-time governance. Under a public order policy and noise control regulations, for example, governments try to frame and discipline street music. Usually restricted to daytime and business hours, street music has limited space for performance after dark. Many musicians playing and passing the hat in the streets or subways also perform in closed venues during the night, from restaurants and wedding parties to concert halls. The rhythms of the city are still quite connected to daylight, and the regulation of street music weighs heavily on noise control policies (Keller 2010; Bass 1864; Picker 2003). From the limitation of performance time for each artist to the prohibition of using amplifiers or percussion instruments, all the aspects involved in playing in public spaces are subject to public order scrutiny. Most municipal laws and norms related to street performance set a period in which the performances must take place above the ground. In Montreal, the current regulatory framework for street performers allows these activities to happen between 9 a.m. and 11 p.m. and the use of amplifiers is allowed (if they cannot be heard 25 m from the artist), while percussion instruments are forbidden. Rio de Janeiro's Street Performer's Law limits the performances up to 10 p.m. and amplifiers should not be over 30 kW.

Temporalities associated with everyday life rhythms, such as commuting, working hours, school periods or leisure activities usually influence the way musicians use streets, plazas and squares. The donations to the musicians' hats depend on the patterns of people moving around the city in their daily schedules. The songs being played, how the musicians are dressed and the background noises are also crucial factors in this equation.

These interactions between the built environment, people and music are crucial to understanding the power dynamics presented in this chapter. Given how intertwined the history of busking is with regulating public spaces, the discussion that follows will look at some key aspects that have been unfolding since the nineteenth century and influence how we govern street performance in contemporary cities.

Nuisance and control

Street performance has been seen, throughout history, as entertainment for the masses, especially the working class and those with less access to certain circuits of art. Simultaneously, it also faced opposition from so many different sectors of society, such as public authorities, professional associations, residents or even other artists. Because of the need to manage the conflicts that emerge when a busker plays at a street corner, the history of street art became intrinsically intertwined with regulatory efforts, control tactics and law enforcement, greatly covered by studies carried out by Sylvie Genest (2001) and Sally Harrison-Pepper (1990), for example. This trend of regulating and strictly controlling busking in favor of public order was strengthened in the nineteenth and twentieth centuries. Notable examples of countries in the Global North dealing differently with the issue are England, France and the United States.

England

In England, we can find records of the disputes between buskers, residents, police officers and local governments in the nineteenth century. An emblematic case is presented by Michael Thomas Bass (1864) in his work *"Street Music in the Metropolis,"* in which he reports the conflicts between street musicians (especially organ players and brass bands) and residents of Victorian London. Bass was a brewer and member of parliament who took up a battle against street musicians of the period, representing the artistic, scholarly and ecclesiastical classes. His report, which also presents the point of view of several residents of London— such as Charles Babbage and Charles Dickens—and the local media about the unwanted presence of these musicians, at various times, sheds light on issues that today we characterize as xenophobia, racism and classism. Bass (1864) documented—and supported—the legal and political attempts to end the nuisance of busking in London:

> I [...] move for leave to introduce a Bill for the better Regulation of Street Music in the Metropolitan Police District. This public intimation gave rise to a more varied and voluminous correspondence than I could have believed possible. Nothing but a careful perusal of their letters could convey any idea of the anxiety felt by so many persons for some effectual check to the daily increasing grievance of organ grinders and street music. The petitions for presentation sent to myself and other Members of Parliament have been numerously signed by all the learned professions. I have received letters and memorials from the most distinguished literary and scientific men. One very remarkable memorial has been addressed to me, signed by the leading Composers and Professors of Music in the Metropolis, and supported by upwards of 200 signatures; it is headed "THE STREET-ORGAN NUISANCE."
>
> (Bass 1864: vi)

This collection of letters, opinions and the like has the main function of supporting the dispute that Bass wages against street music in London, supported by various segments of society so that he could modify the current legislation through a bill, punishing and further criminalizing street musicians in order to "demonstrate what great obstacles are opposed by street music to the progress of science, art, and literature; and what torments are inflicted on the studious, the sensitive, and the afflicted" (Bass 1864: vii). The law in force at the time (The Act of Parliament which constitutes the existing Law touching Street Music in London, is the 2 and 3 Vict. c. 47, s. 57, intituled "An Act for the further improving the Police in and near the Metropolis") that dealt with the regulation and enforcement targeting street musicians was controversial because it only allowed homeowners, personally or through their servants, to ask street musicians to leave the neighborhood due to the illness of a resident of the house, or other reasonable reason; musicians who refused to leave could be fined or detained, as long as they were seen committing the offense by a police officer (Bass 1864: 1–2).

The central point of Michael Bass's (1864: 2–5) argument revolves around the fact that little or no compensation can be obtained by those who are bothered by street music since the musicians must be playing on a public road and close to the residence, but if they touch an alley or garden, for example, even close to the residences, it is up to other people to find the necessary causes to file a complaint. In addition, the issue of reasonable cause was also seen as a problem, since it is a subjective concept, which was at the discretion of the police officer responsible for dealing with the musicians when called upon by the people who could legally do so—and there were instructions so that the police would not remove the musicians directly, but would report the problem to their superior. Another problem pointed out by Bass concerned the wording of the current law saying that only the owner of the home could enforce the law, excluding any tenants and people who did not own their homes from asking the police to remove the musicians. Furthermore, the law required that the police officers see, with their own eyes, and hear for themself the offense being committed so that they could act.

Feeling not enough was being done to alleviate the collective anxiety, Bass used his position as a representative of the people to "remedy the evil" that was street music (Bass 1864: 5). Chapter 2 of his work is dedicated to giving visibility to those who "suffer" from street music and brings letters and memorials from people "who have evidently been severe sufferers from street music" (Bass 1864: 6) and who praise measures to regulate street music in London. These reports present the opinion of intellectuals, artists, clergymen and other people from the wealthier classes, who say they are seriously affected by the music of street organs and brass bands, to the point of interfering both in the health and in the work of these individuals. In one of the letters collected by Bass and written by Mark Lemon, there is the following statement: "The objection to street noises is not a matter of taste, it involves the progress of honest labour, and the avoidance of great mental affliction" (Bass 1864: 7). Thus, the work of street musicians is not seen as an honest way to earn a living, but a way for profiteers to earn money while afflicting parts of the population. Many of them speak on behalf of people who are sick, or on the verge of death, for legislators to take a decision that favors residents:

> Those who want to hear barrel-organs, should think it no hardship to have to call the grinder into their houses, and give him a few pence to play for them; but in a well-regulated country, it is a disgrace and an anomaly that one inhabitant of a square, by giving money and encouraging these pests, should have it in his or her power to make 300 or 400 people more or less uncomfortable, miserable, or frantic, according to their nervous disposition.
>
> (Bass 1864: 9)

Among the various new kinds of noise that emerged after the industrial revolution, one controversial noise was deemed to cause physical effects on people in Victorian London: the songs played by street and itinerant musicians (Picker 2003). Because some believed that busking could cause physical damage to people, an intense public debate was generated around the issue, usually linked to xenophobia in relation to those who exercised the profession:

> The objection to street noises, after all, literally is not a matter of taste but of hearing. Street music generated xenophobic and aesthetic debates, to be sure, but it had damaging impact as a corporeal problem, an urban disease that disturbed not only the duties of middle-class professionals but also their well-being. That Victorians cast the street music problem as one relating to the body is not surprising, given the pervasiveness of illness during the period and the resulting cultural emphasis on the healthy body as indicator of moral and mental fortitude. Critics have approached literary manifestations of illness from feminist perspectives to demonstrate "the persistent attempts by Victorian writers and physicians to define the terms of human physicality, to locate in the body the source of sexual and social divisions, to create a physiological blueprint that would explain the meaning of racial difference and restore a sense of social and material order."
>
> (Picker 2003: 65)

In one of the letters addressed to Michael Bass, the Queen's harpist J. Balsir Chatterton says that these men playing in the streets "torture London society with the dismal strains of their organs, and other instruments, are not bona fide beggars, but the hired servants of some speculating individual in the City, who provides the instruments" (Bass 1864: 9). The letters reflect divided opinions between people who advocate for the eradication of street musicians or greater regulation and enforcement of laws and those who appreciate the musicians' presence in the city. However, the latter group has no voice in Bass' work.

Many of the letters speak on behalf of the poor, saying that even though they don't appreciate these musicians, hope that the "Bill for the regulation of street music" would be strengthened, because "every time a Bill is brought in, and fails, the hands of the musician are strengthened" (Bass 1864: 12). In addition to appealing to health cases and speaking on behalf of the poor, there are xenophobic expressions throughout the documents, such as saying Italians (frequent buskers) "were generally persons of very bad character and most immoral habits [...], wherever Italians congregate there is a fearful amount of vice" (Bass 1864: 13).

One of the letters presented by Bass in defense of regulatory intervention in the activity of street musicians, written by Charles Babbage, shows us data collected by him on the number of interruptions caused by organ players, brass bands and monkeys: In 90 days, there were at least 165 interruptions. In another letter, the sender complains that there is no possibility of the population not hearing the noises caused by the musicians since the sound permeates the city—and that it is possible to listen to music in London for a trifle, not justifying the existence of these musicians playing on the streets. This last argument is reinforced in other letters, stating that music is available to anyone who wants to look for it, and not being necessary for it to exist in the streets, since it encourages laziness in idle servants (Bass 1864). Buskers playing organ grinders were also seen as vagrants without any talent:

> [A]ny vagabond who carry one can play it—that is, grind it by turning the handle, and therefore can continue the annoyance longer than any other street musician, without having been at the pains and trouble of acquiring a certain degree of musical skill.
>
> (Bass 1864: 31)

In the records of the parliamentary procedures of this debate on street music, from 1863 onwards (Bass 1864), the arguments of the opposition to such strict regulation of musicians are laid out, claiming that they continue playing because there are people who appreciate the music and that there are other noises that can annoy London residents too:

> Lord Fermoy maintained that the existing law was sufficiently stringent. Mr. Babbage had put it in force on several occasions, and had punished, he thought unjustly, a great many poor musicians. There could be no doubt that if street music were not enjoyed, it would not be provided; the fact that the bands were

paid proved that they were liked by large number of people, and no person had a right to interfere with the innocent tastes of his neighbour. If street bands were put down, many other things must follow. Huge drays full of beer-barrels, even though the name of "Bass" might be inscribed on them, were a serious annoyance and inconvenience, and some people might say they ought not to be allowed to pass through the streets in the daytime. The fact was, however, that the streets must be free for all legitimate occupations. He hoped that in another Session a measure would be brought in, not to suppress street music, but to provide places of recreation in the metropolis to which the lower and the middle classes could go to hear bands play.

(Bass 1864: 85)

The debate was intense, with opinions often opposed, in parliament, in the media, among citizens. It was about keeping everything as it was, demanding a total ban or stricter regulation, containing time and place: "[S]ome fear that nothing short of prohibition of all street music will afford relief; others advocate the restriction of street music to certain areas and within certain hours" (Bass 1864: 99).

Paul Simpson builds his research upon these reports that historically, musicians connected to the courts had a certain stability and recognition, while musicians who played in the streets, street vendors and nomads did not share the same fate. In a lecture given in July 2015, Simpson states that this way of seeing street musicians has not completely changed:

[I]tinerant performers were and are still very often viewed suspiciously by the authorities, and society as a whole, for their very mobility. Being perpetually on the move can mean that these individuals do not obviously fit within common social structures based around belonging and boundaries. [...] Further, associations between such performers and beggars or vagrancy recur through this history of street music. Where the act's quality did not meet an individual's taste, a common response has been to dismiss a performer as "basically a beggar" or "little more than a vagrant". [...] Due to a variety of reasons (Victorian London) is by far and away the most extensively documented period in the history of street music. The "street music problem", as it was then called, emerged in light of the growing class of musical, medical, legal, and literary professionals—individuals with means and opportunities to voice their concerns, if not to escape them—for whom street music disrupted the quiet tenor of their home-working lives.

(Simpson 2015: 2–3)

This dispute around the profound "discomfort of street music" portrays the dramatic changes in the soundscapes of the United Kingdom in the eighteenth and nineteenth centuries, marked by the industrial revolution and the increase in population density in cities—generating a significant increase in noise and all sort of sounds that were unfamiliar to the public. Many people moved to cities in search of factory jobs, leading them to inhabit increasingly crowded and noisier spaces, and busking was added to the daily noise of the city:

> [S]treet music represented a festive disruption of disciplines—in this case, those of middle-class work and leisure—and in its very status as "hackneyed slang," it presented a provocative other, an alternative to acceptable middle-class definitions of music. Just as the itinerant performer came to symbolize an invasive affront to professional labors, so his music became a "lawless" other, a threatening double to the respectable concert or drawing-room recital.
>
> (Picker 2003: 63)

Given this scenario, Michael Bass's Bill was seen as an important regulatory mechanism—and the publication of the book *Street Music in the Metropolis* in 1864 played a key role in the approval of the (modified) Bill. According to Picker (2003: 64–65), "Bass's act sought through legal means to establish such a distinction between professionals and intrusive outsiders, but only by facilitating professionals' greater meddling in those outsiders' affairs." However, the approval of the "Street Music Act," despite all the efforts of Bass, Babbage, Dickens, Leech and others involved, ended up having little effect on the disappearance of street musicians in London (Picker 2003: 77). Many years later, in the pre-war period, T. S. Eliot wrote about urban noise with a very different view of the relationship between noise and the city: "describing the noise of prewar London, T. S. Eliot noted 'many babies, pianos, street pianos, accordions, singers, hummers, whistlers,' yet concluded: 'I find it quite possible to work in this atmosphere. The noises of a city so large as London don't distract one much; they become attached to the city and depersonalize themselves'" (Picker 2003: 79).

Bywater (2017) discusses the marginal musician through visual comments, such as the engraving "The Enraged Musician," by William Hogarth, made in 1741, which shows the soundscape of London at that time in the form of chaos, with assorted instruments, screams, confusion and, at the window, a musician who covers his ears in fury, silenced by the noise that comes from outside.

Often, disputes around the issue of noise can assume characteristics of cultural control focused on specific segments of society (Bywater 2017; Genest 2001; Picker 2003; Reia 2019), or take political biases, from private interests that undermine public spaces and the cultural nightlife of the city through laws of silence and truculent enforcement (Talbot 2007). England has disputed the uses and appropriations of public space with street artists over time and these conflicts persist in several cities.

In 2014, the public debate revolved around a belief that the intense regulation of street performances was killing busking in London. In an article written by Munira Mirza for *The Guardian* newspaper on April 23, 2014, a need to balance interests without suppressing the vitality that street performances historically brought to London spaces was highlighted. According to Mirza (2014: n.pag.),

> local authorities are imposing licensing fees which can make it prohibitive for many musicians. Buskers complain that certain parts of the capital have become no-go areas and they are sometimes moved on by the police even when they know they are not breaking any rules.

The heavy penalties that go as far as selling off instruments to pay for them pose a worrying trend, given that "busking is a crucial part of the music eco-system in the capital; a chance to develop and grow in front of the public" (Mirza 2014: n.pag.).

In 2015, the Mayor of London launched the Busk in London project to support, facilitate and encourage performance in the city's streets. The project has an online platform, ambassadors, supporters and a partnership with a contactless payment platform.[1] In addition, the platform provides useful information for artists, such as a code of conduct ("Buskers' Code") that presents the regulation of the activity, possible penalties and other delimitations of street performance, by region and presentation condition. For musicians, for example, it provides recommendations on the volume of presentations (which should be kept slightly above the street noise level) and guidance such as not repeating the same song in the same place, as well as providing safety rules (like not placing the equipment in places where people can trip) and leave the space clean and tidy, without damaging any physical structure. Artists can pass the hat and receive donations, but they cannot sell CDs, for example (they need a specific license for that). There is a special section for law enforcement, which emphasizes where it is legal to perform and under which conditions, how to avoid problems with the police and neighbors and, in the last part, defines that street performance is not begging: "Busking shouldn't be confused with begging. Buskers put a lot of effort into their act, give a performance and entertain the public" (Busk in London, n.d.).

The growing importance of busking in the United Kingdom is also reflected in the scholarship and exchanges between researchers and practitioners. In May 2019, the first "Street Music Conference" took place in Norwich, UK and brought together specialists from all over the world to talk about urban musical practices that have the street as their primary platform. During the conference, a comprehensive report on street music in the United Kingdom was launched (Bennett and McKay 2019). It features historical accounts and notes on the recent domestic and international cultural policy and legislation landscape. One of the main takeaways is the central role of advocacy and campaigning to safeguard the rights of buskers in increasingly contested public spaces.

France

In France, the regulation of the activities of street performers began in the Middle Ages. One of the first records of regulation concerning jongleurs in France dates to 1321 (Fournel 1863). This regulation was adopted by the jongleurs, and it divided them into masters and apprentices, reserving to jongleurs who were part of the guild the privilege of performing at parties, detailing who could perform, under what circumstances, and the penalties for the offenders.

In 1407, the guild extended its jurisdiction not only to Paris but to the entire kingdom. The jongleurs saw the heavy regulation of their practices as progress in the pursuit of an income, but in the end, regulation turned out to be a major obstacle to the development of the profession with all its rules and statutes (Fournel 1863). Despite the protection of the kings (Charles VI and Louis XI), the profession of jongleurs and minstrels was transformed after the regulation, as some activities of the profession that were not part of the guild disappeared, leaving them only the function of "playing their instruments," because "of the historic juggler, this complex, universal artist, only the musician remains standing, and soon there will only remain the fiddler of the balls, the violin that makes people dance" (Fournel 1863: 171–72). The guild of minstrels, like all guilds, lasted until the end of the monarchy and was suppressed by the edict of 1776 and the decree of 1789—and the decline of the profession was even recorded in the compositions of the musicians themselves.

More than 200 years later, between November 1997 and April 1998, an exhibition called "*Musiciens des rues de Paris*" ("Street musicians from Paris") was on display at the *Musée National des Arts et Traditions Populaires* in Paris. The exhibition resulted in various materials covering its relevance, such as the text by Florence Gétreau, the exhibition's organizer: "*Le son dans l'exposition Musiciens des Rues de Paris*" (2003). The exhibition was created from archives, documents, fieldwork with street musicians and collections held by associations such as "*Ritournelle et manivelles*," which tried to show the great continuity, through the centuries, of social aspects, regulatory frameworks and civil disobedience inherent to the buskers' occupation of urban spaces. Gétreau highlights the regulation of street music throughout history as a perennial force, which strengthened in the early nineteenth century as the growing number of street musicians led the Paris police department to regularly update governance mechanisms that were spread throughout the territory, leaving traces over the years:

> The authority has left many marks of this omnipresence, both in the censorship files of the peddling commission which controls the printed songs, and in the police

archives which define the places, issue permissions and trade medals [...], and control the repertoire.

(Gétreau 2003: 125)

Even with a modest budget, the exhibition managed to bring out an important approach to music in French public spaces, covering relevant topics of regulation and control. Eliane Daphy (1997) writes about traveling singers in "*La gloire et la rue: Les chanteurs ambulants et l'édition musicale dans l'entre-deux-guerres.*" Daphy states that there were many people earning a living in the streets of Paris during this period and differentiates the street musicians and singers from the traveling musicians:

The first are beggars who beg after their performance. The latter are merchants or sellers of songs. They are paid on a percentage basis on the sale of the sheet music they sell to the public after their performance. They benefit from a special legal status: they must have permission from the Paris prefecture and have their traveling book stamped by the commissioner of the chosen location.

(Daphy 1997: 95)

Traveling musicians must have licenses issued by the Paris City Council to sell their songs, and it is estimated that there were more than 200 licenses issued between 1900 and 1950. Street musicians were seen as beggars, who passed their hats after their performances, becoming a real nuisance for publishers and songwriters—since they did not pay royalties for songs performed in the streets. The traveling musicians, on the contrary, sold the songs and, therefore, the public performance they performed in the streets was seen as advertising for the products (Daphy 1997). In addition to selling sheet music and interpreting the songs being sold, these street professionals should have a deep knowledge of the urban space, since in order to earn money, it was necessary to know the good places, which varied according to the acoustics, season, day of the week and public events—demanding professionalism from musicians and singers, which also translated into knowledge of the streets and the city. The institutionalization and (self) organization of these artists was such that in 1906 they created a union, the "*Syndicat des chanteurs et musiciens marchands de chansons*," with 43 members, three of them women. One of the objectives of this organization was to recognize the quality and morality of the artists, differentiating these people from vagrants and beggars who sang in the streets. The other was to have negotiating power with the publishers (Daphy 1997).

At one point, traveling and street musicians and singers became part of Parisian folklore, appearing in songs and other media such as films (René Clair, "*Sous les toits de Paris*"; Marcel Carné, "*Les portes de la nuit*") and magazines ("*Paris qui brille*").

They go down in history as a collective character—not as real individuals, although some gain notoriety, such as Piaf, or even Lily, *"dernière chanteuse des rues"*— battling between having the street as a transitory place for glory or a residence for those who had no choice (Daphy 1997).

Florence Gétreau, in the text "Street Musicians of Paris: Evolution of an image" (1998), offers a perspective on the regulation and visuality of street music in the French city over several centuries, through images collected from archives, engravings, illustrations, texts and documents. According to Gétreau, nineteenth-century street musicians and singers had to operate under the new legislation: it was necessary to have a license ("permit") issued by the police agency and use a token with a registration number; only a few places were allocated for performances. There was also censorship of the songs' contents, and the representations of the period showed the nomadic musicians of the Baroque period, primarily organ players and one-man bands, in a derogatory way, unlike the musicians of the corporations, who had official authorization and government recognition:

> The guild of instrumentalists and dancing masters enjoyed a monopoly in playing for urban ceremonies, festivals, dances, and public festivities: street musicians, not being members of the guild, were viewed as disloyal competitors, or as beggars. Hardly tolerated, they were also a worry to respectable people and the police. They were indeed often represented as maimed, blind in one eye, drunkards, robbers. In the middle of the seventeenth century, engravers liked to describe misshapen, somewhat terrifying, creatures, associating music with debauchery, as explained in the verses printed with the engravings and intended to provoke laughter.
>
> (Gétreau 1998: 68)

Barrels and organ-grinders were present in other European locations since the eighteenth century and their performances were also subject to local laws, such as the regulation that included traveling musicians sanctioned in 1822 (Gétreau 1998: 70). This was the first ordinance that addressed all street singers and musicians in France, called *"Ordonnance de la Préfecture de Police de Paris du 2 septembre 1822"* (Moyencourt 2015). Despite the relative continuity of the activity of street musicians and the control of these practices, the visual language that represented them was changing, revealing

> not only an evident evolution, albeit very slow, but also variations in the production and dissemination processes, and in the textual commentary. Progressively, one can detect the development of stereotypes. The street musician is certainly an emblematic figure of the city.
>
> (Gétreau 1998: 71–72).

During the twentieth century, the French public space continued to be highly regulated and controlled for street performances, as can be seen in the work of Gétreau (2001: 17), who places the Parisian street as a "regulated musical space," from the seventeenth to the twentieth century. The analysis of these four centuries of street music regulation in Paris shows striking issues, such as fear—of musicians in a situation of begging and their proliferation, as well as the propensity they had to transgress the rules and compete with each other—and the use of regulation as an instrument of censorship and control. At all times, it was the associative movement of artists that sought to negotiate with the authorities in search of better conditions and legitimacy.

In France, from the nineteenth century onward, there was an evident intensification of the rupture with the idea of an ancestral legacy of street performance, as artists sought legitimacy and worked toward the institutionalization and formal recognition of busking as a part of the cultural sector. Although there seems to be a perception of continuity and homogeneity of the festive occupation of public spaces under the generic term "street performance," this perception is illusory (Chaudoir 1997).

Street performance is an artistic movement that has a specific purpose, gaining visibility through some groups and shows in the second half of the twentieth century (Chaudoir 1997). The apparent resurgence of festive urban manifestations that seem to descend directly from an ancestral, traditional approach but under new forms is inserted in a context of crisis (urban, social and political). Based on the idea of reviving the street and giving new meaning to urban life, this mode of intervention in the street takes up the idea of public space as a communicational support for exchanges (Chaudoir 1997).

Significant changes took place in street performance from the 1970s onward, a period in which cultural facilities, regardless of their form, entered into a voluntary logic of symbolizing places and festive spaces; simultaneously, they help in the construction—even if momentary—of the collectivity. In addition to ancestry, Chaudoir (1997) believes that other possible origins and affiliations of cultural intervention in public space can be sought in three axes: the agit-prop, the happening and the American radical theatre. Therefore, the complexity and multiplicity of street performance influences will shape its contemporary configuration and its movement in search of legitimacy.

One cannot minimize the role that institutionalization played in street performance for its legitimacy and recognition as an artistic sector in France, with the French Ministry of Culture and Communication (renamed Ministry of Culture after 2017) as one of the main institutions involved:

> One will be struck to note that the terminological fixation ("street performance", in a single word [...] goes hand in hand with the recognition by the institution

(the Ministry of Culture, in particular) of a phenomenon which escapes them and of which they perceive, through multiple filters, the relevance and topicality.

(Chaudoir 2003: 168)

Britta B. Wheeler (2003) discusses the recent institutionalization of art, which can serve to reflect on the issues of institutionalization faced by street performance in the past decades: "institutionalization, in a conventional sense, is a process by which a new kind of activity in the arts becomes more or less routine as it is accepted by a wider audience" (Wheeler 2003: 491). Therefore, the increase in venues for performance, specialized magazines, organizations, categories for government funding, and departments in universities, all indicate institutionalization.

In the case of buskers, the 1970s stand out as the decade in which new modes of intervention in the public space erupted for artists of a new generation, who sought to work outside the consecrated places of art and who found in the public space an expressive platform for the right to "(re)find" the city (Chaudoir 2003). The emergence of seminars, meetings of artists who worked in "free" spaces, debates on the terminology of artistic practice and the gradual recognition of the media and society showcase the growing mobilization of busking around shared practices. Most of these results were achieved because of the artists' efforts, such as the "integration of street performance to the institutional landscape [...]. The price to pay is based on what has been achieved: spontaneity recoils before subsidies" (Wallon 2001: n.p.). Certain documents point out the high institutionalization of street performance in France (such as the proceedings of the colloquium "Diversity of Street Arts in Europe" from 2007 and the comparative work by Karniewicz from 2004), stating that it is probably one of the most institutionalized in Europe, thus finding itself in a "privileged" position (speech by Stéphane Simonin in Floch 2007: 7).

Specialists affirm that street performance as we know it today began to take shape as a field in the 1960s and 1970s in Europe (Stoffel 2011). In France, this process intensified in 1968 in the context of a political upheaval the country was going through. During the 1970s, some groups of artists started to look for the public "where they are," and throughout the 1980s, these groups experimented with new ways of producing shows, new relationships with the public and different ways of exploring public spaces (Stoffel 2011: 2). It was in the 1990s that street performance consolidated and legitimized itself in France and Belgium, for example, from the increase in the number of companies and the recognition by public authorities, the media and cultural networks. As the sector consolidated and increased its audience, the scarcity of financial resources became evident.

By the end of the 1990s, street performance was finally recognized as a sector, alongside other sectors such as dance, theatre and music, and this recognition was followed by the establishment of a department within the Directorate General for Culture of the French Community (*"Direction Générale de la Culture de la Communauté française"*) and by the allocation of a specific budget (Stoffel 2011: 3). Even if the budget available at that time was not able to cover all the demands, the identification of the sector by the public authorities is an important step for its consolidation, in addition to guaranteeing its inclusion with full rights in the cultural network, as a specific professional sector. From this, it is necessary to create and maintain policies that allow the sector to strengthen and maintain itself.

The approach of the French Ministry of Culture to street arts began in the 1980s, mainly through support for Lieux Publics[2] and policies for the sector that were implemented in 1993 through national centers (such as Lieux Publics and HorsLesMurs until 2016) and distributed regionally to festivals and companies. Karniewicz (2004) and Dapporto (2000) affirm that Lieux Publics was one of the main organizations to contribute to the institutionalization of street performance in France, having been created by Michel Crespin in 1982. However, the symbiotic relation between public power and busking is intertwined with many challenges:

> Street performance cannot exist without public authorities. In addition to the relationship of interdependence that exists between these entities, street performers quickly express their desire to be recognized as belonging to a sector in their own right. In response to artists' desire to be legitimized as performing arts professionals, the Ministry of Culture is putting measures in place, albeit timidly. The ministerial attention paid to the street performance develops after that of the local authorities. For the public authorities, it remains difficult to take street performance into account in their disciplinary and aesthetic complexity, and for artists to fit into the boxes of the ministry. The multidisciplinarity that qualifies the field does not facilitate its official definition.
>
> (Rousselin 2013: 19)

Aiming to gather data and amplify its understanding of the emerging sector, the French government commissioned various materials throughout the 1990s and 2000s on street performance. Many of these documents tried to map and hold a grasp of the sector, such as the study carried out by Franceline Spielman (2000), at the request of the Ministry of Culture, *"Les questions de formation, qualification, transmission dans le domaine des arts de la rue."* Spielman mapped the context and approaches of busking, discussing professionalization, aesthetics, originality, formation and dissemination. Also in 2000, The French Ministry of Culture launched a bulletin on the "street performance economy" (*"L'économie des arts de la rue"*). At the time, there were around 800 French street art companies listed by HorsLesMurs, which mobilized between 3500 and 4000 people, being a sector of constant renewal, in which only 17 percent of the companies had more than fifteen years of existence. The sector was characterized by great diversity and heterogeneity, with theatre and dance as 48 percent of companies, followed by circus (27 percent), music (18 percent) and visual arts (7 percent) (Ministère de la Culture et de la Communication 2000: 1).

In 2004, a major intervention plan was launched by the Ministry of Culture for the period 2005–07. The "Temps des arts de la rue" was a three-year plan for structuring the street performance sector, whose mission was to carry out studies to improve aid instruments, as well as the creation and dissemination of street performance. The early years of the plan served as a test, which little by little brought spectators into dialogue with the construction of a cultural policy for street performance. The 2000s saw increased financial support by the government for various street performance initiatives (Rousselin 2013). In 2010, following the findings of "Temps des arts de la rue," inspired by the National Federation of Street Arts, several existing places of creation and production were labeled as National Centers for the Street Performance ("Centres nationaux des arts de la rue"—CNAR) by the Ministry of Culture.

The legitimization of busking as an autonomous and consolidated field, recognized by public authorities and society, can be seen in the increase of scholars studying the subject, in its insertion in the academic environment through courses, and in the overlap of academia and the street performance sector (Boulanger 2002). In addition to academic legitimation, it should be noted that this process takes place simultaneously with governments (via regulation and funding), the media (presence of the topic in public debates) and society in general. The creation of associations also plays an important role in the process of legitimizing and institutionalizing street performance, such as the emergence of "*La Féderation—Association Professionelle Française des Arts de la Rue*" in France in 1997, which aimed to advocate for the interests of its members (Boulanger 2002). In the 2020s, most of these organizations and associations are still active, working in networks or under a new arrangement.

United States

Some books on buskers—street musicians, specifically—were crucial to the development of this work, as they portray in-depth research and lived experiences about several ramifications of street performance. Three of these emblematic books focus on the U.S. context: Patricia J. Campbell, who wrote *Passing the hat: street performers in America* (1981); Sally Harrison-Pepper, who studied street performers in New York and wrote the book *Drawing a circle in the square: street performing in New York's Washington square park* (1990) and Susie J. Tanenbaum, who looked at New York's subway musicians for the book *Underground harmonies: music and politics in the subways of New York* (1995).

Lily E. Hirsch (2010: 352) believes that the existing academic literature on street performers has responded to the historic devaluation that this profession faces by romanticizing the artists, rather than taking into account many of the contextual and identity issues. Hirsch highlights some exceptions to this trend, such as Michael Bywater (2007) and Paolo Prato (1984), and claims that both Tanenbaum (1995) and Campbell (1981) present partial and overly positive views of buskers, a celebration of the existence of these practices and how they are important for cities. In view of these criticisms, it must be said that all these works mentioned, even though they have an often-idealized vision of what it is to be a street artist, contribute in an essential way to the understanding of these (fairly undocumented and non-quantified) practices.

Patricia J. Campbell's book covers four cities in the United States: New York, San Francisco, Boston and New Orleans, showcasing the buskers' various trajectories, interests and motivations. Some of the characteristics and stories told by Campbell were still present in the narratives told to me by my subjects.

> Other than the love of freedom there are no common characteristics of personality, background, or life-style that describe the average street performer. Men in their late twenties and early thirties predominate, but my interviewees ranged from five to seventy-five years old, and there were a number of women among them. Some performers have never worked the streets anywhere but in their home cities. Others wander the whole country or travel a consistent circuit between two or three cities. [...] Not all love the street—a few spoke bitterly of their life as outcasts. Not all are committed to it for life or make their whole living from it. But in every city I visited I found a hard core of people who had dedicated their lives to the street, who saw themselves as bearers of tradition, and who were articulate and thoughtful about their place in the world.
>
> (Campbell 1981: 12–13)

An interesting point raised by Campbell is the buskers' territorial occupation of the city; they will seek the "good places" to perform and pass the hat, reflecting "not only the density and receptivity of pedestrian traffic but an uneasy mental map of truce between performers and civic authorities. The good places within each city are part of the folklore of the road for performers" (Campbell 1981: 18). Campbell also addresses the fact that merchants can be hostile to artists based on a feeling they drain money that could be spent in stores in the region, especially in tourist areas, leading to—often regulatory—clashes between shopkeepers and artists. One case took place in San Francisco, where stages were created in the port area, frequented by many tourists, and artists needed licenses to perform there—which generated heated discussions between artists, many of whom opposed the idea of stages, auditions and licenses to perform in a space that is public. Harrison-Pepper (1990) also affirms that shopkeepers and business owners can be major historical enemies of street performers, seen as people who would disturb the orderly image of the place and competitors. Campbell points to San Francisco as a place where being a street performer was not well regarded by the police:

> Everyone agreed that the situation now is not as bad as it is used to be, but almost every San Francisco performer I interviewed who had been at it for more than two years had spent at least one night in jail.
>
> (Campbell 1981: 23–24)

In New York, pedestrians were more accustomed to buskers and understood that they were part of a kind of "street scene." However, unlike other cities with milder weather throughout the year, New York's street performance season only lasts a few months (from May to October), when temperatures are ideal. During the rest of the year, the artists have to find other ways to make a living (Campbell 1981: 25). In the study, New York City police officers were quite lenient with buskers. Interactions were limited to police officers asking the artists to leave the places they were performing, and arrests were rare. Central Park was one of the favorite places for artists to perform. If an artist wanted to perform on the Staten Island Ferry, it was necessary to have a special license—but even so, the license did not guarantee that they could perform in peace, pushing them to civil disobedience:

> Performers are only allowed to play the ferry once a month, and the permit is no guarantee of a hassle-free performance—the boat people sometimes invoke the fine print that forbids solicitation of money. For these reasons most performers don't bother with official permission: they simply work the ferry until they are caught and told to leave.
>
> (Campbell 1981: 27)

Boston, on the contrary, was mentioned by Campbell as a good city for street artists, since it had a licensing system that legalized performances in almost any place. Stephen Baird, a troubadour, was partially responsible for the regulation and legitimization of busking in Boston. In the 1970s rescued an almost forgotten law of 1878 that allowed the licensing of street performers. However, he soon discovered the law only allowed performances in some of the few blocks in the center and prohibited the artist from receiving payment for his performance. Later on, in 1973, he managed to modify the law, which then allowed licensed musicians to receive voluntary donations: "The open guitar case had become legal, a situation that existed in no other major city in the United States"; after these efforts, it was necessary to educate the officers about the law, which took approximately three years (Campbell 1981: 31). At the time, for USD10 a year, musicians could perform in most public spaces in the city, but police conducted background checks on musicians who applied for a license, although they tended to turn a blind eye to offenses involving soliciting money and performing in the streets. One of the problems with the law at that time was that it only included street musicians, leaving out other types of performance and artistic practices out of the authorization system, but not necessarily forbidding them either.

New Orleans, as portrayed by Campbell (1981) in the 1980s, was the hometown of street performances in the United States, mainly due to the feeling of camaraderie and respect among the artists. This feeling of proximity was due to the fact that artists could only perform in three places in the French Quarter. This vision of a scenario free of conflicts and camaraderie is an example of the romanticization mentioned by Hirsch (2010). At the time this book was written, The Music and Culture Coalition of New Orleans (MACCNO) developed a "Guide to New Orleans Street Performance" intended "not just for performers, but also for enforcement agencies, businesses, residents and neighborhood organizations" (MACCNO n.d.). The document introduces the regulatory framework, drawing from the existing City Code of Ordinances, and clearly explains the existing law in a user-friendly format.

Campbell devotes an entire chapter of the book to the annoyances faced by artists and issues of regulation. When working on the streets, artists are subject to many annoyances on all sides; the hopelessness of this context begins to dissipate with recognition through legal frameworks that point to a new way of accepting street performance. To be on the streets is to be open to interactions with all kinds of people, as well as being susceptible to confrontations with individuals taking advantage of the crowd around the artist. Street vendors, notes Campbell (1981: 224–29), despite being in a situation very similar to that of artists from a legal, regulatory and informal labor point of view, do not see them as allies. In addition to these obstacles, artists also constantly have to deal with the police and their different forms of repression so that "the busker can never be sure what to expect from the local cops" (Campbell 1981: 231). The basis for this randomness in the treatment of street art in different locations is related to its legal status:

> The basis for all this patternless and unpredictable torment is that busking is not illegal but extralegal. Nowhere does the law say that a person may not perform on the street, nor does the law usually admit that a person may perform on the street

within certain limits. This lack of legal status leaves busking open to interpretation as begging, obstructing traffic, or disturbing the peace.

(Campbell 1981: 233)

As in France and elsewhere in the world (Rio and Montreal included), artists' response to the encroachments and suppression of rights in the United States was to organize and join forces to bargain for better working conditions, in the form of associations, protests and in volunteer work to safeguard their rights.

Sally Harrison-Pepper (1990) looked at street artists in New York, specifically in Washington Square Park, located in Greenwich Village, between 1980 and 1984, highlighting the hostility toward buskers. By looking at the regulation and control mechanisms of busking, one can understand the opportunities and limitations of the practice, and how it interacts with urban life. Harrison-Pepper's work focused on varied artistic manifestations, but all have as a common denominator the use of public space and the practice of passing the hat, in a specific square.

The main competence of the busker for Harrison-Pepper (1990: xv–xvi) is to be able to transform "city space" into "performance space," turning stairs into benches, or turning street furniture into decoration that is part of the show. Street musicians have other specificities, such as the question of the sound that spreads throughout the city and annoys people (Trotta 2020), as well as the need to transform the "place into a stage," ignoring their surroundings as much as possible. Harrison-Pepper (1990: 10–12) quotes Ray Jason, a famous street juggler from San Francisco in the 1970s, who lists three main categories and motivations for artists to be on the street: (1) People who perform in the streets because they can't find a job anywhere else; (2) People who appear in the streets hoping to be "discovered" and (3) People who choose to perform in the streets because they enjoy being there. Harrison-Pepper adds a fourth category and motivation: people who perform in the streets because they like the freedom it provides, being outside the "system" and being self-sufficient, "they said their shows presented alternatives to the existing system of governance or conventional ways of living" (Harrison-Pepper 1990: 10–12).

Few major cities throughout history have treated buskers as assets to urban life, cultural scenes and tourism. Harrison-Pepper states that part of this rejection by cities and public opinion is related to the issue of public image, as well as the irrelevance of these practices from an institutional point of view. New York, for instance, saw a perennial presence of street performers that increased throughout the nineteenth century. Around 1897, the media portrayed the proliferation of street musicians, with the presence of organ players. The feeling in the city during this period was increasingly one of rejection of these musicians, who were seen as beggars.

A decade later, around 1945, musicians and singers would gather in Washington Square Park on Sundays after lunch. They received permits from the (then) Parks Department, which were affordable and could be renewed monthly. They sang and played in a specific place in the square, while other groups, in search of silence, went to other parts, with people "self-regulating" the space. However, in March 1961 licenses were banned, with the justification that "unpleasant-looking" musicians were playing in the square and asking for money. This measure led to protests from artists, who gathered in the square to demonstrate and ended up being repressed by the police—with ten people arrested and many injured on the day (Harrison-Pepper 1990: 25).

People from the community—reverends and lawyers—volunteered to help the musicians who were opposing the measure; one of the lawyers, Edward Koch, would become mayor of the city and later sanction frequent arrests of street performers in New York. A few days later hundreds of musicians gathered in the square to protest the ban and what followed was a legal battle and more protests by musicians, who circumvented the ban by singing a cappella:

> On Sunday, May 7, 1961, six hundred folk singers, led by Reverend Moody and Israel Young, again assembled in Washington Square. On this occasion, however, they sang a cappella, having discovered that the Parks Department ordinance required permits only for those singing with instruments.
>
> (Harrison-Pepper 1990: 26)

After the conflicts, it was decided that the musicians could perform with their instruments first, and the municipal public authorities should receive the registrations for the musicians' permits. In the 1980s, the period when Sally Harrison-Pepper's fieldwork was conducted, laws continued to link busking to begging and arrests were frequent; a busker in San Francisco ranked cities according to the average time an artist could perform before the police arrived. In New York, that interval was only twelve minutes. Faced with this challenge, the artists had to negotiate various limitations and earn a living within the conditions given to them, and it was always necessary to know the laws in force.

Having to deal with this complex context and regulatory framework, busking became an extralegal activity in New York and as long as the artists remained within certain rules and in some places in the city that "accepted" this type of activity, the police would leave them alone (Harrison-Pepper 1990: 39). The struggles for musicians to perform in the New York subway system were also remarkable and interestingly studied by Susie J. Tanenbaum (1995), who mapped the actors involved in subway music:

> There are the musicians, who want to earn money, express themselves, reach out to New Yorkers, or use the subways as a stepping stone to greater fame. There are

the riders, who may welcome the pleasant sound or resent the additional "noise." There is the Metropolitan Transportation Authority, which sponsors acts through the Music Under New York program, and its subsidiary, the New York City Transit Authority, which authorizes musical performances, both sponsored and spontaneous, underground. There is the court system, which prompted these quasi-governmental authorities to change their policies by affirming subway music as a form of free expression, but which also upheld their right to regulate it. There are transit police officers and station managers who, charged with maintaining order, silence musicians for breaking rules that may not even exist. And there are TA employees (other than transit police) and concession stand workers who have many opinions about music that some of them have to listen to all day long.

(Tanenbaum 1995: x–xi)

Tanenbaum (1995) sees the subway musicians as extraordinary, admiring their courage and believing that the songs played underground are a pleasure and a relief for all discomfort of being in transit, "a wake-up call from the mindless rush of the subway routine." It is a romanticized view that Tanenbaum casts on subway buskers, almost homogeneously, which is criticized by Hirsch (2010) and Chatterjee (2022). Although essential for understanding the New York subway music ecosystem in the 1980s and 1990s, the book addresses some issues with enthusiasm that are not reflected in other contexts—such as in Rio and Montreal.

The origins of music on the subway trace back to the creation of the system's first tunnel in 1900, when bands played at subway celebrations, seen at that time as a huge public event. From the beginning, what Tanenbaum (1995) calls "freelance subway music," was present in the subway system in a spontaneous, diverse way with varied motivations and non-authorized existence until the 1980s. Busking has since persisted in the subway system until the present day, passing through processes of regulation and control.

In 2022, buskers can perform in NYC under certain conditions. Buskers normally do not need a permit; however, a permit is required if they intend to use a sound device (loudspeaker, megaphone or stereo) or perform in or next to a park. The local police precincts are in charge of permits for a sound device, which cost USD45, and the Department of Parks and Recreation issues permits for performances in or next to parks for USD25 (valid for a month). Artists are not allowed to use park benches, tables, ping-pong tables and other urban furniture during their performances, and some parks in NYC have specific spots for buskers, identified by a medallion.

Underground, musicians can play in NYC subway stations without a permit. Only acoustic performances are allowed on subway platforms and, if the musicians want to use an amplifier, they should use the subway mezzanines. Performances inside subway cars are not allowed—but happen regardless. Safety must be a priority and musicians need to be careful not to block any access, stand 25 feet away from booths and 50 feet from offices. The music should never be above 85 decibels, so people can hear the announcements. Similar to other cities, the subway in NYC has a program called "Music Under New York—MUNY"[3] that is dedicated to promoting buskers and scheduling performances at prime locations. The process involves applications and auditions, earning them a membership, customized banners and invitations to perform at events.

The following chapters present detailed stories about busking and its regulatory frameworks in Montreal and Rio de Janeiro, both above and below ground. Some similarities and challenges are unique to these locations, but the overall conversation can benefit cities worldwide.

NOTES

1. See: https://www.foundinmusic.com/busk-in-london. Accessed June 9, 2024.
2. Historically the leading national centre for creation in public space in France, Lieux publics was awarded the label Centre National des Arts de la Rue et de l'Espace Public (CNAREP) in 2017. See: https://www.lieuxpublics.com/en. Accessed June 9, 2024.
3. See: http://web.mta.info/mta/aft/muny/. Accessed June 9, 2024.

PART II

ABOVE GROUND
AND BEYOND REGULATION

3

Legitimation:
The Blurred Boundaries between
Policy and Control

Much of the history of street performance [...] is found in laws that prohibit it.

Sally Harrison-Pepper, *Drawing a Circle in the Square* (1990)

The voyage across the dual city is indeed a familiar feature of Montreal literature. The trajectory is often along the east-west axis of Sherbrooke Street or Sainte-Catherine—and the direction of the walk often indicates the emotional temperature. Going east means exploring the density and colour of an endless proliferation of shops and houses; going west promises a grander and more varied landscape, the attractions of downtown, the monuments of the city core.

Sherry Simon, *Translating Montreal* (2006)

During the U.S. prohibition, Montreal was a well-known destination for people seeking a vibrant nightlife, entertainment options and alcohol consumption. In 1920, when the U.S. Congress passed a constitutional amendment prohibiting the production and consumption of alcohol, the city "became a centre for culture and entertainment for all North America. [...] A veritable oasis for anyone seeking to escape the policies of the prohibitionists, Montreal quickly built up an attractive reputation for tourists, investors, gamblers and raqueteers" (Bélanger 2005: 18–19, translation added). Located not too far from the Canada–U.S. border, the city has been home to a variety of music scenes, disco cultures (Straw 2022), nighttime economy activities (Straw and Reia 2021; VibeLab 2023), creative industries, art and festivals (Bild et al. 2022) over the last century. Part of the province of Quebec, Montreal (also known as Tiohtià:ke) is a fluvial island home to around a million people in its metropolitan area, located on unceded Indigenous lands (Kanien'kehá:ka Nation). French is the official language of Quebec, but Montreal has a multiplicity of languages thanks to its historical and contemporary communities that immigrated from all over the world. Neighborhoods such as Little Italy, Little Portugal and Little Magreb coexist with Hasidic families and the diaspora from Chile, Brazil and Greece. The map of the city might confuse those who first arrive, given that East is not really East, nor is North (Figure 3.1). Fragmented by languages, administrative disputes and an ever-changing cultural landscape, the city thrives through its loud summer and long, silent winter.

To better understand Montreal, we should consider that language plays a central role in everything we do. There, traveling means translating and walking

FIGURE 3.1: The city of Montreal, QC, Canada. Source: Map data from OpenStreetMap, City Roads on GitHub by Andrei Kashcha, 2023. http://openstreetmap.org/copyright.

through the streets of the city implies a combination of familiarity and strangeness. From the 1980s onward, Montrealers realized that the barriers of historic communities were more fluid than previously believed:

> Many Montrealers came to realize that the official voices of Montreal's historic communities became more diverse and less easy to define according to strict linguistic or ethnic categories. Neither the positions of the francophone nationalists nor the anglophone opposition reflected the everyday life of Montreal. This consciousness was dramatized in 1992, during the commemoration of the 350th anniversary of the founding of the city. Innovative celebrations brought many new groups onto scene— the varied populations of the industrial south-west, native peoples, immigrants— groups whose existence had been obscured by the hoary battles of the national epic. All of a sudden the variety of the communities sharing Montreal burst into visibility.
> (Simon 2006: 7)

Annick Germain (2016: 4) writes about these communities from the perspective of immigrant neighborhoods in Montreal, using the idea of neighborhood in a specific way: "as a territory of collective urban life, as distinct from merely the immediate surroundings of a place of residence," which does not necessarily respect official and administrative divisions. For the author, neighborhoods in Montreal are the ideal scale to analyze the issue of immigration in the city and influence the construction of a cosmopolitan city. In addition to intercultural policies, it is the daily life of Montreal that ends up shaping the multifaceted complexity of the city. Although quite specific in the past (Chinese, Greek, Portuguese, Italian neighborhoods, etc.), the territories of immigration in Montreal become quite fluid, meaning that on the island of Montreal, there is less and less evidence of a city divided into two (one multiethnic and the other homogeneous) since there is a dispersion of immigration (Germain 2016).

In addition to immigrant neighborhoods and communities, it is important to look at Montreal's administrative division because it shows us the complexities behind any regulatory effort that shapes the city's territory. The entire administrative structure of Quebec and Montreal is quite complex, especially with regard to the division into metropolitan communities, cities, boroughs, neighborhoods, city halls and councils. According to Raphaël Fischler and Jeanne M. Wolfe (2012), the spheres of power deal with varied subjects, depending on the necessary instance: the federal government deals with matters of national importance (such as foreign relations, defense, monetary and fiscal policies, transport and communication nationalities, the northern territories and immigration) and is based in Ottawa. Below are the provinces that take care of aspects of local government such as education, health, social services, land-use planning and transportation. Local governments are completely under the control of the provinces, which can create or abolish municipalities and dictate development policies, with municipalities being responsible for much of their own financial sustainability—and also managing issues such as infrastructure, parks, economic development, public safety, social housing and cultural venues (Fischler and Wolfe 2012: 532–34). Three important aspects of the municipal reform that the government of Quebec promoted in the early 2000s in the Montreal region deserve to be highlighted, the first being about the Montreal metropolitan area and its administrative specificities:

> The city of Montreal itself is located on an island that until recently it shared with twenty-seven other municipalities. Between 1979 and 2001, the central city and its near suburbs were members of the Montreal Urban Community, a regional body in charge of planning for the island as a whole and of administering shared infrastructure and services, such as main roads and cultural facilities, policing, and property valuation. In 2000 the Quebec government, then run by the Parti Québécois, introduced sweeping and radical local government reform to the major cities of the province. The arguments presented for the reform were both greater efficiency and greater equity [...]. In the region of Montreal, the reform first meant dissolving the Montreal Urban Community and replacing it with a more extensive metropolitan body. The Montreal Metropolitan Community [...], which has been in operation since January 1, 2001, is made up of eighty-two municipalities and has jurisdiction over an area of about 18.6 miles (30 kilometers) in radius, roughly contiguous with the Census Metropolitan Area.
>
> (Fischler and Wolfe 2012: 536–38)

Montreal's metropolitan community was given responsibility for issues that affect the region, from waste management to cultural development. The second important aspect of the municipal reform promoted by the Quebec government at that time was the merger of the 28 municipalities on the island of Montreal to become the "megacity" of Montreal—and the merger of six south coast municipalities to form the city of Longueuil—allied to the efforts of the mayor, Pierre Bourque, whose slogan was "one island, one city" (Fischler and Wolfe 2012: 538). He lost the race in the first election of the new megacity to Gérald Tremblay, who opposed the centralized model that had been imposed.

The third aspect of the reform was, then, the redesign of Montreal's city administration into 27 boroughs ("arrondissements" in French), nine originating from the old downtown area of Montreal and eighteen representing the annexed municipalities. The forced merger began on January 1, 2001, raising the ire of several sectors of society and giving the Liberal Party the opportunity to capitalize on the discontent to win the 2003 elections, promising (among other things) to allow municipalities on the island of Montreal to step out of the merger. By then, "fifteen municipalities elected to reconstitute themselves, even though they would not get back all their original powers. Merged services would remain regional in scale and would be run by an island-wide body, the Agglomeration Council" (Fischler and Wolfe 2012: 539).

For Pierre Delorme (2009), Montreal is one of the most managed cities in the world, referring to government decisions that, seeking to simplify management, end up making it even more complex. The various administrative, legislative and public policymakers make understanding issues in the city of Montreal a difficult task, full of challenges and possible paths. With all its historical complexity, cultural diversity and the constant idea of learning to live together, Montreal ends up occupying an interesting place as an object of study, on the one hand, and a catalyst for urban life studies, on the other, serving as an exemplary "school" of urban studies in North America (Germain 2013). Accepting a less rigid version of the concept of "school," Germain (2013) believes that studies on Montreal can offer interesting perspectives on being a city of "in-betweens," based on a wide variety of research done on urban life, showing the exchanges and differences that cohabit the city, with special attention to public spaces and sociability.

An emblematic symbol of Montreal is the Mount Royal ("Mont Royal"), a mountain just west of downtown that is also a public park. Throughout the eighteenth century, the original name of the city, Ville-Marie, was gradually replaced by the designation that referred to the mountain, creating the city itself: "without Mount Royal, so it seems in these popular narratives from around 1900, Montreal would never have been" (Kopfler 2009: 140). In the present day, Mount Royal Park occupies a prominent place in the city's imaginary, from postcards to the meaning it has for residents, featuring several artistic performances throughout the year, scheduled or spontaneous, such as the weekly free festivals on summer Sundays called Tam-Tams and general busking.

Many of the city's public spaces are occupied throughout the year, including the winter, even if less frequently. Montreal has countless festivals, parties, ephemeral artistic installations, spontaneous occupations, street fairs, temporary open-air markets and ice-skating rinks that encourage its residents to participate in activities collectively. Montreal has several public spaces that have been built and reshaped over the years. Dagenais (2002: 352) presents data on the evolution of new leisure spaces (from parks to squares and playgrounds) in Montreal between 1880 and 1940, showing that in 1880 the total of these new spaces was 28, but after 1940 they totaled 108.

Public spaces in Montreal are highly regulated, controlled and surveilled. Parks close overnight, and buskers cannot use any street or square available. Regulatory grey areas create confusion, and while major festivals occupy public spaces every year, smaller festivals focused on busking struggle to secure funding. These contradictions are relevant to the discussion presented here because they put street performance into the broader context of the city's governance mechanisms and policies.

Spectacular city

Other than being known for its harsh winters—that affect busking in extreme ways—and confusing administrative layers, Montreal is also world famous for its festivals. The Montreal International Jazz Festival started in 1980 and holds a Guinness World Record as the largest jazz festival in the world. Osheaga is a music festival that brings international musicians to the city. The Mural Festival is focused on graffiti, and Mutek is focused on the promotion of electronic music and the digital arts. POP Montreal brings together hundreds of musicians every year and Suoni per il Popolo is rooted in exploratory musical forms. The Montreal First Peoples Festival engages the artistic creation of indigenous peoples, the *Festival international des arts du cirque* showcases circus performances and Piknic Électronik is a weekly electronic music festival that takes place every Sunday during the summer. Les Francos de Montréal features French-language performers from all over the world, and Nuit Blanche à Montreal takes people outside for an entire night of cultural programming in the dead of winter. There are also many other festivals that feature a diverse range of music and performances.

Montreal has been a city of festivals since the nineteenth century. One example was the Montreal winter carnival, which lasted a few years and offered the residents opportunities to practice winter sports and visit ice castles (Dufresne 1984). In the twentieth century, the city hosted Expo 67, bringing attention from the international community. The city invested in public infrastructure to receive visitors, building the metro system that opened to the public the year before. In 1976, the city hosted the Olympic Games and faced the typical challenges of hosting a mega-event, such as corruption scandals, delays and debt (Todd 2016). The Olympic Stadium, which became an architectural landmark, has been repurposed and incorporated into the local imaginary, standing in the east of the island, near the Botanical Gardens, as a reminder of the mega-event aftermath. The metro turned into a stage for disputes between buskers and the public transit agency, later becoming a place for the legitimation of street musicians. In the twenty-first century, the celebration of the 375th anniversary of Montreal took place. The local government spent years planning the celebration, which included major events, interventions in urban design and infrastructure, along with various cultural activities. There is often a spectacle going on at any given time in the city, all year round.

Anouk Bélanger (2005) analyzes how these urban spectacles have been forming the imagination of Montreal based on an analysis of the Faubourg Saint-Laurent, one of the oldest neighborhoods in the city:

> Montreal, and its particular festive history which is still rooted around the Faubourg Saint-Laurent, becomes a privileged place to grasp the constitution of the urban imagination as it is expressed through the processes of spectacularisation of the city. It is clear that the imagination worked by the spectacular participates in the transformation of urban space through its dialectical relationship with the vernacular and not through simple processes of fusion and assimilation.
>
> (Bélanger 2005: 32).

According to Bélanger, Montreal's imagery has always been linked to that of an open-minded city (unlike other North American cities, seen as cold and puritanical). For her, the Faubourg Saint-Laurent has and continues to contribute to the image of Montreal as a festive place that concentrates an important part of a "myth" of the diverse, plural, tolerant and festive city (Bélanger 2005: 17). Loison and Fischler (2016) state that Montreal still has an important area of commerce, residences and various activities in its central region. It survived the modernist urban renewals of the 1960s–1970s and the many parking lots that occupied the region in the 1980s, combined with the use of private cars as the main means of transport. In the 1990s, the projects for the region changed:

> After the recession of the mid-1990s, when the future of downtown seemed compromised, the City of Montreal launched a series of ambitious plans and projects to boost its vitality and stimulate private development. The main idea behind this policy is well known to those who have studied revitalization efforts in Western cities: an attractive public realm and a concentration of similar activities can create a social and economic dynamic of urban (re)development.
>
> (Loison and Fischler 2016: 349)

One of the first projects that implemented this perspective in the early 2000s was the Quartier des Spectacles. Based on a coalition between property owners and government representatives, the city created and redesigned buildings (with provincial funding) and public spaces, using local talents to develop these spaces and street furniture. The region was seen as problematic, revolving around nightlife, addictions and sex work. Efforts to revitalize the area were part of a campaign to strengthen the central region and position Montreal as a creative city with global appeal (Harel et al. 2015; Loison and Fischler 2016).

Montreal has played several symbolic roles in the Canadian social imaginary. It was the Canadian "sin city" (Straw 2014), configured as a cosmopolitan city in which the universes of sex, sin and leisure found literary, musical, art and cinema scenes. Montreal has been properly "mythologized" in several media: "The corrupt yet compelling worlds of the thirties, forties, and early fifties in Montreal have been more than adequately eulogized and mythologized in a number of book and films dedicated to showing the city's once seedy glamour" (Stahl 2001: 100). This era used to be seen by the English-speaking elite as a period in which Montreal stood out as a cosmopolitan and modern city, followed by a period of decadence.

The Quartier des Spectacles is part of what is historically known as Faubourg Saint-Laurent, one of three suburbs that developed outside the walled city of Montreal, which formed around the former Chemin Saint-Laurent, now Boulevard Saint-Laurent (also known as "The Main"). By the beginning of the twentieth century, especially around the 1920s, Rue Sainte-Catherine had become one of Montreal's main entertainment hubs, with its bars, restaurants, clubs, cabarets and theatres. Americans would come to the area during the U.S. prohibition period, and it was known as a notorious region of illicit activities:

> The rise of illicit and criminal activities, together with the growing obsolescence of the building stock, drove the middle class away from the Faubourg Saint-Laurent in the 1940s and 1950s. [...] Criminal activities drew attention of reformist officials, including a young lawyer named Jean Drapeau. In 1954, Drapeau successfully ran for mayor of Montreal on the promise of ridding the city of prostitution and crime and ending collusion among the mob, police, and officials. He wanted to "clean up" the city while at the same time maintaining its standing as a tourist destination, a dual objective that would be echoed half a century later.
>
> (Loison and Fischler 2016: 351)

The fact that Faubourg Saint-Laurent emerged beyond the walled region and on a path that generated commercial and cultural exchanges contributed to its configuration. With the demolition of the wall in 1801, Boulevard Saint-Laurent became the main street of the new city and its residents, and the "Lower Main" region became a reference in the Montreal imagination, with its myriad of day and night activities (Bélanger 2005).

This period is known as the golden age of Montreal nightlife and provincial authorities turned a blind eye to illegal activities taking place in the region. There was even an intertwining of the legal authorities with the illicit world, evidencing systemic corruption (Bélanger 2005). The stock market crash of 1929 had a significant impact on Montreal's entertainment industry, followed by the end of prohibitionist policy in the United States and the post-war morality campaign spearheaded by then mayor Jean Drapeau, which aimed to end the region's "moral chaos" through a "public morality" committee to clean up the city—mainly the Faubourg Saint-Laurent (Bélanger 2005). New regulations and control of activities in the region reduced profits and led it toward a certain decay.

The period in which Drapeau was mayor (1954–86, with a hiatus between 1957 and 1960) greatly affected the central area of Montreal. Through "cleansing" efforts, moral campaigns and regulatory efforts to eliminate illicit activities, the public imagine of the city in printed media also changed:

> The image which attached itself to Montreal in the mid-1960s involved a revised view of the city's pleasures which cast them now as sophisticated and European. This new image was interwoven with that transnational cultural sensibility of the 1960s which emphasized tastefulness, cosmopolitanism, and technological progress.
>
> (Straw 2014: 138)

The city's print media included cheap and sensationalist "*journaux jaunes*," tabloids sensitive to the issues of the time and magazines that sold an image of Montreal as a modern metropolis to international visitors (Straw 2014). The changes were also shown in the construction of buildings such as the Place des Arts, the largest entertainment center in Canada, and structural changes in the design of the streets. From the construction of the first concert hall in 1963 until 2012, when a new symphony hall was inaugurated, the Place des Arts underwent profound transformations and became a space for hosting large cultural and "high culture" events, where marginalized and "low culture" activities had previously taken place. Montreal ended up following the path of several cities (a little belatedly, perhaps) of placing culture as an instrument of economic development (Loison and Fischler 2016). The design of the Quartier des Spectacles shapeshifted throughout its planning and implementation phases, and from a certain stage, the Partenariat du Quartier des spectacles became attached to the city, becoming

> a representative of local stakeholders [...]. From this point onward, the Quartier des spectacles would serve the broader goals of selling Montreal to the world as a creative city, strengthening Montreal's downtown, and broadening the city's tax base by means of private real estate development.
>
> (Loison and Fischler 2016: 355)

The centrality of culture in promoting Montreal as a vibrant, modern, metropolitan and creative city extends to other realms, such as policies for cultural development. Ambitious plans have been developed to situate Montreal locally and internationally as a "cultural metropolis." A significant example is the "Cultural

Development Policy Project 2017–2022" ("*Projet de Politique de développement culturel 2017–2022*"). The 123-page plan points to the challenges and opportunities for cultural policies in an ever-increasing context of digitalization and the search for the transversality of culture in society. The premise of living together is present throughout the action plan, which places the cultural policy acting as a "catalyst of human encounters, promoting diversity and innovation" (Ville de Montréal 2023: 18).

One of the key actors in this ecosystem is the Conseil des Arts de Montréal, a private organization founded in 1956 and funded by the urban community of Montreal. According to their website, "The Conseil des Arts de Montréal scouts, guides, supports and recognizes the creation, production and presentation of professional arts in Montreal." According to Christiane Bonneau, cultural advisor at the Conseil between 2013 and 2018, about her role:

> What sets us apart is that we want to finance creation, production, and artistic dissemination; we only fund organizations and artistic collectives. Individual artists are not funded, apart from certain residency projects. And our support is mainly concentrated in the city centre.
>
> (Bonneau 2016: n.pag.)

Despite the concentration of festivals, activities and funding in downtown Montreal, there is an extensive network of people and venues created far beyond the central areas. Since the beginning of the 2000s, Montreal has been notorious for its independent music scenes, away from the limelight of the Quartier des Spectacles and downtown. The city could be seen in a different light, combining two images of decay and resilience:

> Nowadays, the city is more likely to be conjured up as a complex milieu marked by a starker contrast: on the one hand, it is the epitome of the fallen and ruined city, a once robust financial and transportation hub whose glory days have long since waned; on the other, it is a city whose diminished economic status has fostered among local and non-local artists (and others) an image of a still vital cultural centre. These are not incommensurate images of the city. In fact, they inform two complementary narratives: one of economic decline and weakness marked indelibly by language tensions and sovereignty debates, and the other, a narrative of resilience as expressed through the mythical character of its enduring cultural life.
>
> (Stahl 2001: 100)

Montreal still resonates with a mythical aura, being seen as "a positively charged city-as-sign rendered in such a way that it remains a privileged locale for social and aesthetic activity" (Stahl 2001: 101). Montreal has been seen as the cultural hub of Canada, also positioning itself as a "city-as-scene," promoting and maintaining an idealized vision of centralized urban cultural life, with artists attracted by cheap rent, decent leisure at low cost, underemployment and open minds.

For years, music scenes and networks (Straw 2014a, 2002; Costantini 2015) played a very important role in Montreal and were present in different contexts: concert halls, shows, record labels, festivals, as well as on the streets and in the subway. The Anglo-Québec independent music scene was consolidated in the neighborhood known as Mile End:

> Since the late 1990s, Mile End has been considered the most vital area for rock-based music in Montreal and probably in Canada. It is the home of the influential group Godspeed You! Black Emperor, of their record label Constellation Records, of house music label Mile End Records; it is the "birthplace" of Arcade Fire, the location of Casa del Popolo, probably the most important venue for alternative rock-based forms of music in Montreal, and of the important venue Cabaret du Mile End; and it is the neighbourhood in which dozens of bands and other musical configurations started and in which some continue to live.
>
> (Straw 2015: 404)

The Mile End is slowly losing its musical centrality, mainly due to the gentrification that affects the area. The neighborhood became well known for the occupation of warehouses by artists, record labels and ateliers. However, it has suffered from regulation (requiring authorizations and licenses), enforcement (inspection and fines) and institutionalization (through government intervention) that led to the closure of certain establishments and that work together with other mechanisms to change the neighborhood and the activities carried out there (Bedford 2015). The situation has been drastically changing; real estate development and gentrification play a significant role in the decline of the Mile End as a hub for music scenes in Montreal. Smaller music venues struggle to remain financially sustainable among fines due to noise complaints and rent hikes. The situation was exacerbated by the pandemic (Straw and Reia 2021), leaving the future of many small venues uncertain.

At the same time, festivals that happen in non-central areas or with less visibility than the most established ones also face difficulties. One of the most relevant street performance festivals in Montreal is the Lachine Street Theatre Festival ("*Festival de Théâtre de Rue de Lachine—FTRL*"), created in 1997 (Figure 3.2). It claims to be the only one of its kind in North America with over 100 artists and creators transforming squares, streets and parks via temporary stages (Ville De Montréal 2015: 14).

Since it was established in the late 1990s, the FTRL attracted thousands of spectators and brought together over 250 collectives and companies of professional artists.

FIGURE 3.2: Festival de Théâtre de Rue de Lachine, August 14, 2015. Source: author's personal archive.

In the mid 2010s, the festival's main sponsor was Loto-Québec, a government agency created in 1969 to oversee the lottery and gambling in the province of Québec. On its webpage,[1] Loto-Québec presents itself as a mechanism the government created to contain organized crime and re-invest the gambling money back into society. By looking at the sponsors of festivals, we can start to understand where the money for cultural activities taking place in public spaces in Québec comes from, and also the power dynamics that influence street performance. Loto-Québec was created in the context of the upcoming 1976 Olympic Games in Montreal as an effort to tackle illegal gambling operators and organized crime. Over the past decades, it has been criticized for many reasons, especially as an enabler of the social damage caused by compulsive gambling. The institution annually allocates a considerable part of its budget[2] to sponsor festivals in public spaces (such as the FTRL and major festivals at Quartier des Spectacles), which also serves as a branding strategy.

Sponsorship of events is important to cultural policy as it pertains to the financial sustainability of creative practices. An interview with Lucie Lamoureux, director of the social responsibility sector, or "engagement sociétal," at Loto-Québec in 2016 exposed how the mechanisms of sponsorship for cultural events in public spaces in Montreal worked, especially for festivals like the FTRL. The interview exposed, in many moments, the logic of this type of sponsorship—based on the visibility of the brand—which imposes limitations on support for smaller festivals and cultural events. Overall, Loto-Québec sponsors some of the biggest festivals and events in public spaces in the province, many of them in Montreal, mostly free to the public, unlike in other regions of the province (Lamoureux 2016).

This kind of sponsorship has as its main objective and driving force not the promotion of arts and culture, but the visibility of the corporation and the invitation for people to consume Loto-Québec products and services, mainly casinos and lotteries. "The idea is to be present in events that generate economic and social benefits, and which allow […] the organization to convince citizens and the public to obviously invite them to visit our establishments" (Lamoureux 2016: n.pag.). The choice of events and festivals to be sponsored follows this logic of visibility and profitability for the sponsor, which places small and medium-sized street performance festivals in a rather complicated position, as they do not always attract crowds, especially when they take place outside the central areas of Montreal. According to Lamoureux (2016), Loto-Québec tends to invest in large events following four specific criteria: events must attract a large crowd of adults; sponsoring events for minors and children is not allowed; the events need to be already established in the city; and the events that offer the possibility of leading the public to participate in activities at Loto-Québec outlets like casinos. In the interview, Lamoureux (2016) affirmed that there are many funding options for festivals and smaller events— information that was disputed by the artists interviewed—so Loto-Québec prefers to focus on those who need the most money and attract the largest audience.

Lamoureux (2016) also stated that other major sponsors of festivals in public spaces in Montreal that sometimes work with Loto-Québec are telecommunications companies (such as Bell and Telus), banks, breweries and the Société des Alcools du Québec (SAQ). For the interviewee, it is increasingly necessary to bring the investments that Loto-Québec makes in cultural activities closer to the needs of the organization. For her, the corporation "cannot simply be generous for being generous," and must work to bring people to their casinos after the festival ends at 11:00 p.m., stating the fun "continues at the casinos" (Lamoureux 2016).

In addition to questioning whether these festivals will continue to be free, the director mentioned that the budget for sponsorship of these activities has decreased (it used to be CAD 14 million, and at the time of the interview it was CAD 11 million).[3] With a smaller budget available to invest in cultural events and festivals, Loto-Québec decided to prioritize large events. In this process, according to Lamoureux, Loto-Québec would have chosen not to sponsor the FTRL anymore since it is not able to offer the structure considered adequate for the visibility that is expected in return for the investments. No matter how "beautiful" or "attractive" the festival is, it does not provide what the sponsor expected:

The Lachine Street Theatre Festival is a very beautiful festival, ok? The problem for us, for a sponsor, is that it is difficult for us to be recognized that people are aware that we are sponsors, given the type of festival which has very little infrastructure [...] and it has a lot of mobile, public entertainers; on the site, nobody really knows that we are associated with this.

(Lamoureux 2016: n.pag.)

This interview excerpt touches upon topics that are transversal to this book. Primarily, how unreliable (and unavailable) private funding can be for cultural activities that are marginalized and do not have a massive appeal. Other than that, it portrays how the legitimation and institutionalization of street performance have its limitations: even when it gets closer to governments and corporate power, its survival and continuity are not guaranteed. This situation worsens if the street performance festival is held in the outskirts of the city, in public spaces that are not seen as valued as the central ones.

The FTRL also received money from the local government, as shown by the information available on the open data portal of the City of Montreal under "support for artists, cultural organizations and boroughs" ("*soutien aux artistes, organismes culturels et arrondissements*"), in the section "society and culture" ("*societé et culture*"). In 2015, the eighth edition of the FTRL received CAD 10,000 in support of festivals and cultural events in the range of up to CAD 500,000 (the total amount for that year was CAD 219,500). The same amount has been paid to the FTRL organization since 2011, according to data available on the portal. The funds available for this type of support have slightly fluctuated in recent years and represent a small portion of the municipality's budget for cultural events and organizations. In 2011, for example, the total budget ("*Grand total culture— Direction de la culture et du patrimoine*") was CAD 27,545,900.72, while the item in question supported 23 organizations with a total of CAD 274,500, of which CAD 10,000 was transferred to FTRL.

In the FTRL's 2015 edition, the Loto-Québec logo was still displayed in the program, on banners, and was projected after dark onto one of the walls in the park where the event took place. Other partners were the borough of Lachine, Bureau des festivals et des événements culturels de Montréal, Desjardins Bank (Caisse de Lachine), Groupe CLR, Conseil des Arts de Montréal, Conseil des Arts et des Lettres du Québec and the Patrimoine Canadien. The organizers also included a message in the program stating that voluntary contributions from the public were welcome so that the festival could remain free and accessible.

The FTRL featured diverse programming with multiple shows frequently scheduled at the same time and often interfering with each other, especially those with music playing loudly. People could walk from one show to the other without ever being too far from everything taking place simultaneously.

Festivals such as the FRTL are important platforms for buskers to bring accessible culture to the city, mostly to those who normally would not have access to theatre and musical performances in their neighborhoods. The regulatory frameworks designed to contain and organize buskers in Montreal take place far from Lachine, primarily in the downtown area, which will be explored next.

Permits, auditions and seasonality

Street music in Montreal is mostly concentrated in areas of the Plateau-Mont-Royal borough and, in a much more prevalent way, in the Ville-Marie borough (Figure 3.3). If one goes for a stroll in the central region of the city—mainly along the commercial Sainte-Catherine Street—and through the historic area, close to the Vieux-Port and Place Jacques-Cartier, it is possible to get an idea of the dimensions of street performance. The metro also serves as a stage for many musicians at designed spots. Encounters with music in public spaces are common, even if the reception varies a lot among residents.

Street performance in its various forms has existed in Montreal for years (Genest 2001)—and so have the strict regulation of these activities. Regulatory frameworks trying to tackle noise and enforce public order have been in place for over a century in Montreal, such as the rules established in the regulation n. 333, adopted on June 19, 1905 ("*Règlement pour empêcher que les piétons ou la circulation ne soient obstacles et la paix publique troublée dans les rues, ruelles et places publiques de la Cité*"). Section 2 prohibited disturbance and noise in streets, alleys and public squares, including shouting or disorderly music, for example. Sections 2a and 2b stated that people found loitering or drunk in public spaces or wandering after dark without a justification would be punished according to the law. The noise concern is still an important aspect of Montreal's regulatory framework—see, for example, the reports commissioned by the city in the cadre of the nightlife policy (Bélanger et al. 2020; Reia and Rouleau 2021). Currently, the law that defines and regulates noise in the city is the By-Law concerning noise (B-3),[4] which establishes maximum sound levels depending on the context and time of day, including limits for sounds emitted by musical instruments.

There are few historical studies and documented records on street performance in Canada—even fewer in Montreal. The number of scholars and experts looking at busking has increased over the last three decades, but few projects analyze the broader social and regulatory frameworks. As previously mentioned, the lack of data about street performance is surprising, be it in Canadian or

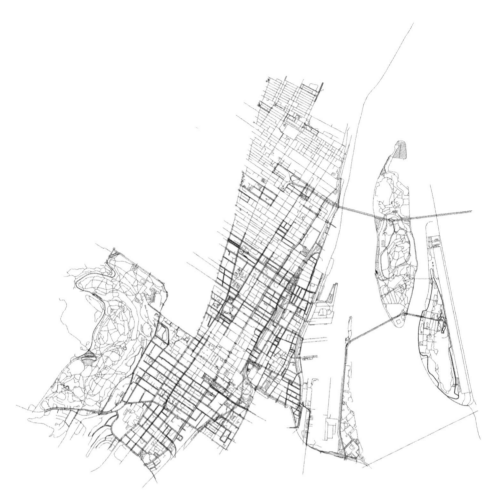

FIGURE 3.3: Ville-Marie borough in Montreal, QC, Canada. Source: Map data from OpenStreetMap, City Roads on GitHub by Andrei Kashcha, 2023. http://openstreetmap.org/copyright.

international archives, libraries, museums and open datasets. Murray Smith (1996) argues that the reason for the scarcity of information about buskers is twofold:

> First, in view of its low, often criminal, status throughout history, busking frequently has been either ignored by historians or treated in a perfunctory or romantically sentimental manner. Buskers have been portrayed as passive inheritors of predictable, i.e., stereotypically represented, musical traditions, and their role as active agents in the construction and reconstruction of their own historical identities has

not been emphasized. Second, [...] Canadian music history is, on the whole, somewhat sketchy.

(Smith 1996: 6)

As already stated by Harrison-Pepper (1990) and reiterated by Smith (1996: 8), many of the references and documents dealing with street music can be found in laws, trial records, police reports and other legal sources. This reality is no different in Toronto, where street musicians have been present since the beginning of the nineteenth century (around 1830), and their presence was linked to waves of immigration—mainly Italian (Smith 1996). It is possible that the public debate around the activities of "beggars and vagabonds" (categories in which street musicians were usually classified) was consolidated around the 1860s, a time when strict laws indicated a growing intolerance to vagrancy and its aftermath. The first reference to street musicians in Toronto is from this period. Other Canadian cities also featured buskers:

> Another early reference to musical busking in Canada concerns the city of Ottawa. For instance, we know that as early as 1872 at least three musical acts were performing in the streets of our nation's capital: an organ grinder and his monkey, a blind accordion-playing gentleman who sang "arias from various operas" led by a little girl who accompanied him on the "French fiddle," and a German band from New York.

(Smith 1996: 9)

The fact that in 1877 there was a high number of itinerant musicians in Ottawa indicates that street music had become relatively common in Canada at the end of the nineteenth century. Judging by the dates (1860s and 1870s), the types of instruments used, the age of the musicians (including children), repertoire and place of origin (Italy and New York), it is likely that most of the Ottawa musicians at that time were part of the same group originating in the South of Italy who migrated to various places around the world in search of a better life opportunities (Smith 1996).

While street music became less ubiquitous in Europe and North America in the 1900s due to legal restrictions, social disapproval and economic decline (Smith 1996), photographs show that organ-grinders persisted until at least the mid twentieth century in Toronto. In the 1970s, street musicians are drawn to the pedestrian Yonge St. Mall and, especially, underground—illegally playing in the city's subway system. In 1979, after being fined several times, one of the subway musicians, named John Musgrave, challenged the current law that prohibited music in the city's subway system and, with support from the local media, his campaign ended up forcing the subway administration to authorize musicians to perform on its premises.

Following a similar playbook of legitimization of busking worldwide, there was a need to prove the musicians were actually talented. For this reason,

> in 1981 a vinyl LP recording was made of the eight chosen subway acts. Called Music for Subways the album was recorded in the studio "as a test" to dispel what the producers considered to be a popular opinion that street musicians were not legitimate artists.
>
> (Smith 1996: 14)

During the 1990s the program expanded and faced protests from artists (known as "Troubadour Day"), led by violinist Ezra Azmon in 1991, who viewed the system of auditions and permissions to play on the subway as elitist. Despite not being able to make the subway spots available on a first-come, first-served basis without auditions, they gained extra spots to play in more stations, totaling 74 venues in 1993.

The idea of ancestry and continuity of the profession also played out in Ontario. The street musicians that Smith (1996: 15) studied until the 1990s identified with the stereotypical image of medieval troubadours and minstrels, which is not only an image that brings personal empowerment but also helps to create a political strategy through ancestry and the tradition of playing music in the streets.

Street musicians faced similar issues in Montreal. Efforts to regulate street performance in the city, aimed primarily at street musicians, began in 1857 (Genest 2001: 31). It was an intervention by a city councilor at a meeting that marked the beginning of the discussion and implementation of regulatory frameworks and law enforcement that condemned these cultural practices, leading to an almost complete exclusion of buskers from urban life. However, street musicians were an important source of entertainment and joy, especially for lower-income classes:

> At a time when there were few ways to be entertained in Montreal, singers, above all barrel organ players, assumed the role of broadcasters and promoters of light music to the mass of low-wage earners and even the Montreal elite. [...] Despite their poverty and their status as beggars, street musicians enjoyed the prestige of true artists with the people who listened to them.
>
> (Genest 2001: 31)

Genest (2001) considers a "street musician" to be any musician playing "outdoors" in public spaces, including traveling and nomadic musicians. Between 1850 and 1920, the press portrayed these practices as "marginal," outside the traditional system of cultural production. This marginality was also related to ethnic, cultural and physical specificities (illnesses), or even to age and economic status (unemployed, poor or so-called unskilled people). Musical practices in public spaces were an accessible means of being reintegrated into the economic system and earning a living.

Leisure and entertainment options began to multiply at the beginning of the twentieth century in Montreal, mainly through the expansion of parks and public spaces, reducing the population's interest in street musicians. The decline of busking was intensified by the growing availability of radio sets at more affordable prices, reducing the need for the presence of the artist in live performances as the only way to listen to music.

In 1937, the city government passed laws that challenged all sound sources, including traveling musicians. By 1940, the musicians who performed in the streets were no longer described as characters of urban folklore by journalists, who often looked at them with nostalgia and wrote about the possible "last" traveling musicians in Montreal.

Laws were also changing. The 1937 noise regulation was amended in 1976 and the fee musicians had to pay to obtain permits rose for the first time since 1889, from CAD 50 to CAD 100 in 1979 and to CAD 120 in 1985. Sylvie Genest, who conducted research on archival materials spanning 350 years of Montreal's history, identified that the municipal regulation of street musicians acts in two ways. On the one hand, as a "mechanism of the process of exclusion" of these musicians, and on the other hand, as "a tool of social condemnation of the marginality that characterizes them" (Genest 2001: 32).[5] Street music as a pathway to be informally reintegrated into the economy persisted in the early 2000s, as the marginality of street musicians was expressed through the distance they had in relation to the formal network of culture and leisure in the city:

> From the middle of the 19th century until today, the street has therefore enabled people suffering from different forms of social exclusion to take part, through music, in urban economic and cultural activity. It is from this angle that we must examine the issues of municipal regulations aimed at containing musical practice in the public domain.
>
> (Genest 2001: 34)

By the time Genest's work was published, Montreal was undergoing considerable administrative changes, which had an impact on the organization of the territory and the laws that governed the city and its boroughs. Until 1994, musicians were the only category of street performers who needed police approval to get a permit to play. The excessive persecution and control of street musicians in Montreal's public spaces came from regulations dating from the end of the nineteenth century. Such regulatory frameworks had taken shape through noise control efforts and, indirectly, poverty, an urge to contain informal activities in a period of crisis, in which the number of beggars increased (Genest 2001). Faced with strict regulatory systems, musicians engage in civil disobedience, contesting or ignoring the rules imposed by the authorities.

Even though much has changed, ambiguous regulation and civil disobedience are still part of a busker's journey in Montreal. Today, it is common to find street performers around the city, mainly in the boroughs of Ville-Marie and Le Plateau-Mont-Royal (Figure 3.4). In general, artists tend to be concentrated in the busiest streets, avenues and squares, close to subway stations, with shopping and leisure options that attract more people and, therefore, increase the chances of receiving donations in their hats and cases. Each borough can have its own regulatory mechanisms, but the only one in Montreal that regulates and controls busking through auditions and official authorizations called permits ("*permis*"), which function as licenses, is the borough of Ville-Marie, in the central region.

Lucas, part of the band Street Meat, addressed the confusion generated by the issuance of permits by only one borough, which combined with the lack of knowledge by law enforcement agents in the city, creates a scenario that is hard to navigate:

FIGURE 3.4: Busker performing from a van in the Plateau Mont-Royal, Montreal, September 26, 2015. Source: author's personal archive.

Everyone tells us something different. So, when we got the permit, the Ville-Marie borough said: "We are the only borough that emits permit, so your permit is good for the entire Island of Montreal. It is recognized by all the other boroughs." And then, we got stopped in the Plateau once by cops and they were like: "No, this is for Ville-Marie." And then we were, like: "Ok, but the people at the Ville-Marie told us it was good for everywhere." And then they said: "No, no, it's only good for Ville-Marie." So, there's this whole thing going on where the cops don't know the rules. A lot of the musicians don't know the rules. And even the people who emit the permits don't seem to know the rules. So, street performance is regulated, but it's not very well regulated. It's sort of just a big mess.

(Lucas 2015: n.pag.)

The growing number of street performers applying for a permit to use the public spaces in Montreal, in addition to the complex administrative organization of the municipality, shed light on the rigid governance and incongruences within public administration in the city. Ville-Marie, located in the city center, is known for its specific and detailed regulations for street musicians, public animators and balloon sculptors (CA-24-006). For many years since the adoption of the CA-24-006 norm, the Ville-Marie administration issued the permit based on the artists' talent recognized through auditions and professional associations, and frequently updated the rules and norms regarding how artists should proceed to obtain—and keep—their permits. Once approved, the permit was given to artists who pay all the fees and is valid for one year.

Penalties, mostly in the form of tickets and also part of the governance process for anyone who infringes the law, with fines ranging from CAD 100 to 1000. Recidivists could also lose their permit and the right to get a new one the following year. In 2017, for example, musicians needed to pay to open a dossier at the borough (CAD 55), plus CAD 150 to issue the permit (if they passed the audition). In 2022, the fees were slightly different: CAD 61 for the dossier and CAD 85 for the permit (and CAD 61 to replace a lost permit).

The penalties are based on strict rules that buskers must follow. Rules are often unclear and changed on a frequent basis. The broader regulatory framework encompasses laws about noise, public order and street performance in different locations of the island. The main legal framework for these practices is listed on the City of Montreal website, with selected examples in Table 3.1.

As Table 3.1 showcases, the regulatory framework a busker needs to understand and navigate the city is complex. The municipal online platform where legislation is available is not user-friendly and can be confusing even for people who lived in the city for many years. In 2022, the Ville-Marie borough prepared a simplified two-page guide for street performers. It contains the locations where

TABLE 3.1: Regulatory framework for buskers in Montreal, 2022.

Number	Who is responsible	Subject
CA-24-006	Ville-Marie	Regulation relating to musicians and public entertainers carrying out their activities in the public domain. See also: Administrative Codification 2018-04-14 and CA-24-006.3—By-Law amending the By-Law on musicians and public entertainers working in the public domain (2007).
CA-24-006, o.38	Ville-Marie	Ordinance relating to the code of ethics for musicians and public entertainers carrying out their activities in the public domain.
CA-24-006, o.49	Ville-Marie	Ordinance on the exercise of activities by musicians and public entertainers on public property (2016 season).
CA-24-006, o.61	Ville-Marie	Ordinance on designated locations and the exercise of the activities of musicians, entertainers and balloon sculptors in the places d'Armes and Jacques-Cartier and their surroundings.
P-1	Municipality	By-Laws concerning peace and order in the public domain.
T-3	Municipality	Regulation concerning special taxes on businesses, occupations and activities.
B-3	Municipality	Noise regulation.
C-3.2	Municipality	Regulation concerning the certificate of occupancy and certain permits.
CA24-006 o.46	Ville-Marie	Composition and operation ordinance of the joint committee of musicians, public entertainers and balloon sculptors.
CA24-006 o.62	Ville-Marie	Ordinance on the exercise of the activities of musicians and public entertainers and balloon sculptors on public property.

Source: Created by the author based on legislation available at: https://montreal.ca/ and the "guide des musiciens, des amuseurs publics et des sculpteurs de ballons."

they are allowed to perform at Place Jacques-Cartier and the surrounding area, laws and rights they need to be aware of, COVID-19 safety measures, their responsibilities and specific guidance for performing in the Old Montreal area.[6]

One of the most relevant ordinances is the CA-24-006. It offers guidelines, rules and penalties for street performances in the Ville-Marie borough. Organized in sections and subsections, and until 2018, the ordinance detailed the types of activities that could be considered street performance under the regulation and, most importantly, described the audition process to obtain a permit and who would be part of the evaluation committee. Article 12 describes how the committee will be appointed by the responsible department. The committee must contain three voting members, two of whom were members of corporations or professional associations that have competences related to the exercise of the activities evaluated and one is an employee of Ville-Marie. Additionally, there must be two observers representing the artists, chosen from among those who already have a permit. According to the version of CA-24-006, the term of office of the committee members was three years (Article 14) and the committee was responsible for giving a "notice of conformity" ("*avis de conformité*"), which attested to the approval of the artist to request a permit from the government. It also specified that the authorization was given to the musician or public entertainer who paid the official fees stipulated in that year, being restricted to one authorization per person to perform activities in public spaces in the region, and is valid for one year (from January 1 to December 31).

Guylaine Girard, the cultural agent of Ville-Marie, was a key actor during fieldwork between 2016 and 2017. At the time, she was responsible for all cultural programming that took place in the "public domain," that is, in the public spaces of that borough, including street musicians and entertainers.

As the sole borough issuing permits, it involved a lot of work for Girard: all the bureaucratic tasks, the inspection of the streets and, at the time, managing the whole system of auditions that would legitimize the artists, separating them between legal and illegal performers. The ordinances serve, according to Girard (2016), to better fit the practices in the public space, and this whole system is complemented by other regulations, laws and ordinances that act more generally in the organization and control of urban life, such as the code of ethics and the noise regulation. The issue of noise is key to street musicians, and the use of amplifiers by artists ends up generating numerous debates and disputes with the local government:

> This year we have limited not the wattage of the amplifier, but the distance that the noise must not be heard. Before, we limited the amplifier to a maximum of 25 watts. But we realized that there were people who were tampering with their amplifiers and it was too loud, so in 2016, there was a modification to the ordinance which effectively says that the use of equipment of sound should not exceed more than 25 meters. So that's an order that is revisited, monitored and filed every year.
>
> (Girard 2016: n.pag.)

Other kinds of disputes happen around territories and regulatory grey areas. While Ville-Marie is the only borough that issues permit for street performers, it creates generalized confusion about its scope. Some musicians affirmed they usually play in other boroughs without any permit, while others show Ville-Marie's permit when approached by inspectors or police officers. Even with this intricate governance process, the Ville-Marie borough cannot fully control legal and illegal performances all the time nor can it monitor whether musicians are respecting the limits of time or duration of presentations (up to one hour at the same spot). According to Girard (2016),

> we do not have an inspector on every corner, and we are aware that artists, when they are in an extraordinary spot, making lots of money, do not want to leave it. They can stand there for three, four, five hours.
>
> (Girard 2016 : n.pag.)

The disparity between strict regulation and loose enforcement creates a scenario of uncertainty for street musicians.

Until 2018, if the artists were not part of any professional association they needed to go through auditions in order to obtain an official permit from Ville-Marie. If an artist did not renew their permit, even if only for one year, they would have to go through the auditions again before getting a new one. Auditions are controversial and seen as a form of gatekeeping since they narrowly define what talent means:

> The auditions have been going on since 2008, exactly. The person goes to the *Accès Montréal* office and fill out the form to pass an audition at the Culture Division. We have specific dates, because it's not every day and not every week—we have about 5 auditions a year. They have 30 minutes to perform; sometimes we ask them for another song because we want to see their ability, technique, quality of the music, approach to the audience. We have sheets to complete there, to make a tally. About 70% can succeed, there are not many failures. People, for the most part, pass, and then, afterwards, when they have passed the audition, they can pay for a permit valid until December 31 of each year.
>
> (Girard 2016: n.pag.)

There was no maximum number of artists who could apply and obtain a permit, and auditions were not open to the public.[7] The audition application form for those wishing to obtain a permit requested personal information from the candidate, such as name, address, email, phone number and language. It also had a specific box for the person to indicate if they already had a permit to perform in the streets. Finally, the person had to mark which type of permit they wanted: musician, balloon sculptor, public entertainer or public entertainer who uses fire—to use fire in public spaces, it is necessary to have other authorizations and certificates. In attendance at the audition that took place on June 17, 2017, was Guylaine Girard, representing the Ville-Marie borough, four experts (two of them were current buskers who held permits), and myself, as an observer.

Many buskers auditioned at the theatre at Maison Frontenac that day, showcasing a wide variety of music genres, styles and approaches to busking. They were judged according to the criteria mentioned in Table 3.2, presented in a form that was given to each of the evaluation committee members (and later shared with me).

Each criterion receives points according to the following evaluation: insufficient (0–17 points), good (18–21 points) or very good (22–25 points). The maximum number of points for each criterion was 25 and the minimum total sum to pass the audition was 70 (from a maximum of 100). In the form, there was also a space for general comments. During the selection process with musicians, many said that they perform on the subway and in the streets as well—and they all claimed to have the proper authorizations—a fact that I was able to confirm during the interviews.

In general, auditions and permits can be seen as a way of pre-screening people according to vague notions of talent, class, nationality and legal status in the country, since only citizens and permanent residents could have a yearly permit.

TABLE 3.2: Categories evaluated by the evaluation committee during auditions.

Criteria	Description
Technical skills	Training, mastery of skills, experience in the field of performing and performing arts, etc.
Diversification of practice	Variety of repertoire (distinguished by a wide variety of themes or musical genres), variety of numbers and/ or proposed performances (circus, dance, theatre and balloon sculpture)
Originality	Original animation or innovative artistic proposal, relevance of the proposal or animation to the public space
Quality of the presentation and the contact with the public	Ability to maintain the public's interest during the presentation, the artist's personal ability toward the public, quality of accessories and costumes

Source: Ville-Marie, shared with the author in 2016.

The auditions can also exclude people because they require registration and performance during business hours (which can be difficult for those with other day jobs). Then artists need to pass them and, especially, pay for the permit fees annually. For Girard (2016: n.pag.), the need to request permits from artists revolved mainly around the differentiation between artists and beggars: "Because the regulation of ways to occupy the public domain prohibits any form of solicitation. So, to solve this problem, it was necessary to determine that they had to have a permit."

In 2018, ten years after the auditions were established, the Ville-Marie borough decided—for the first time—to stop holding auditions to evaluate the artists' talents. According to the local press, the costs of getting the committee together every year to evaluate the candidates' performance before issuing the permit were too high and did not pay off, while the number of artists performing without the permit enraged the ones who went through the whole process (Normandin 2018). Four years later, auditions are still not required and the regulation was amended by an administrative codification in 2018[8] to reflect this change; the entire section on the evaluation committee was repealed.

The current ordinance, still under the CA-24-006, called "*Règlement sur les musiciens et amuseurs publics exerçant leurs activités sur le domaine public (codification administrative)*," presents the "*amusers publics*" as a juggler, a mime, a singer, a magician, a dancer, a clown, a poet and a balloon sculptor. It states that "it is forbidden to exercise, on the public domain, an activity of public entertainer or that of a musician, without a permit" (Ville de Montréal 2018: n.pag.). The ordinance provides guidance for requesting a permit (Section II), receiving the permit and abiding by the rules (Section IV) and penalties for infractors (Section V). The fines can be steep. The first infraction receives a fine from CAD 100 to 300; recidivism can result in a fine ranging from CAD 300 to 500 and multiple infractions can result in fines from CAD 500 to 1000. If the buskers keep getting fined, they may also lose their permit and the right to obtain a new one the following year.

Other ordinances presented in Table 3.2 detail decisions by the competent authorities and provide updates on matters already regulated. CA-24-006, o. 38, for example, is a June 2012 ordinance concerning the code of ethics for musicians and public entertainers who carry out their activities in public spaces in Montreal, referring to paragraph 15 of Article 28.1 of regulation CA-24-006. Having only one paragraph, the code of ethics is based on the idea that musicians and public entertainers who are authorized to perform in the streets must adhere to four rules: number one, "to animate the public domain while respecting the tranquility of the residents and without hindering the activities of other users"; number two, contribute to the quality of public entertainment and therefore must adopt an attitude that respects the work of his colleagues ([…] and) not to hinder or denigrate the work of their colleagues, to address the general public by avoiding targeting a particular individual and not to solicit children;

number three, recognize "that each permit holder is an ambassador for the City of Montreal [… who] demonstrate good citizenship […] and to speak in French to their customers"; and number four, "to participate and collaborate in the development of a convivial public space" (Ville de Montréal 2012: n.pag.).

To perform at Place Jacques-Cartier (Figure 3.5) and its surroundings—one of the busiest and most touristy areas of the city—artists must follow specific rules and ordinances for that region, such as CA-24-006, o.61. This ordinance stipulates the time when street performers are allowed, the conditions for performing in the square, the seasonality of performances and the penalties for those buskers who do not follow the rules, in alignment with ordinance CA-24-006.

Additionally, broader municipal laws have a significant impact on the activities of street artists. One example is the P-1 by-law on peace and order in public spaces, which prohibits, among many things, the consumption of alcoholic beverages in public spaces, vagrancy and the buskers' performance in some places. Other

FIGURE 3.5: Busker performing at Place Jacques-Cartier, Old Port, Montreal, July 28, 2015. Source: author's personal archive.

examples are the T-3 on fees and commercial activities, the C-3.2 regulation about permits in general, and the aforementioned B-3 By-Law on noise regulation.

The number of buskers seeking permits has been increasing, even when they had to go through auditions. There are currently three categories for the permit: musician, public entertainer and balloon sculptor. They can obtain annual permits or a temporary permit, which is valid for three consecutive days (only one per artist per year was issued and it was non-renewable). However, it is hard to measure the size of the busking population (even under such strict conditions) or the efficiency of regulatory frameworks that supposedly ensure people abide by the governance measures in place. For example, how many artists have a permit in Montreal? This data is not publicly available, and had to be requested from Ville-Marie's employees every year. The numbers from 2015 were written down on a post-it note during the interview with Girard in 2016. Later, in 2017, an email follow-up managed to get the numbers from 2016 (see Table 3.3). Afterward, numbers would only be known if requested by the employee in charge of permits or by filling Freedom of Information Act (FOIA)-equivalent requests. The lack of data makes it hard to understand the dimensions of busking in the city and how to better draft policies for them and for the residents living in the area.

Beyond the regulatory frameworks, other tactics are used by the city government to contain buskers in specific locations. In the streets, passages and squares, the physical and symbolic structures of the city can encourage or prevent the presentation of artists. For example, in the Champ-de-Mars station tunnel, there are signs that prohibit loitering and vagrancy on the premises. This tunnel connects the area close to the Old Port and Place Jacques-Cartier to the Champ-de-Mars metro station. In it, there are loudspeakers that play music at a considerable volume, making it impossible for street musicians to perform. The instrumental music coming from the speakers directly competes with other types of sounds and noises that could emerge in the tunnel. Thus, it is important to think about how barely noticeable factors shape busking and are shaped by busking.

TABLE 3.3: Number of permits issued by the Ville-Marie borough, per category, 2015–16.

Category of permit	Total in 2015	Total in 2016
Street musician	134	164
Public entertainer	35	41
Balloon sculptor	8	9
Temporary (up to three consecutive days)	20	8

Source: Created by the author with information provided by staff at the Ville-Marie borough.

LEGITIMATION

Daily life and occupation of the city

Street performers occupy Montreal's public spaces in various ways, but there are some common threads. For instance, most subway musicians also played in the streets—and vice versa—and almost all of them claimed to have authorization to do so. In addition, they all played in public spaces and indoors, some traveling to other locations with their bands. The climatic conditions influence the way artists occupy the city based on seasonality. During the warmer months, they play in the streets, squares and public markets. During the cold months, they need to find alternatives—the subway is one of them, but even the subway gets too cold sometimes—that's when concert halls, cafes, bars and restaurants appear as not only profitable alternatives but also quite welcoming during the winter. According to Caroline (2015: n.pag.), "it's rare for musicians to play outside in the winter. I sometimes played outside for too long in the fall and my fingers froze. I no longer play below a certain temperature; I go into the metro." Artists will also adapt their performances according to the venue. For Philippe Mius d'Entremont (2015: n.pag.), even though he plays often in concert halls when he does, "it's going to be with others, it's not the same as what I do in the metro." Grégoire (2015: n.pag.) said buskers always try "to get contracts, to get gigs, playing in places—we do the best that we can. Nobody said it was going to be easy (laughs)."

Some buskers have favorite spots, be it the street or the metro. Jocelyne (2015: n.pag.) prefers to perform in the subway, instead of performing in more formal music venues:

> I don't really like structured performances, because there is a barrier between me and the audience. That's why I like the metro so much. It's very intimate. It feels like a genuine exchange. Whereas if you are up on a stage, there's a barrier.

FX Liagre also prefers to only perform in the subway system. He believes that the street is not the ideal environment to sing his songs, since he must compete with other noises:

> I consider myself mainly as a songwriter and the lyrics are of great importance to me. [...] And when you are outside, the noises you have to fight against are much more numerous and I think it's the place for artists making money with the songs that everybody knows. Ok, let's go for Stairway to Heaven, for the fifth time in a row!
>
> (FX Liagre 2015: n.pag.)

Musicians will also adapt their performance according to the environment, time of day and audience. There seems to be a consensus that original songs might not be the go-to option for buskers trying to pass the hat. Jesse affirms that

> in the metro we play covers, but sometimes we play our own stuff [...] as performing musicians we play more covers. As artists and "creative musicians" it would be more towards our original music. And sometimes when we play in bars, they ask for covers.
>
> (2015: n.pag.)

Lucas said he and his band

> don't play as much original music on the streets. We do sometimes if we want to practice it, and it's just us three. There's also what makes more money, I find it much easier to just play gypsy jazz. Instrumental music, more than to sing.
>
> (2015: n.pag.)

FX Liagre talked about having patience and consistently showing up are key elements to succeed as a busker because

> you have to make people get used to you. [...] It's also one of the great rules I learned there. It's not enough to arrive somewhere and begin to play. You come there, earn some money. Come twice, two weeks, three weeks, five weeks. When the regular people passing there at this time get used to you, you get an income raise.
>
> (FX Liagre 2015: n.pag.)

Being visible in these public spaces is crucial for musicians—not only because it allows them to receive donations in their hats, but also might lead to contracts and invitations to perform in other venues: "These are visibility opportunities for us, I have already had contracts for weddings. People can ask us for a business card or have a project, [...] we can do all sorts of things, family events, shows, circus" (Caroline 2015: n.pag.).

> I really try not to be invisible, but I try to be very discreet, I tell myself I don't want people to feel obliged to give me money; I don't want to impose myself. [...] it happened to me two or three times to have small contracts. The STM people, because they work in collaboration with the metro musicians, sometimes gave us small contracts, especially when they wanted to promote the transport agency.
>
> (Jamie 2015: n.pag.)

Sometimes we take advantage of it for promotion; but for me, professionally, what I do is a little different. For people who play all the time it can create a real visibility.

(Mius d'Entremont 2015: n.pag.)

I have had people asking me to do various little things and I have done it. I played before a theatre performance once—and that was somebody who just came along and asked that. And somebody else's asked me to do a project in January, just from having seen me in the metro. I love to do that because it's something different.

(Jocelyne 2015: n.pag.)

Many musicians agree that both the streets and the subway are not good places to play and sing their own compositions, as passers-by prefer popular songs— known hits usually make them more money. Thus, they prefer to use the public space as a space for visibility, an opportunity to make a living, or even to rehearse. For Lucas, one of the main reasons for his group to continue playing in the streets is the opportunity to practice, combined with the money that goes into the hat:

Since I play a lot of different instruments, if I want to practice one, I might as well practice two hours in the metro and get a bit of money for it, than practice two hours at home and get nothing. So, practice is a big part of it.

(Lucas 2015: n.pag.)

A similar opinion is shared by Juliana, who sometimes performs alone and so does her brother, to "make a little bit more money that way. And it is good practice, we can both sing" (Juliana 2015). Boetzkes makes a similar point that recycling forgotten songs is facilitated by the ephemeral stage that is created on the subway platform before the crowd disperses:

Performances that recycle long-forgotten songs are made easier by the fundamentally ephemeral stage that emerges on the site at particular moments in the movement of subway cars and people. [...] The performances are usually synthesized versions of musical clichés that convey a sense of cultural degeneration. Indeed, because of the limited amount of time between trains, the music must be reprocessed in such a way that the temporality of the situation is creatively integrated into the performance. In the most interesting cases, buskers choose familiar songs so that in spite of the necessary adjustments in rhythm, they can capture the continuously shifting attention of the audience before its imminent dispersal.

(Boetzkes 2010: 139)

Another transversal issue affecting buskers below and above ground is safety in public spaces. The feeling of safety is largely shaped by gender identity and expression (Catterall and Azzouz 2021; Bain and Podmore 2023; Navarrete-Hernandez et al. 2021; United Nations 2023), race and ethnicity (Gray and Lin 2021), and legal status in a country. As an informal activity historically criminalized, busking also has to confront these issues. When playing in public spaces, artists are subject to all kinds of interaction with people, in an environment not necessarily designed for artistic performances, and encounters are not always pleasant for everyone.

Contrary to the current situation in Rio, the musicians in Montreal rarely mentioned disputes or confrontations with the police in the past decade. When musicians must deal with the police, it is usually because of authorizations (or lack thereof) and noise complaints:

> [S]ome of the street musicians sometimes have difficulties with the police. They are playing in an area of town where somebody might complain. Then the police come and tell you that you must move or, you know, go to another part of the town. Other than that, most of the time it's pretty good.
>
> (Mius d'Entremont 2015: n.pag.)

Artists also mentioned issues with the city inspectors responsible for ensuring public order—Lucas, for example, received tickets for playing with musicians who did not have a permit, even though he had one:

> For a while, my entire band had a permit. This summer we started playing with a lot of musicians who were just coming to town. And we were eight or nine people playing in the street sometimes. And sometimes, I was the only one with a permit. Towards the end of the season, this guy came to talk to me. He gave me a ticket— I had a permit!—because everyone else who didn't have a permit refused to be identified. So, he gave me a ticket because, even if you have a permit, you are not allowed to play with people who do not have a permit. The person who was following the rules got the ticket. [...] But there's this whole interesting thing too: you don't have to identify yourself to municipal inspectors. You have to identify yourself to a police officer, but not municipal inspectors. [...] There is also the crack down before the 375th anniversary (of the city). They've gotten stricter over the last year to prepare people for that. Sort of like what they were doing in Rio probably for the Olympics and probably like they did before FIFA too, I imagine.
>
> (Lucas 2015: n.pag.)

Regulation is a controversial topic among buskers. Most fully support having a regulatory framework that makes their work legal and sets guidelines for what busking should be in the city. Others criticize the confusing system, the arbitrary law enforcement and the barriers it imposes on artists who just want to do their jobs. Among those who see regulation as crucial, Jocelyne (2015) says she "wouldn't play as much, just because I would have to find a spot and be inspired to do it; and the metro provides a consistent audience." Caroline (2015) also appreciates having a structured schedule and reserved spots: "I like having a schedule, because I have children; it's more practical, it also assures me that at such a time I have a place reserved for me instead of waiting for musicians to finish their show." Beyond practicality, Clément also addresses that "the regulation can make things more equitable for everyone, and that works out" (Clément 2016: n.pag.), otherwise, musicians would play for eight hours in the most profitable spots.

On the one hand, for buskers like FX Liagre, Montreal is an example to be followed when it comes to the regulation and organization of street performance, as the regulatory framework allows musicians to work in a more orderly way, with their rights guaranteed, avoiding disputes between them:

> The system is not perfect but I have to agree that Montreal is probably one of the best places for buskers because of the long tradition of busking in the metro and squares. But also it is something quite organized. We do not rely on arbitrary decisions. [...] for me, the kind of regulations we've got here in the metro or outside are quite good ones, making people work properly, without any kind of problem and having also a positive effect [...] Because not all the buskers are educated people, not all the buskers are healthy people, especially mentally healthy people [...]. And I think both regulations and the fact that there's a part of the responsibility for the buskers not to make trouble.
>
> (FX Liagre 2015: n.pag.)

On the other hand, for buskers like Lucas, regulation—as is done in Montreal—can be very strict and even harmful. He talks about his experience in other cities, such as São Paulo, and regrets that musicians in Montreal have not fought for more freedom. Raising the question of musicians' freedom of expression being hampered in the face of all the regulation and control exercised by a program like the "*Étoiles du Métro*," which ends up excluding those who cannot adapt to the rules, he says:

> I have a lot of respect for the people, the volunteers who are also musicians who put that system in place because they didn't have a choice. The Société de transport de Montréal (STM) required them to put the system in place. But then I look at other places like Sao Paulo, like New York City, where buskers, when faced with new regulations, fought back with protests; they actively tried to keep their liberty and

freedom of expression. And I find it is just sad that here there's none of that. When-ever there's new regulations to put us more in a box, we just accept it and go with it. [...] And just in general, I think rules relating to busking are ridiculous. Shouldn't anyone be able to just play music or perform art wherever they want? What if you are not doing it for money? If you are doing it for money, but not actively soliciting money; there's just a case there and people are putting money on it. So, you are telling me that people are not allowed to throw money on the ground and other people aren't allowed to make strings and pieces of wood vibrate, it just doesn't make sense to me.

(Lucas 2015: n.pag.)

It is hard to balance legitimation and freedom. This more perverse side of regula-tion, especially as it has been done in Montreal (through auditions and permits) ends up segregating artists who do not fit into strict rules and guidelines. When you charge for annual permits, for example, some people might not be able to afford those fees. Caroline told me how, during a particularly difficult year, she decided not to renew her permit because it would put a financial strain on her, an immigrant single mother:

Last year, I didn't renew because I couldn't afford it. It was around CAD 125 per year. [...] That's a lot of money for some musicians, we're not really rich. When we have a contract we take it, but then when we find ourselves in the metro, during the winter, we have to get by.

(Caroline 2015: n.pag.)

She believes that we must find ways to respect musicians who wish to have more freedom:

It's a bit like finding a good environment to respect our way of life too, because we're not conservatory musicians who play in symphony orchestras, we're street musi-cians—it's not that we play worse, it means that the environment we have chosen to play in is free.

(Caroline 2015: n.pag.)

These stories shared by musicians are important information for policymakers, urban planners and researchers who try to understand their role and impact in public spaces. Their lived experiences fill out certain gaps that the lack of data and evidence-based policy are currently not covering. As these reflections on infor-mal urban work advance through conflicts and legitimation, they reveal common threads in global cities. Some of the discussions addressed in this chapter are also relevant in Rio de Janeiro, as we will see next.

NOTES

1. See: https://societe.lotoquebec.com/en/corporation/about-us. Accessed June 19, 2024.

2. According to the annual reports made available by Loto-Québec, a portion of the profits obtained is used by the social responsibility sector to sponsor cultural and sporting events, as well as to try to minimize the negative impacts of gambling addiction. In 2015–16, for example, 11.5 million Canadian dollars was allocated for sponsorships, 16.4 million for non-profit organizations and 27.1 million for what they call "the fight against excessive gambling," in a free translation—in a context where gross profit exceeded 3 billion Canadian dollars.

3. According to Lamoureux, Loto-Québec's profits have been declining, largely due to generational changes—young people do not gamble as much as previous generations, prompting the corporation to look for alternatives, such as investing in online games (Lamoureux 2016).

4. For more information, see: https://montreal.ca/en/reglements-municipaux/recherche/60d7607bfd653124d4577c25. Accessed June 19, 2024.

5. Building upon these two takes on regulatory frameworks and drawing from my own fieldwork, I have identified the other aspects (and consequences) of regulating street music previously described in Chapter 2.

6. See: https://portail-m4s.s3.montreal.ca/pdf/vm_guide_musiciens_amuseurs_sculpteurs_2022.pdf. Accessed June 19, 2024.

7. After a productive interview with Girard, she invited me to attend the upcoming audition, on June 17, 2017, with buskers who applied for a permit to perform in the Ville-Marie borough.

8. Available at: https://montreal.ca/reglements-municipaux/recherche/60d7caa6fd653112af59b639. Accessed June 19, 2024.

4

Disputes:
Busking as Public Service and Lawmaking

Culture, or the forms through which people and groups communicate with the universe, is inherited and also relearned through the profound relations between people and their environment.

Milton Santos, *The Nature of Space* (2021)

All the musicians have returned. The city has not renounced its musical vocation—Rio, where everything is music, from the harmony of kisses to the strident dissonance of brawls.

João do Rio, *The Enchanting Soul of the Streets* (1908)

In November 2009, the British newspaper *The Economist* featured a cover of Christ the Redeemer ("*Cristo Redentor*") at Corcovado—a famous tourist destination part of UNESCO's World Heritage list in Rio de Janeiro—being launched into the sky. The headline was "Brazil takes off," highlighting a 14-page special report on the successful story of the Latin American country (*The Economist* 2009). A month earlier, Rio was announced as the host city for the 2016 Olympics, after competing in the bidding process with other global cities such as Madrid, Tokyo and Chicago. The city would also host the 2014 FIFA World Cup. For almost a decade, Rio was in the spotlight due to mega-events, transnational investments, smart city awards, political scandals and controversial policies to prepare for international visitors—and deal with the aftermath.

The city of Rio de Janeiro is the second most populous in Brazil and its metropolitan area is considered a megacity by United Nation's metrics.[1] Located in the southeastern region of the country—and the capital of the state that bears the same name—Rio had just over 6.7 million inhabitants in 2022. Rio used to be Brazil's capital, until April 21, 1960, when former President Juscelino Kubitschek moved the capital inland to Brasília—a city built from scratch in the middle of the country.

Today, the Metropolitan Region comprises around 22 municipalities, including the capital, whose total population is around 12.2 million. This is by far the highest population density in the State of Rio, given that the population of the State is just over 17.4 million. The city of Rio de Janeiro was founded, according to official data, on March 1, 1565, on the shores of Guanabara Bay, facing the Atlantic Ocean. The date refers to the moment when the Portuguese colonizer Estácio de Sá arrived at the bay and built a small fort. Before that, however, various indigenous communities already lived in the territory—such as the tamoios and the temiminós—and were subject to the cruelties of the colonization process. Administratively, the city of Rio (Figure 4.1) is divided into five planning areas: North Zone, West Zone, Jacarepaguá-Barra, South Zone and Centre.[2] These, in turn, are divided into 33 administrative regions. The administrative regions cover the 164 neighborhoods of the city.

Rio is globally known for its beautiful beaches, vibrant music and art scenes and breathtaking landscapes that combine mountains and architecture. Rio is also known for the brutality of its police force, historical inequalities deepened by elitist urban planning, and a lack of adequate public infrastructure throughout its territory. Resilience, a word commonly associated with cities that endure challenges and keep on thriving,[3] is often used to describe Rio in its hundreds of years of existence. Resilience is also part of the ever-so-present smart city agenda (Reia and Cruz 2021, 2023), another aspect that is vital to understand the current issues in Rio and the disputes around (dis)order in public spaces. Rio won awards

FIGURE 4.1: The city of Rio de Janeiro, RJ, Brazil. Source: Map data from OpenStreetMap, City Roads on GitHub by Andrei Kashcha, 2023. http://openstreetmap.org/copyright.

in smart city expos worldwide and was one of the first cities in Brazil to deploy facial recognition cameras in its public spaces.

Under the mandate of Eduardo Paes as Mayor between 2009 and 2016,[4] Rio implemented an IBM flagship control center ("*Centro de Operações do Rio—COR*") and underwent a process of "smartification" (Morozov and Bria 2018; Reia and Belli 2021; Sadowski and Bendor 2019) and datafication (Baibarac-Duignan and Lange 2021; Brandusescu and Reia 2022). A huge emphasis was put on tracking and understanding the city in real time, with terabytes of data being collected and used every day. Still, several aspects of city life and activities taking place in public spaces remained invisible to the government. As Paes led City Hall, Rio hosted mega-events, created a hub for the creative economy and re-urbanized parts of its territory in controversial projects, such as the Porto Maravilha and Boulevard Olímpico.

Hosting mega-events always transforms the host cities according to the frameworks of the governing institution (such as FIFA or IOC), and these processes can be characterized by the incorporation of mechanisms of power in social and spatial forms, with economic rationality and social control as their objectives (Gaffney 2010). Rio has hosted mega-events since the beginning of the twentieth century, such as the 1922 World's Fair (Gaffney 2010). The trend has intensified in recent years and many researchers have studied the impacts and legacies of mega-events in Brazilian cities—specifically in Rio de Janeiro (Jennings et al. 2014; Freitas et al. 2016; Oliveira 2015; Mascarenhas et al. 2011; Cardoso 2013; Faulhaber and Azevedo 2015). One of the main arguments of these studies is that these megaprojects often leave municipalities with large debts and reduced public space (Gaffney 2010).

The benefits of mega-events end up going to more affluent areas and residents, as well as international tourists looking for this type of entertainment. Thus, "the increased security apparatuses that have become defining features of global mega-events effectively privatize public spaces in the city, installing surveillance mechanisms that continue operating long after the Games are over" (Gaffney 2010: 18). In Rio, surveillance of public spaces under the excuse of preparing for mega-events increased with the use of balloons and high-definition cameras (Coding Rights n.d.). The consequences of these processes continue even after the events are over and the tourists leave. The population still suffers from the loss of public space and the use of technology that controls the streets and the city's daily life.

When talking about the norms and public policies that impact the use of public spaces by people, it is necessary to dive deeper into the process of institutionalizing (and enforcing) public order in Rio de Janeiro. In 2009, Eduardo Paes created the "Municipal Department for Public Order" (*Secretaria Municipal de Ordem Pública—SEOP*) whose main purpose was to maintain a specific vision of what "order" should look like in a city's public spaces. SEOP staff worked together with other municipal departments, such as transportation and facilities management, and with the Municipal Civil Guard force to maintain said "order" through "Operation Shock of Order" ("*Operação choque de ordem*"). The "shock of order," as it became widely known, reignited debates about the right to the city and the occupation of public spaces in Rio, especially by individuals who use the streets to earn a living and survive. Street vendors, unhoused communities and street performers were particularly impacted by this new approach that some specialists called the "criminalization of poverty" (Laignier and Fortes 2010).

An article published in November 2010 brought to light the "shock of order against popular culture" in the city of Rio, referring to buskers and carnival blocks being persecuted by the municipal government. Protests claiming the operation's unconstitutionality and the attacks on freedom of expression in public spaces arose, with artists and carnival blocks taking up the streets to voice their disagreement with the new requirements for authorization before any performance. This context is connected to a broader political framework seeking control instead of fostering cultural activities:

> The experience with police repression and the privatization of public space that restricts the freedom of expression of popular theatre has become widespread throughout the country. [...] There is no culture or education policy. It only has a control policy.
>
> (Vaz 2010: n.pag.)

Based on an agenda that framed informality and poverty as "disorder" in public spaces, the people in charge of the operation also persecuted street performers—especially musicians. As much as performing in public spaces was not an illegal activity per se, it was not legal either. The blurred boundaries of illegalism (Telles 2010) in the use of public space make it difficult to assert the rights of street vendors and street performers to occupy streets with their businesses and crafts. Precisely because buskers occupy these liminal spaces (Bywater 2007) that escape simplistic binaries of formal and informal, legal and illegal, these artists in Rio were subject to the arbitrariness of those responsible for enforcing the law and maintaining their so-called public order. Paes' administration staff followed a strict conception of what an orderly existence in a megacity should look like, negatively impacting all individuals who used the streets to make a living (or survive).

This narrow-minded view of public order goes against the history of cultural effervescence Rio has always fostered. With a vibrant urban life that features a globally notorious carnival and numerous street parties, the city has centuries of lively music expressions taking place in the streets. Recently, a diverse range of studies have looked at music-related parties and artistic expressions in the streets of Rio, speaking about its "sonic-musical territoriality" (Herschmann and Fernandes 2012), contemporary official and unofficial carnival (Belart 2021; Barroso and Fernandes 2018), spoken poetry and saraus (Cura 2019), Baile Black (Xavier de Oliveira 2019), *passinho e funk* (Pereira de Sá 2019) jazz (Herschmann and Fernandes 2014) and the annoyances of music in public spaces (Trotta 2020a).

After a long period of socio-economic, political and cultural decline, which began with the move of the country's capital to Brasília, Rio de Janeiro began to recover in the mid 1990s and gradually regained a certain role in the national scene and greater prominence internationally. The aforementioned cover story in *The Economist* showcases the shift in the perception about not only Brazil but Rio as well. Herschmann and Fernandes (2011) believe that public and private investments directed to the city before the mega-events, as well as artistic activities that take place on the city's streets, played an important role in the reversal, at least momentarily, of the negative image the city gained nationally and internationally. Nonetheless, after the games were over, both the State and the city of Rio de Janeiro have been facing enormous economic and political crises, uncovering old issues that were overshadowed by an ever-changing landscape. Opposition to mega-events by the population took great proportions, occupying the streets in 2013 (Maricato et al. 2013). The dissatisfaction is related to anxieties and concerns about the right to the city. It raised questions as to who would actually benefit from hosting these events in Brazil. Afterward, the situation got worse. Brazil went through a coup in 2016, elected a far-right government in a tight election in 2018, and faced constant attacks on its democratic institutions (Pinheiro-Machado and Scalco 2020).

This context is relevant to frame the political and sociocultural conditions that buskers have been dealing with over the last decade. Back in 2012, they were facing police repression and an absolute lack of support from City Hall. To counter these issues, while advocating for funding and cultural policies, buskers decided to advocate for a law of their own. A group of artists mobilized city council members and other artists to convince the mayor that street performance not only mattered but also deserved consistent cultural policies that considered the intricacies of the activity. The fascinating process, which will be discussed in detail later in this chapter, culminated in the approval of Law 5.429 on June 5, 2012, known as Street Performer's Law. With just three articles, this law formalizes busking and provides guidance on the requirements for all performances taking place in Rio's territory, with no previous authorization requirements, and preventing them—at least on paper—from being harassed by the police.

Following Rio's example, other Brazilian cities and states drafted laws and decrees to regulate the activity of street performers. However, Rio's process was emblematic of having a bottom-up approach initiated by the artists; other municipal governments did not offer meaningful civic engagement opportunities for buskers and ended up with much-criticized laws.

In Rio, the law emerged from a collective endeavor of many groups and individuals who were actually involved with drafting the law and negotiating its terms with authorities. The Street Performer's Law was not an imposition of public power onto citizens; it was created in conversation with the artists. Later on, funding opportunities and cultural policies were designed to finance street performance in the city's public spaces. Beyond talking about the intricacies of the buskers' law, it is also necessary to discuss the background in which it was created, as well as the movement to claim street performance as a public service. The groups that led the lawmaking process started to frame their work as "public art" in a political move to seek validation and legitimation from the government. It was in this context that buskers decided to conduct an informal census, request funding for a festival and promote themselves as a service to the residents of Rio. Below, the mobilization around laws, cultural policies and community-based data collection are detailed.

Busking as bottom-up lawmaking

Buskers' daily activities imply continuous negotiation with legal norms that span way beyond the very nature of their performances. Regulations about silence and noise, street commerce, permits, video surveillance, public safety, public order and many others shape how, when and why they can or cannot perform in the city. In Rio de Janeiro, one needs to consider the municipal laws, state laws and federal laws that are related to the use of public spaces for performances (see Table 4.1). And, beyond the regulatory framework, urban infrastructure zoning and the privatization of spaces will define where and how buskers are allowed to perform.

Navigating this regulatory framework and disputing premium spots with other buskers and street vendors add layers of uncertainty to the practice of street performance. The artists wanted to have one simple legal mechanism that allows them to perform without being bothered by the police while establishing the guidelines by which they must abide in public spaces. In Rio de Janeiro, the process of making such a law is quite unique.

The Street Performer's Law did not emerge as a top-down initiative; it was built based on demands and mobilization of buskers who saw in the law a possibility of legitimation and respect. The artists saw a window of opportunity in the mandate of elected official Reimont from the Worker's Party ("*Partido dos Trabalhadores*") to the City Council. Together, they started a dialogue with the municipal government (especially the City Hall, the Municipal Civil Guard, and

TABLE 4.1: Selected legislation and draft bills related to busking activities in the city of Rio de Janeiro.

Number/Year	Who is responsible	Subject
1.876/1992	Municipality	Law concerning street vendors in Rio de Janeiro
3.628/2001	Municipality	Law concerning noise pollution in Rio de Janeiro
779/2010	Municipality	Draft bills further regulating street vendors based on Law 1.876/1992. The last activity was in 2017
5.429/2012	Municipality	Street Performer's Law
6.235/2017	Municipality	Law that establishes the Special Public Order Fund
126/1977	State	Law regulating noise and silence in the State of Rio de Janeiro
8.120/2018	State	Law regulating busking in trains, subways and ferries. Revoked in 2019
6.149/1974	Federal government	Law concerning security measures in the subway transportation system
Federal Constitution	Federal government	Article 5, IV, IX and XVI

Source: Created by the author with information available on governmental web pages.

the Municipal Department of Culture), trying to make themselves heard in the process of regulating and legitimizing busking in the city.

The law soon is usually referred to by the artists as "the law that works," alluding to the improvement (at least in some specific circumstances) of buskers' working conditions and the reduction of police repression that contested their right to perform in the streets. The first article states that presentations of street performers in open public spaces (such as squares, amphitheatres and boulevards) do not require prior authorization from the municipal public bodies, provided that the artists and their performances fall within certain criteria and follow determined guidelines: (1) performances must be free for the spectators, but spontaneous donations are allowed; (2) buskers need to allow the free flow of traffic; (3) performances should allow the circulation of pedestrians as well as access to public or private facilities; (4) buskers cannot use a stage or any other structure that needs to be previously installed on site; (5) the maximum sound power must be below 30 kVAs; (6) the maximum duration for each performance must be up to four hours and never extend beyond 10:00 p.m. and (7) buskers should not have private sponsorship characterizing the performance as a marketing event, but projects supported and funded by municipal, state or federal laws or cultural policies are allowed (Rio de Janeiro 2012).

The first paragraph of the law provides that the person responsible for the performance must inform the Administrative Region of the day and time of the presentation in order to make the sharing of space compatible, if applicable, with another activity of the same nature on the same day and local, which, in practice, leaves the request (or not) for authorization up to the artists' discretion. The second paragraph states that the artists do not benefit from tax exemptions. During the performance, artists can sell certain goods, such as CDs, books and paintings.

In its second article, the law offers a framework for what can be considered as "cultural activities of street performers": theatre, dance, capoeira, circus, music, folklore, literature and poetry, among others. These delimitations can be narrow or too strict, circumventing what can (and cannot) be considered a valid form of art. Therefore, the option of creating rigid limits for busking through a legal mechanism ends up including (those who fit) and excluding (everyone else), possibly generating numerous problems when enforcement agents enter the picture. In other words, the decision of whether or not a practice falls within the legal protection provided by the Street Performer's Law will be made by whoever is enforcing the law at the moment—police forces, inspectors and other civil servants—which can cause ambiguity and arbitrariness. The aforementioned "Shock of Order Operation" offered the artists a glimpse of what arbitrary notions of public order and repressive law enforcement looked like.

Even with street performance receiving more attention from the media, governments and academia over the last three decades, the marginalization faced by many artists is still rooted in a perception of busking as culturally irrelevant, a transitory condition or a last resort. Although these perceptions are not completely true and do not cover the multifaceted artistic practices that take place in the streets, the informality intertwined with busking pushes them to a liminal condition (Bywater 2007). In this context, it is understandable that artists see regulation as a way to prevent police abuse and guarantee the right to occupy urban public spaces with their art.

In Rio, the law and policymaking processes were seen as a path toward respect and financial sustainability—but they were neither quick nor simple. For both the law and the festival funding, the artists had to engage in ongoing dialogues with the City Hall, find political supporters among elected officials, and question what was being offered to them by the public authorities.

The first proposal from the city government came in the form of a decree, which was rejected by the artists for not guaranteeing the continuity of certain rights since the decree can be signed by one mayor during their mandate and discontinued by the next elected mayor. Therefore, the artists wanted, at least, a municipal law—which would be more difficult to be extinguished by whoever had a seat at City Hall. According to Richard Riguetti—a member of the group Off-Sina and the "Brazilian Street Theatre Network" ("*Rede Brasileira de Teatro de Rua*"—RBTR) who participated in the mobilization for the law—the efforts started within the Network and found resonance with the local buskers in Rio (Riguetti 2015). The law had the support of various artists, but the street theatre assumed a central position in the political articulation with different stakeholders. Based on discussions that had been building up for years among the artists, a draft bill was introduced to the Municipal Chamber of Rio de Janeiro under the leadership of Reimont.

However, at first, when it came time to sign the bill into law, Eduardo Paes vetoed it, causing indignation among the artists. Then city councillor Reimont invited the mayor to join his mandate and several groups of artists for a conversation about the law and its purpose. This event took place at the Tá na Rua building, in Lapa, with the goal of changing the mayor's mind:

> We did a very meticulous, surgical operation, which involved putting the mayor Eduardo Paes in a circle and asking him to justify the veto in front of many artists. We called Eduardo for a conversation—he thought he was going to talk to some 10 or 15 artists and, when he arrived, there were more than 300 of us. Then he said: override of my veto.
>
> (Reimont 2017: n.pag.)

> Then we started a movement against the mayor's project and he came to Tá na Rua's headquarters in Lapa for a large, broad, democratic discussion. We debated the issue and the mayor, in front of hundreds of street performers who were gathered together, lifted his veto. So the law came into force.
>
> (Haddad 2014: n.pag.)

City Councilor Reimont also described his role in this political process, including how his mandate approached the public art movement anchored on the notion of the right to the city (Lefebvre 2001; Harvey 2014; Maricato 1985; Tavolari 2016) as a force that opposes the privatization of public spaces:

> The right to the city is a theme that permeates several policies, with existing legislation throughout the country that says everyone has the right to the city, such as in the "*Estatuto da Cidade*"[5] ("City Statute") and other local laws. However,

public authorities still end up understanding the city as a space to be privatized. In this sense, I understand that public art is the expression of greatest resistance to this dismantling of the public realm and to this embrace of the private. [...] I had contact with the public art folks at the beginning of my first mandate, back in 2009 or so, when we realized that the city of Rio de Janeiro was curbing, prohibiting and persecuting buskers. The artists were already mobilizing at that time and tried to start a dialogue with the City Hall, notably with the Municipal Department of Culture, so that legislation could be prepared for them [...] Then a working group was established to think about legislation [...] and a public art project—we created a special commission in the Municipal Chamber to deal with the democratization of communication and culture, made up of more than 26 city councillors. In the end, we consolidated a very simple law, which later became Law 5.429. In summary, it reads like this: public art can express itself in the city without asking for permission.

(Reimont 2017: n.pag.)

The clash between the "Shock of Order Operation" led by Mayor Eduardo Paes and the entire mobilization for the law's approval that involved various levels of government is a remarkable sign of how complex the political context buskers must navigate to safeguard rights. The fact that a law makes their life easier is interesting from the legal point of view, given that public art would be a guaranteed constitutional right, not requiring previous authorizations or licenses, according to the interpretation of those who created the Street Performer's Law in Rio de Janeiro. Nonetheless, artists need to keep fighting for policies and mechanisms that allow them to continue using the street.

The narrative surrounding the process of approving the Street Performer's Law is centered on Tá na Rua and its supporters. That does not mean all buskers in the city are on board with it, or that there was a lack of resistance. The division of opinions on the regulation of busking and the control of public spaces exists. On the one hand, there is a debate based on the assumption that public spaces can and should be used for artistic expression without the need for laws because they are public and belong to everyone. On the other hand, there is the need for laws that regulate the activities of street performers—allowing them to work without being repressed by the police—as well as provide protection of rights and the recognition of busking as a legalized job.

The leadership stewarding the public art movement tended to diminish the antagonism of other artists to the law and proximity to the local government. Haddad also got defensive several times during our interactions, as if asked the wrong questions. The informal census of street performers was a particular sensitive topic:

We intend to solve each problem in its time, we have nothing planned, we are not that kind of mind [...]. Here we work with Paulinho da Viola, "I'm not the one who navigates me, it's the sea who navigates me" which is a wonderful thing. I let things happen, following the events. This movement has grown a lot because we just follow what happens, we don't try to determine them in any way, to maintain a contemporary feeling, an attunement with history and not with ideology, whether on one side or the other. [...] We made a long report about the Festival, which is in the hands of the Secretary of Culture, it's in the hands of the City Council, it's in the hands of the mayor. And we are working now with a final conceptualization of what public art is and what public policies for the public arts would look like.

(Haddad 2014: n.pag.)

To say the public artists are not determining what happens is not only an understatement but also a contradiction since they worked actively to shape and approve a municipal law. And not disclosing the plans for such an effort as mapping buskers in the city might be a strategy that keeps relevant information behind closed doors. The findings of the sole major data collection task force on street performers in the city are not publicly available and the goals are opaque. Not much is known beyond the number of performers. Issues related to their motivations, labor conditions, or expectations are not consistently mapped or disseminated.

The precarious labor conditions faced by buskers exacerbate the need to focus on their interests and display support for the mechanisms that keep them afloat. Every year, street performers organize a birthday party for the law in June. For instance, on June 5, 2013, buskers got together in Cinelândia, downtown Rio, to commemorate one year of the approval of Law 5.429. It began with the Municipal Civil Guard band playing in front of the City Hall while one of the leading artists of the movement told the audience: "The Guards that used to beat us now beats drums!" Meanwhile, several street performers arrived in a procession, dancing, with fireworks and banners featuring slogans such as "Long live public art." They got together in the square's center to hear Reimont give a speech, and then several presentations began, lasting all afternoon. Dissident voices criticized the fact that artists were celebrating a law that legitimized the "Shock of Order Operation," as well as the lack of critical perspectives from the groups behind the party organization. At some point, birthday cake was served to the audience. In June 2014, a new commemoration was held when the law had been in place for two years, and other celebrations followed until at least 2020.

This kind of formal regulation of busking gained strength in Brazil in the following years. Shortly thereafter, the city of São Paulo approved a similar law that regulated the activity of street performers in public spaces. Since late 2010, the police had already been acting with truculence and targeting musicians, clowns, live statues and jongleurs. This program is based on a partnership between the City Hall and the Military Police of São Paulo to maintain public order in public spaces. "All of them [buskers] are now subject to police intervention; the main objective is to curb and frame illegal street commerce on the city's main roads" (Salmen 2010). Specialists interviewed by the reporters affirmed this operation was an "abuse of power."

In emblematic cases, the abuse of power by the government was evident, with the seizure of musical instruments and physical aggression of artists. These operations ended up generating protests and fostering a public debate on busking and the right to the city. In the following year, the Decree 52.504 was approved on July 19, 2011 as an experiment to allow the regulated presentation of some street performers in the city of São Paulo. However, in 2012, there were still complaints about police brutality targeting buskers, disregarding the decree and the legality of the presentations. It was only on May 29, 2013 that the City Hall approved Law 15.776, which provides a legal framework for the presentation of street performers in public places. The law consists of six articles that provide similar guidance (while expanding the criteria) to the pioneering law from Rio de Janeiro (São Paulo 2013, 2014). As it happened in Rio, the law in São Paulo divided opinions about whether it was necessary, on the one hand, and the selective protection of buskers (but not street vendors and other informal laborers) as unfair on the other.

Other localities have also discussed the matter of busking and approved laws that regulate the activity. In some cases, they generated controversial results, such as in the state of Pernambuco. The state law 15.516 led to protests in June 2015 as it restricted the performances (including traditional presentations such as maracatu parades) to specific times and prohibited the participation of children under 14 years of age in presentations. Artists organized a demonstration via Facebook to protest in front of the Legislative Assembly at 10 p.m. (the time when silence should prevail over artistic performances, according to the law). A few days later, Congressman Ricardo Costa, author of the bill, revised his position and admitted the mistakes, filing a request to revoke the effects of the law and initiating a conversation with buskers to draft a new proposal. Costa used the laws from Rio de Janeiro, São Paulo and Porto Alegre as justification for the regulation. There were also laws that framed street performance as begging and a threat, forcing artists to wear badges to be able to perform, especially at traffic lights—under the excuse of ensuring the safety of drivers (G1 SC 2017).

On June 6, 2015, the newspaper *O Globo* published an article about several bands that play in public spaces in Rio de Janeiro: Astro Venga, Ma Non Troppo, Bagunço, Beach Combers, Dominga Petrona and Os Camelos. The article highlights the increasing visibility of this type of presentation while portraying the difficulties faced by musicians when trying to play in music venues. For these bands, playing in the streets and selling CDs directly to the audience improves their financial revenues. Astro Venga sold CDs for BRL 20 each and Ma Non Troppo claimed to receive around BRL 50 per day. The topic of competition is also covered in the article, as there were more bands in the streets of Rio. But, for one of the interviewees, Bernard Gomma, the competition for public spaces became a "street music scene," even if that was not the initial purpose:

> We went to the street because the band was limited to the bars where we played, not because a scene was emerging. It was a way to continue our work. And what we saw was that a scene actually emerged.
>
> (Essinger 2015: n.pag.)

Coincidentally, in that same week, EBC published an article in which the reporter discussed the three years since the approval of the Street Performer's Law in Rio, featuring an interview with Amir Haddad. Haddad says the law had improved the situation of artists, but they still faced resistance and difficulties, suggesting the need to rethink the concept of "public order" in the city so that it is not associated with the absence of people.

During the Olympic Games in 2016, Haddad and Tá na Rua curated a program with buskers who performed at Olympic Boulevard (Figure 4.2), a recently renovated strip in the Port region.[6] The curatorship was coordinated by RioTur (according to information from an interviewee) and with remuneration available to the artists. The Olympic Boulevard featured a new boardwalk, the Museum of Tomorrow designed by Spanish starchitect Santiago Calatrava, and huge graffiti murals, quickly becoming quite popular during the Olympics. It attracted millions of visitors and, consequently, many artists who were not part of Tá na Rua's curatorship came to Rio to benefit from the circumstances. In early August 2016, the media reported that street performers earned up to BRL 2000 a day in the area of the Olympic Boulevard:

> Walking on the Olympic Boulevard during Rio 2016 is a guarantee of fun and meeting street performances. On the surroundings of the Museum of Tomorrow, at Praça Mauá, in downtown Rio, buskers arrive very early to set up camp and guarantee generous tips from visitors this Saturday. Valdir Dantas, 41, from Ceará, woke up at 5 a.m. and left Campos, a city in the North, to work from 10 a.m. to 10 p.m. and make sure he gets the extra income in this busy season. Valdir, who works dressed as a clown, celebrates: "I've been working in the streets for 10 years and I've never made so much money. I want the Olympics every year in Rio de Janeiro. It's been wonderful to work here, because the City Hall has freed up the space for us, as long as it doesn't interfere with the event. I earn at least BRL 400 per day. Foreign tourists are very

FIGURE 4.2: Musicians performing at Boulevard Olímpico during the 2016 Summer Olympics in Rio de Janeiro, Brazil. Source: author's personal archive.

generous, they give dollar and euro bills. On the opening night I got almost BRL 2,000, I'm very happy." To save money, he said he brought water and snacks from home.

(Rodrigues 2016: n.pag.)

Quickly, the local media started to write about the growing interest in busking during the Olympic Games. In another article, the reporter argued that many more buskers were coming to Rio to perform since word of mouth and articles featured impressive donations that artists received on their hats, as rarely seen before. Quickly, the streets had various musicians, living statues and one-person-bands: "every day, new street performers discover that the Olympic Boulevard, in Rio's Port Zone, is an excellent—and profitable—stage to showcase their work" (Lins 2016, n.pag.) Another factor that may have driven the increase in buskers was the approval of the law that regulated their activity and safeguarded their rights, protecting them against police brutality—at least in front of international cameras.

Despite the popularity and profitable busking activities during the Olympics, the dispute for the right to perform in public spaces has been contested by legislators before and after the mega-events. In May 2015, the Street Performer's Law started

TABLE 4.2: Comparison between Article 1 of Law 5.429/2012 and draft bill 1.267/2015.

Law 5.429/2012, Article 1	Bill 1.267/2015, Proposed Article 1
"Art. 1° The cultural manifestations of street performers in open public spaces, such as squares, amphitheatres, largos and boulevards do not require prior authorization from municipal public bodies, provided that the following requirements are observed: [...]"	"Art.1° The realization of cultural manifestations by street performers are restricted to open public spaces, such as squares, amphitheatres, largos and boulevards that do not have residences in their surroundings, and may be carried out without prior authorization from municipal public bodies, provided that the following requirements are met: [...]"

Source: created and translated by the author.

to be attacked by other city councilors concerned about disorder and noise in affluent neighborhoods in the South Zone. City Councilor Leila do Flamengo—the same elected official who was responsible for the bill that intended to put fences and close São Salvador Square to the public[7]—proposed the bill 1.267/15, which aimed to amend Article 1 of the "Street Artist Law" in the following way as given in Table 4.2.

The reason behind this change, according to Leila and her mandate, was to minimize the nuisance of nocturnal presentations at squares that attract crowds, disturb the neighbors and reduce the price of real estate in the region. She called the musical presentations a generalized mess in the streets of the Marvelous City in an attempt to prohibit a cultural activity guaranteed by law. By allowing musical presentations only where no residences exist, it becomes virtually impossible for buskers to perform anywhere in the city. Reimont's mandate summoned the artists as soon as they realized that this bill would be voted on in the municipal chamber. The artists were quick to mobilize overnight to occupy the city council during the voting as a way to put pressure on the bill not to be approved. The collective action worked out; the bill was archived in 2017 and did not come into force.

For Richard Riguetti (2015) from the group Off-Sina, this persecution of buskers was unfounded since bars at São Salvador Square were open until later than the time limit imposed on buskers. According to him, it was always necessary to fight against these setbacks, because they were "a horrible approach, and we're mobilizing to defend ourselves. You have to fight, it's like sleeping standing up with one eye open."

The strategy to stop this type of setback was to promote a multi-stakeholder dialogue, safeguard the rights established by the Street Performer's Law as well as to follow the guidelines listed in the legal text, fostering a respectful cohabitation in urban public spaces:

We have a lot of frictions and tears in representative politics. Either we take a step further in the construction of participatory politics or we have no way out. When

> Leila presents a bill that will hinder the rights guaranteed but the law 5.429, we make a movement centred in debating in the plenary, and we look for city councillors interested in acknowledging that this bill conflicts with the existing law. [...] There are public artists in the city who are pretty vigilant of their legislation. [...] They say: "I am a public artist, so the law is mine." The person carries the law under their arm, inside their bag, in a plastic cover, ready to be presented to authorities.
>
> (Reimont 2017: n.pag.)

While interviewing buskers, various musicians said that they carry the law "in their pockets" or on their phone's screen. This was an ongoing practice, years after the law was approved. The subsequent mandate of Marcelo Crivella which started in 2017 cracked down on informality and reduced the budget for cultural policies in the city. At the time of my interview with Reimont, he expressed his concerns about the creation of a "Public Order Fund" in partnership with the private sector. Crivella shielded the municipal government and appointed a coronel tied to the dictatorship (Duarte et al. 2016)—coronel Amêndola—to head SEOP and invitations for interviews, demands for data and access to information requests went nowhere.

The aforementioned bill—Projeto de Lei (PL) 87/2017—reinforced the ongoing privatization of public spaces in Rio. It instituted the "Special Public Order Fund" ("*Fundo Especial de Ordem Pública*"—FEOP), without legal personality and of indefinite duration. It is linked to SEOP, which saw its scope and influence expanded with the purpose of "providing resources to meet investment expenses and funding [...] of activities of interest to the public order in the City of Rio de Janeiro." Article 3 of the bill stipulates that the fund may receive contributions from individuals or legal entities. Paragraph 2 contained the following information: "The Management Board, to be regulated by the Executive Branch, will promote the disclosure of the FEOP to the private sector, with the purpose of raising donations and sponsorships for the purposes provided for in this law." One of the counterparts featured in Article 5 is that companies that donate resources to the fund would be able to have their names or brands advertised by the municipality. The bill's proposal and configuration set the tone for the beginning of Crivella's take on the role of public order and public services, with blurred boundaries between public interest and corporate power, and was signed as Law 6.235 in 2017.

The legality of busking in Rio is always uncertain. Crivella's mandate was a disaster on so many fronts, and inequalities were extremely exacerbated by the COVID-19 pandemic. Artists struggled during the lockdown, facing financial constraints and being pushed even more to the margins of society. Financial aid and policies to relieve the situation came in late, after much pressure from artists (Amoêdo and Oliveira 2020). Whenever the administration changes, buskers are left wondering if their rights will be safeguarded and enforced—and this is why buskers try to present themselves as a proposal of continuity, rooted in a public service.

"We are not a protest; we are a proposal"

The interest in understanding buskers in Brazil has increased recently. Around 2013, it was difficult to find various resources and research projects about street performance—with exceptions such as the work about street musicians in Porto Alegre by Celso Gomes (1998) and Rio de Janeiro by Michel Moreaux (2013), a busker himself. Other works explored the practices of street clowns (Santos 2014), street theatre (Saar 2012) and musicians (Cahen 2011). The more robust body of work focuses on street theatre and its ramifications across Brazil (Cruciani 1999; Telles and Carneiro 2005; Alves and Noe 2006; Carreira 2007; Turle and Trindade 2016), and many of them highlight the central role Grupo Tá na Rua plays in shaping street theatre in the country (Turle and Trindade 2008).

Grupo Tá na Rua is centered on Haddad, a respected playwright, theatre director and actor who helped create the group in the 1980s. Since then, he has been working with theatre conceived specifically for public spaces—or open spaces, as they usually call it—and fostering networks of buskers in Rio and beyond (Turle and Trindade 2008). In the 1990s, Tá na Rua occupied a house in Lapa, downtown Rio, as its home. Paulo, a street clown, has been working with the group since the 1990s and spoke about the process of occupying such a marginalized space in the city without public funding:

> [The house] was an empty space, abandoned by the government [...]. We brought light, art, culture. We stayed there, doing street theatre, occupying the space. It has always been a very democratic house. We didn't have any support to maintain the space—we rented it out for parties and used the money to buy a fan, refurbished the flooring, renovated the bathroom. And Tá na Rua offered theatre workshops every Monday; on Friday, there was music. And we did festivals too, opening space for musicians, theatre, and cinema. [...] We started a movement there. And, since the 2000s, Lapa began to re-develop.
>
> (Rafael 2017: n.pag.)

The precarity faced by Tá na Rua, the lack of support from the government or cultural policies, and the connectedness they felt with urban territories were present throughout all fieldwork. A relevant aspect in this context is the constant emphasis on switching the concept of "street performance" ("*arte de rua*") to "public art" ("*arte pública*"). More than a semantic choice, this change bears with it a meaningful process attempting to legitimize busking:

> I'm interested in being here talking to you about public art. It's a story that is in the air but we know little about it, it's a novelty, there are no publications about it, there is no jurisprudence, let's say, no developed thinking about it—although it's a very old thing, art has always been public. But it has been increasingly privatized, becoming a market product [...]. So it became necessary again to tinker with this issue.
>
> (Haddad 2014: n.pag.)

Haddad sees himself and his group as catalysts of the much-needed change in the ways art becomes accessible to city residents. They also claim to be helping to strengthen the dignity and self-esteem of practitioners of street performance in Brazil. One of the most remarkable statements made by Tá na Rua, "we are not a protest, we are a proposal," is rooted in their hopes to build a support network for buskers while serving the population with their "public art." According to Haddad, urban public spaces became hostile, and it is their role—as buskers and creative performers—to change the narrative. By expanding the concept of public art, he wants to foster democratic conditions for their work, offering art that is free to everybody: "When I said 'public art' people thought I was talking about monuments and statues. I said: no, I'm talking about an art that cannot be sold, cannot be bought, that can happen anywhere, with any audience" (Haddad 2014: n.pag.).

Haddad is right—public art is often associated with monuments and statues. While public art remains more institutionalized, publicly and privately funded, street performance has been mostly marginalized, seen as aesthetically and culturally inferior, and alienated from traditional spaces that legitimize art. If we look at public funding available for the arts and culture in Brazil, opportunities for street performance have been almost nonexistent or an afterthought. Haddad raised this issue and questioned how public authorities see the artistic expressions made specifically for the streets that go against the privatization approach of current funding policies:

> Street theatre has advanced a lot, but it has always been treated as a bastard and rejected child, always treated as a second line of cultural production. When we see public funding and call for applications, [...] an amount is offered for an indoors theatre production, but the amount for the group that makes street theatre is dozens of times lower. Because we were always being placed at the end of culture's lifeline.

> We say: we don't want that; we want to make people understand that we are another proposal for cultural life. [...] And I wanted to give the street theatre movement this notion of its importance, to build self-esteem to understand how much future possibility exists in this gesture, apparently simple, but obviously political, of taking cultural activities out of a closed room where you need a ticket to attend and take it to the street for anyone and everyone. The gesture itself already puts in check the whole question of cultural life, of society, of the privatizing capitalist bourgeoisie. This gesture is already a change of attitude, it is contrary to the sentiment of the dominant ideology.
>
> (Haddad 2014: n.pag.)

A similar feeling exists among musicians and all kinds of street performers. The dissatisfaction with the way governments framed busking is omnipresent. It is not surprising, then, that Haddad and Tá na Rua managed to gather an extensive network of buskers involved in different artistic practices around the notion of public art—and law and policymaking—centered on street performers. The mobilization around the concept of street performance as public art turned into the "Public Art Forum," a space dedicated to discussing all things busking in Rio, to articulate campaigns, and to advance the interests of the artists.

The emphasis on the opposition between "protest" and "proposal" is rooted in the activities of the Public Art Forum, placing public art as an alternative for the city. Haddad and the artists in the Forum are always advocating for a re-signification of the concept of public art. It is worth noting this change is loaded with a very well-defined positioning, moving them away from the street and presenting busking as a public service provided by artists to the population. It also represents their political interests, dividing the street performers and organizations into partners and opponents, while participating in the fragmentation of the street performance circuit in Rio.

The analysis of street performance as public art (and vice versa) is important for highlighting the different practices and approaches that constitute the public art movement. The public art movement in Rio believes that an artist who wants to show their work on the streets needs to have a "public spirit," a certain ethic that guides the configuration of the possible uses of public spaces. Here lies the differentiation made between this manifestation of public art and art in the streets: the art that is "made in the streets" is not necessarily public from this point of view since it may have emerged outside the streets, a "private" art that goes to the streets. Art "made for the streets"—public art—is born in the streets based on the public spirit mentioned by the artists, which respects the space in which it takes place, the passers-by, and whoever shares that place to also earn a living.

Patricia Phillips (1998) states public art is not public just because it is outdoors but because of the kinds of questions it asks.

Nonetheless, the approach proposed by the public art movement also presents some problems in relation to the regulatory mechanisms that are being built. Even though regulation can protect street performers in a city like Rio, it also simultaneously excludes other practices. Informal cultural labor is subject to the arbitrariness of law enforcement and the many gaps existing between the law on paper and the reality of the street. The legal norm, in itself, does not guarantee the ability to perform in public spaces or how they are by public agents (from civil servants to the security forces), leading to artists carrying the printed version of the law in their pockets. In addition, having a law that protects street performers and street performers only creates a distance from other informal urban workers operating at the margins of society.

Drawing from this particular frame of mind, Haddad and the Public Art Forum sought the legalization and institutionalization of busking through different mechanisms. Lawmaking was crucial to this process, but the artists also worked hard to have access to continuous funding opportunities designed with the limitations and potentialities of street performance in mind, even considering a specific department in the municipal government focused on these artists. On May 19, 2014, Herculano Dias, a busker who had a prominent role in the group Tá na Rua, published a newsletter of the Public Art Forum, clarifying the political articulation with the municipal government around Haddad's idea of creating a department within the Secretary of Culture for Public Art. According to the information made public, the purpose would be "to catalogue and serve the buskers, under our (Public Art Forum/Tá na Rua) management" (Dias 2014, translation added).

The request for a dedicated sector within the Secretary of Culture to attend to the needs and hopes of street performers is deeply rooted in a history of scarcity, stigmatization and uncertainty. Guaranteeing funding for street performances is not an easy task; Haddad stressed the importance of not being dependent on the market or sponsors to carry out artistic activities, as they would lose their public artists' character. Ideally, artists would secure other sources of funding, both public and through donations when they pass the hat:

> We believe the government has responsibilities, so it has to offer funding and development policies, to cross-pollinate these activities. Instead of issuing a call for proposals, you create continuity for policies, you inject money in groups that are working so they can grow their work, multiply it, then you start promoting, provoking the growth from top to bottom. You are not buying specific cultural products but providing conditions (for buskers).
>
> (Haddad 2014: n.pag.)

According to members of group Tá na Rua, it is also the city's and its residents' responsibility to fund and support buskers as patrons because they are offering their talents for free to the public:

> The city has always had this tradition of funding its bums, […] it should sponsor the artist who is on the streets, the people of the streets. It's as if we were thinking: when are we going to have a city so full of artists one day that we choose the artists and put more in this one's hat, put more in that one's hat? Because if everyone collaborates a little, the city itself—this is an absolute utopia—keeps its artists afloat. And the taste of the city will determine which will receive more and which will receive less. It is a kind of market without currency, depending on the public utility of the work that an artist is doing, if that art there is helping to grow, if the population is interested.
> (Haddad 2014: n.pag.)

This perspective is problematic for a couple of reasons. In general, the public art movement presents itself as a proposal that tries to create a reality in which citizens coexist with street performance in a perennial way. Public artists try to distance themselves from the protests that storm the place, disturbing the order; for them, it is important that the movement be understood as a proposal for the city, not a protest, in order to build a narrative of reciprocity with public spaces and those who occupy them daily. This point of view can be understood as limiting since it diminishes the importance of protests as a way of giving voice to discontent and the denunciation of social injustices, especially in a context such as that of 2013, in which protests made people "return" to the streets, retaking the public space as a place to exercise citizenship (Maricato et al. 2013). At times, the speech of Haddad and the Public Art Forum seems to focus a lot on the Street Performer's Law and everything that orbits around the interests of public artists as a category, leaving aside, or diminishing the importance of several other forms of occupations, narratives, performances and activities that take place in public spaces in Rio de Janeiro on a daily basis.

At the same time, the Public Art Forum and the Carioca Public Art Festival (discussed below) still do not include most of the city's artists. The aforementioned informal census of street performers counted hundreds of buskers, showing a significant number of people dedicated to bringing art to the streets in Rio. However, it is also worth questioning that those who are invisible to the informal counting left out of the Public Art Forum debates, probably presenting themselves in an atomized and dispersed way throughout the city, or even not identifying themselves with the narrative built by the public art movement, for instance.

When the word "street" is removed from the daily practice of art in public spaces and re-signified as a form of public service, it also leaves behind a considerable part of the weight of marginality that busking has always faced. It reappears as something inherently public, for all citizens, and which opposes the privatization and commodification of art. Another key point is the lack of any questioning about whether or not the population wants many "public artists" performing, disregarding the discussion around noise, nuisance and disorder.

The involvement of artists in the policymaking process, and their active participation in proposing public policies that address their interests and needs is relevant to guarantee legitimation (Reia 2017). The inclusion of part of the artists in the political dispute of the city is linked to its institutionalization—which can be proven by the connection with the Municipal Department of Culture and the demand to create a "department" or a "foundation" that is dedicated to public art.

Looking beyond (and reading between the lines of) political articulation, however, it is possible to envision the artists not only acting as citizens and defending the interests of their movement through social participation but also understanding the potentialities of public art in promoting cohabitation in public spaces. The participation of citizens in the artistic performances that take place in the streets (by way of watching, dancing, donating and interacting) is a prerequisite for street art to happen—and many performances bring up current political and sociocultural discussions that resonate with the public after the end of the presentations. It is impossible to have a common denominator in terms of the content of the performances (regardless of genre) given the variety of practices and artists that perform in public spaces. There can be political statements, criticism of the status quo and inequalities or reproduction of oppressive values deeply rooted in Brazilian society (such as racist, LGBTQIA+phobic and sexist content). But, as Haedicke (2013) points out, even if the performances are not political in themselves, just the fact that they occupy public spaces that were not originally designed for this purpose makes them act politically.

The Carioca Festival of Public Art

The proposals, concepts and mottos of Rio de Janeiro's public art movement permeated the approval of the Street Performer's Law and, at the same time, shaped the approach to the Carioca Festival of Public Art. Councilman Reimont was a key supporter of the buskers and an enthusiast of the idea of busking as public art in Rio de Janeiro:

> We believe that public health and public education have to be for everyone. And we understand that public art is not just the street performer—the street performer makes the public art, which is an ancient heritage of humanity. When we base ourselves on the discussion of public art [...] [t]he artist is the one who takes to

the streets with their courage, dialoguing with their audience, who can welcome or react to their art. [...]. So, the definition of public art implies you don't pay for it—it has no price, it is not made to be sold; the artists are there to donate their art to the people passing by and then they propose the hat. The hat is a proposal. In fact, public art is a proposal that is offered to society [...] The people need to live with art, art humanizes our city.

(Reimont 2017: n.pag.)

As mentioned earlier, along with the negotiation of the Street Performer's Law, there was also a concern with funding and the continuity of policies that encourage, support and guarantee the financial sustainability of public art in Rio de Janeiro. After many rounds of negotiation with the public authorities, members of Tá na Rua, together with other buskers, managed to get funding for the "Carioca Festival of Public Art" (*"Festival Carioca de Arte Pública"*) between 2014 and 2016.

The festival's own organization, as well as its articulation with the City Hall and the Municipal Department of Culture, generated several controversies among buskers and other cultural organizations in the city. In 2013, Tá na Rua received around one million Brazilian Reais to create and conduct the Carioca Festival of Public Art. At the time, the Secretary of Culture Sérgio Sá Leitão said the amount was allocated to cover a four-year agreement with groups of excellence and public impact, including Tá na Rua (Tardáguila and Reis 2013).

The Secretary claimed that it is an investment in "continuity actions" that contribute to the "image of Rio" and said that the BRL 13 million for these five groups did not come from the Municipal Department of Culture, but from what he calls "supplementary credits" (such as excess tax collection) that were released by Mayor Eduardo Paes at the request of the Secretary himself. In the meantime, other planned and expected investments were left for the following year. The interview with the secretary ended with a significant affirmation: when asked about the budget for the following years, Sá Leitão stated that it was a promise by the mayor to keep the 2014 budget similar to that of 2013 since "in times of the World Cup and the Olympic Games, defending this budget is a survival tactic" (Tardáguila and Reis 2013).

Haddad did not take long to respond to these remarks by Secretary Sá Leitão, expressing himself through an email to the mayor, which he made public, and saying he was not aware of the four-year agreement:

We were stupefied [...] when we opened the newspaper "O Globo" today and read the interview given by the Secretary of Culture, Sérgio Sá Leitão, stating that we will receive BRL 1,000,000.00, per year, for 4 years, to put together a program with street performance groups from all over the city. [...] We both know this information is false: the project has a duration of three months, the amount of R$ 1,083,000.00 is for Tá Na Rua, Cia. de Mysterios e Novidades, Off-Sina and Boa Praça — that is, for the 4 groups to hold the First Carioca Festival of Public Art. [...] We would like this public information to be clarified, since Tá Na Rua has always been guided by transparency and respect in dealing with public money.

(SRZD 2013: n.pag.)

On December 26, 2013, Secretary Sá Leitão publicly replied to Haddad's inquiry, saying that the continuity of the project had been previously agreed upon and widely shared in front of an audience of 700 people, when the program was launched. According to the Secretary, "Obviously, the intention of the Department, when making an agreement part of a program called 'Continuity Actions', is that there is [...] continuity" (*O Globo* 2013, translation added).

These political misunderstandings and constant negotiations between state and nonstate actors showcase the complexity of navigating the policymaking context in the city, with all the conflicting interests, information shared and agreements requiring time and resources that are not always available to buskers. In this case, there is a central group (Amir Haddad on behalf of Tá na Rua) acting as leadership while taking charge of what street performance in Rio should look like. The Carioca Festival of Public Art is a reflection of the advocacy of specific actors and their interests.

The first edition of the Carioca Festival of Public Art took place in 2014, followed by a second edition in 2015 and the third in 2016—and I conducted fieldwork in all three editions. In 2014, after several impasses between City Hall, the Municipal Department of Culture, and street performers (mostly belonging to the Public Art Forum), the first edition finally happened. It began on January 15, 2014 and lasted for three months, featuring four groups in four different squares in the city: Tá na Rua worked at Praça Tiradentes (Downtown); Grande Cia Brasileira de Mysterios e Novidades focused on Praça Harmonia, in the Gamboa neighborhood (near the Port); Grupo Off-Sina occupied the Largo do Machado (South Zone) and Boa Praça occupied Praça Saenz Peña, in Tijuca (North Zone). Performances included a mix of music, theatre, dance, comedy and interactions with the public.

In 2015, the second edition of the Carioca Festival of Public Art Festival expanded to other regions of the city and included more groups and individuals—especially more street bands and musicians. On Saturday, 18 April, the festival began with an opening ceremony (Figure 4.3) at Praça Barão de Taquara, in the Praça Seca neighborhood, West Zone of the city. In the context of the 450th anniversary of the city of Rio de Janeiro, the festival had activities scheduled from 10 a.m. to 6 p.m., led again by Tá na Rua, Grande Cia Brasileira de Mystérios e Novidades (Figure 4.4) and Boa Praça. Starting that month, the festival's program

FIGURE 4.3: Opening ceremony of the Second Carioca Festival of Public Art, Praça Seca, April 18, 2015. Source: author's personal archive.

FIGURE 4.4: Grande Cia Brasileira de Mysterios e Novidades performs at Praça Seca during the Second Carioca Festival of Public Art, April 18, 2015. Source: author's personal archive.

included concerts, workshops and panels. After Praça Seca, the festival would move to other regions of Rio.

The opening ceremony included fireworks, fanfare and loudspeakers, dance and costumes, as well as a busker procession that went around the public square, in the middle of traffic. The celebration was impossible to ignore. Some people came to their windows with a puzzled expression, trying to understand what was going on. Quickly, many joined the party—one resident, accompanied by their kid, mentioned their love for theatre and the importance of initiatives such as the festival for places that were suffering from violence and abandonment. As a resident of Praça Seca for more than four decades, they remembered the cinemas that closed, giving way to commerce, and the square as a unique place in the past.

Another resident expressed their enthusiasm: "This is the actual Praça Seca, not just criminals or shootings. We need art!" Many local residents looked surprised and followed the procession until it made a complete turnaround and re-entered the square through a big, inflatable portal toward the bandstand. Upon arrival, Haddad—who rode there in a decorated bicycle—began to explain the purpose of the festival, stressing the importance of using art and communication to fight violence in the city. At various times throughout the day, Haddad—who was sitting on the bandstand, with a microphone, commanding the party—would say that "art is worth more than 50 batons, and it educates more than a house of corrections or 40 bullets." Throughout that day, and in the following days of activities, the program included music, theatre, dance, comedy and political satire, among other forms of artistic expression. The Second Carioca Festival of Public Art occupied Praça Seca until June—with the help of local buskers and groups that were also part of the Public Art Forum—when it moved to another location, Marechal Hermes. The following activities at Praça Seca, in May and June, were called "cultural occupations"; they were less busy than the first day but provided an opportunity for the local residents to engage with buskers and workshops that rarely go to this impoverished area of Rio.

In a report published in 2014 as part of the accountability process of those who receive public funding (Tá na Rua et al. 2014), this perspective on street performance has highly influenced the informal census and data collection of buskers throughout the festival. By mobilizing and mapping buskers without a set of criteria or standards on what being a busker means, they cast a wide net. Access to the methodology, the questions asked, or the rigorousness of the process was not available to outsiders. In the end, according to the report (Tá na Rua et al. 2014: 240–243), they counted 760 buskers in Rio in the first edition of the festival, with 160 individual artists and 600 groups. The information available is limited to names, and it was very hard to get any additional details from the organizers.

Informal data collection fills the gaps in knowledge about populations, groups and individuals who are mostly invisible to established power. However, the downsides can be a lack of consistency, opaque (or absent) methodologies that affect or prevent replicability, and the challenging access to the information being collected since, normally, these datasets will not be subject to Freedom of Information Act (FOIA), nor be publicly and freely available. In the case of the buskers, we cannot know more about these 760 entries unless Tá na Rua decides to make the dataset available. Even without the details, here the efforts around the data collection, combined with law and policymaking led by the artists, represent a crucial step in understanding the data invisibility of busking (and other informal labor) in contemporary cities.

The report also featured the bulletins from the Public Art Forum weekly meetings at Tá na Rua's headquarters in Lapa. Usually organized by João Herculano, these bulletins function as informal minutes. In the entry dated January 20, there is a justification for the importance of collecting data about street performers:

> It is important to have documented how many we are, who we are and to know the diversity of artistic expressions in public spaces, because, when the project ends, we will present this material to the public authorities—so that they have an idea of the universe of artists who exercise their craft in the urban spaces of the city.
>
> (Tá na Rua et al. 2014: 23)

On May 12, the artists gathered to discuss tactics for talking with Mayor Eduardo Paes in order to ensure the continuity of public art as a policy in the making. Haddad used this opportunity to deepen the discussion about what it means to be a public artist since many new artists were taking to the streets to perform, and being in the streets does not necessarily turn artists into public artists according to those behind the festival.

In the last meeting registered in the report, on May 19, there was an overview of the festival and a survey of the next steps (Tá na Rua et al. 2014: 59), focusing on the need to further negotiate forms to promote public art with the City Hall that go beyond a standardized call for proposals. Tá na Rua insisted on having a specific area within the Municipal Department of Culture dedicated to public art, despite the resistance from the government. One of the issues with this argument is centering the knowledge and responsibility on the shoulders of the main groups behind the festival, aligned with Tá na Rua, while all dissident buskers or those who are not connected to the public art movement would not be in charge or risk not being incorporated in this process. By trying to fight historical exclusion and stigma, the movement also created exclusionary boundaries.

In the third edition of the festival (Figure 4.5), in 2016, the context was quite different. It was announced toward the end of the year, with a smaller and more

FIGURE 4.5: Artists sitting in front of the municipal legislative chamber in Rio during the third Carioca Festival of Public Art, November 10, 2016. Source: author's personal archive.

modest program that, according to the artists, reflected both the lack of public investment and the post-Olympic political and economic crisis the city was facing. Paes' mandate as mayor was also ending, and a right-wing conservative politician (and also an Evangelical pastor), Marcelo Crivella, had been elected by the time Tá na Rua was wrapping up the festival.

Geographically, most performances took place in the old port and downtown regions of the city between November 4 and November 14, 2016—after the Olympic Games were over. The festival was hampered by bad weather, with heavy rains that forced cancellations and rescheduling. Participant observation included attendance at presentations downtown (Figures 4.6 and 4.7), at Cinelândia (November 10 and 11), and meetings of the Public Art Forum (November 7 and 14), to understand what the recent elections meant for the future of the buskers in Rio.

On November 7, the Public Art Forum brought together special guests and Haddad to discuss the current political situation and economic scenario at the

FIGURE 4.6: CHAP performance during the third Carioca Festival of Public Art, November 10, 2016. Source: author's personal archive.

FIGURE 4.7: Kosmo Coletivo Urbano performs during the third Carioca Festival of Public Art, November 11, 2016. Source: author's personal archive.

headquarters of Tá na Rua. Haddad said he had not seen such a complicated context in many years, but that street artists have always survived and will continue to survive, as they are on the margins of society, acting as a force of resistance in the city. The importance of the festival and advancing the projects of public artists were highlighted throughout the evening as well as the discussion about the precariousness in which the artists were left that year, with the drastic decrease in funding.

A week later, on November 14, various buskers got together to wrap up the festival and discuss the next steps. Haddad arrived after the beginning of the event and spoke again about the importance of the festival to the population, and about resisting in the dark times we were living, reaffirming that street performers always resist and always survive, whether the city wants them to or not. On that day, reflections on the five years since the first meeting of the Public Art Forum were presented, reinforcing the stand of busking as an opposition to the "Shock of Order" and public order operations. The artists also shed light on their tactics of survival as public artists, while recognizing the support from the City Hall and soon-to-be former mayor Eduardo Paes. Ironically, the people congregated around the festival did not question that the same mandate that implemented the "Shock of Order" was the same that funded their activities.

The dreams expressed by Haddad and the Public Art Forum of having a department dedicated to public art never came to life, and the artists continue to fight to build cultural policies and foster the right to the city. If above ground the fight is relentless, things get even more complicated underground, in the metro, in a struggle led mostly by street musicians against security guards and limitations imposed by urban infrastructure.

NOTES

1. The city is part of the Metropolitan Region of the State of Rio, also known as "*Grande Rio.*"
2. The fieldwork conducted for this book took place in all areas except for Jacarepaguá-Barra.
3. See, for example, global initiatives such as the Making Cities Resilient 2030 (UNDRR): https://mcr2030.undrr.org/. Accessed June 27, 2024.
4. Mandates of mayors in Brazil last four years and they can be re-elected for four more years. Paes second mandate was followed by Marcelo Crivella's mandate, considered quite disastrous as he undid several urban policies from his predecessors and underfunded crucial programs in the city. Paes was elected for a third mandate starting in 2021.
5. The "Estatuto da Cidade" is available here: http://www.planalto.gov.br/ccivil_03/leis/leis_2001/l10257.htm. Accessed June 27, 2024.
6. Porto Maravilha is an emblematic example of the urban readjustment works that took over the city before the 2016 Olympic Games and the controversies that involved numerous evictions in the region (Faulhaber and Azevedo 2015).

7. In 2014, councilwoman Leila do Flamengo drafted a bill proposing to enclose the square with fences to limit people from entering into the space, especially after dark, to decrease noise complaints and nuisances in the surrounding area. The bill was received with a public outcry and criticism by several artists and city residents.

PART III

GOING UNDERGROUND, BEING UNDERSTOOD

5

Disobedience:
Lawbreakers and Talented Stars

What does it mean to be above or below in today's rapidly urbanizing world? As humans excavate deep into the earth, build ever higher into the skies, and saturate airspaces and inner orbits with a myriad of vehicles, sensors and platforms, how might we understand the remarkable verticalities of our world?

Stephen Graham, *Vertical* (2016)

Subway music grew out of the ancient art of street performing, whose practitioners regard themselves in plazas, in parks and on sidewalks in towns and cities throughout the world. Despite their long history, however, official government attitudes toward them have rarely been favorable.

Susie J. Tanenbaum, *Underground Harmonies* (1995)

It was one of those cold evenings in São Paulo, in 2014, as I walked in a hurry toward the Paraíso metro station. I entered the station and lined up to buy tickets, while a busker was playing saxophone nearby with the musical instrument's case opened in front of him. We were standing near each other, somewhere between the entrance of the station and the turnstiles. Rather quickly, two security guards approached the musician, asked him to grab his belongings, and leave the station because he was disturbing the passengers. No one asked us about our perceptions, for that matter. The busker slowly collected their belongings, without much resistance, and walked away. In the meantime, the person standing in front of me in line said, angrily: "They can't do that! It's art! He is not just asking for money."

A few months later, I was riding a rather crowded bus stuck in traffic in Botafogo, Rio de Janeiro. A busker wearing shorts and a T-shirt entered the bus and asked the driver if he could sing a few hits to the crowd. He picked up his guitar and started playing a hit; most passengers sang along, seemingly enjoying the interruption. The musician played two songs, passed the hat, and played a third one to a cheerful crowd. He left at the next stop and hopped into another bus.

These two stories are relevant for understanding the relationship between busking and public transit, centered primarily on street musicians. Sometimes seen as a nuisance in stations, trains and buses, but other times celebrated as a relief in the daily commute in big cities, these artists have to deal with challenging circumstances to perform for their audience. Throughout fieldwork, it became clear how various levels of disobedience are intertwined with playing in the public transit system—and disobeying rules can lead to changes in policy and cultural programs.

Rio de Janeiro: Civil disobedience underground

Rio was the first Brazilian city to properly regulate street performance and it did so thanks to the efforts of artists working together with legislators and policymakers. However, even though most street performers celebrated this law as a bottom-up effort that worked quite well for many of them, some musicians highlighted the gaps between levels of municipal authority and enforcement—and how the law does not protect buskers playing in the metro and train cars. In the streets, above ground, buskers said they still must walk with the law printed in their pockets or on their cell phone screens (Reia 2018), to be quickly displayed in case police officers interrupt presentations by questioning the performance's legality. Underground, the situation is more severe, with a long dispute for the right to perform in the metropolitan public transit system.

In Rio, the subway was opened to the public in 1979 and has been operated by the concessionaire MetrôRio since 1997. At the time this research was carried out, after the mega-events, the Rio subway system had 41 stations, three lines and fourteen integration points. The daily use of the subway in the city by street performers, street vendors, panhandlers and preachers is part of the cultural landscape of commuting in Rio. As is the case in the streets, data on the number of buskers and other informal workers is not publicly available; the dimension of this ubiquitous activity continues to be a knowledge gap from the policy and planning perspective.

The discussion about regulation and "irregular" uses of the subway by buskers gained attention in the public debate after a series of violent repressions of musicians. In 2015, videos shared on social media showed security guards pulling two musicians from the cars, by the neck, despite complaints from various passengers. The incident ended up being covered by local and national media outlets, generating a discussion on whether artistic performances inside the trains should (or should not) be allowed (Gomes 2015). MetrôRio prohibits artists from performing in the cars—and, until recently, in any area of the subway system. Busking inside the trains is repressed by staff, sometimes violently. The presence of street performers inside trains has been covered since the early 2010s by local media.

Following the public debate and numerous viral videos featuring security guards violently pushing buskers away from subway cars, MetrôRio finally decided to address the problem: in September 2014, the company created a project called "*Estação da Música*" ("*Music Station*"). However, the project lacked a proper understanding of busking, leading to a generalized indignation among the artists. While buskers would not receive any financial or infrastructure support from MetrôRio, they still had to pass an audition, sing only original songs (or songs already in the public domain), and would be prohibited from passing the hat during their presentations. In the end, artists would have to undergo an unclear evaluation of their talents, without a counterpart other than showcasing their work for free. To make the proposal even worse, the artists would have to sign a consent form releasing their image, voice and name rights to MetrôRio. Local media covered the absurdities of the proposal, adding the voice of other stakeholders as fuel to the fire. Cíntia Cruz (2014), writing for the Extra newspaper, addressed the controversies surrounding the "*Estação da Música*" project, involving the "Union of Professional Musicians in the State of Rio de Janeiro" ("*Sindicato dos Músicos Profissionais do Estado do Rio de Janeiro—SindiMusi*") and opinions that stated that in this project "the musician has no rights":

> According to the rules, those selected will not get paid, will not be able to pass the hat or sell their CDs. The use of electricity is also prohibited, and during the one-hour presentation, the artist will have only five minutes to promote their work. [...] On social media, the project's rules have already been shared by dozens of dissatisfied professionals. The Union of Professional Musicians in the State of Rio de Janeiro (SindMusi) said it is studying the case and may take legal action.
>
> (Cruz 2014: n.pag.)

By the time Cruz's article was published, MetrôRio claimed to have at least 24 musicians registered to perform as part of the "*Estação da Música*" project, highlighting the fact that this was a "cultural project" aiming to offer artists visibility in well-known locations within the subway system:

> As a Public Service Concessionaire, MetrôRio must observe the relevant legislation, as well as the rules contained in the Concession Agreement, and cannot authorize any act that encourages the donation of money by its users, nor allow the practice of any act that may embarrass its users, in addition to not being able to encourage the sale of products illegally and without the relevant tax payments. Considering that we

are a subway transport operation and maintenance company, at the time of defining the spaces for the presentation of the selected musicians, we cannot guarantee that everyone will have easy access to electricity, which is why, in compliance with the operational needs and user safety, this rule was provided for in the regulation. The idea of the project is to present independent musicians, featuring their own works or works in the public domain, to promote the dissemination of new talents, and we must comply with the copyright law in Brazil. [...] Based on the concession agreement, political or religious manifestations are not allowed on MetrôRio's premises. There is no restriction of music genre.

(Cruz 2014: n.pag.)

These different interpretations of what configures busking, framing the activity as mere "donation of money" or the "sale of products in an unlawful way" and "without relevant tax payments," show the gap between reality and norms. Subway musicians end up transgressing these three points, once they pass the hat, they often sell CDs (of their own compositions or covers) and are informal, precarious workers. The lack of knowledge—or even a willingness to understand—and dialogue with artists who know the reality of the streets and cars around the city leads to this type of myopic top-down regulation that crushes nuances and needs of those on the more vulnerable end of transactions.

In August 2014, shortly before the public launch of "*Estação da Música*," the subway system in Rio de Janeiro hosted the Third International Festival of Subway Musicians—Red Bull Sounderground, which featured twelve concerts of musicians from eight countries plus three local artists who played in six busy stations across the system.

An article at the time (Pennafort 2014) mentions the festival's creator and cultural producer, Marcelo Beraldo, who traveled to several cities in 2009, including Montreal, "to meet with artists and discover the rules of each subway system. 'In Montreal, there's a sign to determine where they can play; in Barcelona and London, a marking on the floor'." Beraldo links the regularization of musicians in the subway with their professionalization and cites famous names who began their careers playing in public spaces, further perpetuating the notion that those who are on the street are also waiting to "be discovered." On the occasion of the festival, musicians could not pass the hat but would be paid by the event's sponsor, Red Bull. Among the bands selected was the band Street Meat, from Montreal— whose interview is included in this book.

After MetrôRio canceled "*Estação da Música*," and with the ban on busking in the subway system, musicians kept disobeying the rules and playing in the subway cars. In May 2015, the press was still covering the presence of musicians in the cars despite the ban. One of the articles (Areias 2015) discussed how tough it can be to be a busker in Rio, given the constant aggression, despite the support of most of the audience. In a single morning, eight different performances were spotted in the subway cars, with artists telling the reporters they could make an average of BRL 100 per day, playing for four hours on line 1; they avoid line 2 because the security guards are more aggressive. One of the musicians interviewed for this piece affirmed he was suing MetrôRio because of one violent aggression he experienced (Areias 2015).

Around the same time, a draft bill was making its way into the Legislative Assembly of the State of Rio de Janeiro ("*Assembleia Legislativa do Estado do Rio de Janeiro* —ALERJ"). Known as PL 2.958 and authored by Congressman Andre Ceciliano, the bill was introduced in 2014 with seven articles that finally proposed a regulation for the busking situation in subway cars; it was later approved as Law 8.120/2018. The first article allows "cultural presentations" in trains, subway cars and ferries in the state of Rio de Janeiro. By "cultural presentations" it meant singing, playing instruments, reciting poetry, theatre, dance and other artistic performances. The second article stipulated a registry of buskers interested in performing in the subway, while the third article affirms that offering free admissions to the artists is up to the concessionaires. The fourth article of the bill presented a timeframe for performances, in order to avoid rush hours in the system: buskers could perform between 6:00 a.m. and 11:00 p.m. on weekdays and from 7:00 a.m. to 11:00 p.m. on weekends and holidays. Additionally, artists could only accept donations and must stop if any passengers complained or asked them to stop. The remaining articles introduced exceptions and stated that the law would come into force upon its sanction.

This draft bill would solve one of the biggest impasses between musicians and the subway, which is the demand (and prohibition) to perform inside the train cars. In October 2015, the bill was debated at ALERJ, and "during the debate, proposals emerged such as the creation of exclusive cars for musicians on the trains and subway in Rio. Issues such as the collection of copyright for songs played by musicians were also discussed" (G1 Rio 2015, translation added). The musicians asked for some changes in the proposed bill, such as the centralization of the registry managed by the Secretary of State for Culture (Secretaria de Estado de Cultura—SEC) and free admission to the subway system. The transport concessionaires (MetrôRio and SuperVia, in charge of the metropolitan train system) argued that the ban on cultural performances inside the cars follows governance models adopted in other cities around the world and is mainly based on user safety issues—such as to prevent blocking the circulation of passengers, the inability to hear the announcements or even the risk of falling inside of trains.

While the PL 2.958 was slowly being discussed—and contested—in the Legislative Assembly in Rio, several cases of aggression and brutality against artists who performed on the subway gained greater visibility. On August 14, 2015, musician Carlos Adriano Oliveira, who played the transverse flute, was brutally attacked by a security guard at the Botafogo metro station: he was punched in the face and dragged by his feet. The musician declared that the security guard called him a "beggar and a clown" before attacking him. The aggression caused immense anger among the passengers, who almost attacked the security guard. MetrôRio claimed to have fired the security guard, and the security company was fined by Procon Rio de Janeiro, a branch of the organization defending consumers' rights in the state (Savedra 2015). Another case that received a lot of attention and sparkled protests happened on November 5, 2015, when musicians Thales Browne, Thiago Mello and Yuri Genuncio, who were performing inside the subway car, were aggressively attacked by MetrôRio security guards.

Browne, Mello and Genuncio are part of the "Coletivo AME—Artistas Metroviários," a collective defending buskers' rights to perform in the subway system that was created to engage with policymakers, negotiate with the subway concessionaire and represent the artists' interests in the context of PL 2.958. The collective used a Facebook page as the main source of engagement with the public up until 2020. On October 19, 2015, they published a "Manifesto for the Metro Art" ("*Manifesto pela #Artenometro*") that stated their demands—such as the end of the authoritarianism and violence against buskers, accountability in the face of the violence, and ensuring the buskers have the right to perform without being attacked. The Manifesto also praises what they call "itinerant art" within the subway system and highlights its importance to the city and residents.

On November 18, 2015, following an attack on buskers that was filmed by a passenger and widely circulated on social media, Coletivo AME staged a "peaceful and artistic occupation at Largo da Carioca," a square in downtown Rio (Targino 2015). Other public artists, mostly connected to the Public Art Forum, joined the subway artists, including Amir Haddad himself. The buskers also held an open conversation about public art with representatives of the municipal and state legislature (Reimont, Wanderson Nogueira and Eliomar Coelho). Less than a month later, *O Globo* newspaper published an article titled "The underground battle" (Lichote 2015), featuring the perspectives of artists, the Department of Culture of the State of Rio de Janeiro and MetrôRio in an overview of the escalating conflicts. The Department of Culture was acting as the mediator between musicians and the company operating the subway system.

One of the first actions recommended by the Coordinator of Music at the Department was to conduct a survey and collect data about the passengers' perception of artistic performances inside the subway cars. However, MetrôRio was resistant to the idea and said that, according to the interactions on their social media pages, "62 percent were criticisms of musicians playing in the subway cars"

(Lichote 2015: n.pag.). As the article points out, this number is out of context as we do not know what it represents, the sample, methodology, or any other relevant information. This lack of data does not help policymakers and the government to make evidence-based decisions, and it is difficult to rely on social media interactions without a solid methodology to affirm the passengers dislike the performances. Artists from Coletivo AME screened the MetrôRio Facebook page and confirmed they could not find that many mentions criticizing the buskers. At the same time, Coletivo AME has been keeping track and informally archiving all the police records of artists being attacked by security guards, as well as videos and other media that serve as proof of the violence directed toward musicians in the subway system.

MetrôRio insists that Coletivo AME's demands to perform inside the subway cars are quite unique, without precedent in the world; most global cities that regulate buskers' presentations in their subway systems only allow performances in the station. Facing increasing backlash, especially after the failed *"Estação da Música"* project and the violence caught on camera against buskers, MetrôRio created another program in 2016 called *"Palco Carioca"* (*"Carioca Stage"*) (Figure 5.1). In the beginning, the new program offered only three stations (Carioca, Siqueira Campos and Maria da Graça) for musicians to perform in the entire subway system. The schedule for presentations was also quite strict: from noon to 8 p.m. on weekdays, preventing live music from being part of the subway life and commuting during the mornings, nights and weekends. Some other rules were strict and did not meet the needs of many street musicians, such as the suggestion to avoid public interaction and the prohibition to sell CDs. On the subway website, Palco Carioca was presented as a project that aimed to "encourage talents, carry out cultural exchanges and provide the opportunity for musicians to present their work to the public that walks through subway stations." The website also provides a space for musicians to schedule their performances and display the rules artists must follow.

In 2022, six years after the program was launched, MetrôRio expanded the availability of stations to a total of twelve and the timeframe for presentations from 9:00 a.m. to 8:00 p.m. on weekdays, allocating 60 minutes for each busker. The seven-page regulation document[1] provides guidance for artists and states the rules and restrictions. It is worth noting that buskers need to go through a pre-registration that requires a legal status in the country—thus pushing away whoever does not have a CPF, from undocumented immigrants to traveling musicians from other countries, a common practice in Latin America (Parreira 2014). Buskers had to present their ID to staff upon arrival at the station and have a maximum number of three people in each performance (larger bands are not allowed). All presentations must be musical (no theatre or poetry) and cannot contain religious,

FIGURE 5.1: Palco Carioca, Rio de Janeiro, 2022. Courtesy of Guto Franco. This figure is licensed under the Creative Commons Attribution (CC BY) Licence: https://creativecommons.org/licenses/by/4.0/.

political, obscene or criminal incitement contents. Techno music, DJs and playback are not allowed, as well as the commercialization of merchandise such as CDs and T-shirts.

Wagner José, one of the buskers interviewed in 2017, usually performs in the streets, but he decided to give *"Palco Carioca"* a chance after the program was launched. He played with a colleague as a duo called DuoPlex and told me that they did not like the experience because of both the conditions imposed by MetrôRio and the behavior of the public. Despite saying that the battle to play underground is not his, he understands the importance of this dispute between artists and the public transit system, stating he "never saw people who play inside the subway cars playing at the spots" designed and managed by Palco Carioca (Wagner José 2017).

Even after the implementation and expansion of *"Palco Carioca,"* buskers continued performing inside the subway cars and demanding their right to be there. During fieldwork research, I followed artists getting in and out of the subway cars to perform—and occasionally, I was even able to see musicians performing inside the buses in the South Zone, despite it being an activity with less incidence and mobilization. From time to time, accusations of aggression against artists by subway security guards come to light and foster debates around the subject. Until the approval of the bill or the dialogue and formulation of policies to support subway artists, they performed at the margins, through civil disobedience, or were relegated to programs like *"Palco Carioca."*

It was only on September 25, 2018 that the draft bill 2.958 was signed as state law, as Law 8.120/2018 (Estado do Rio de Janeiro 2018). It regulated busking on-boarding of trains, subway cars and ferry boats in the state of Rio de Janeiro. Highlighting the gap between legislation and law enforcement, in the same week the law came into force, buskers were still facing aggression and expulsion from the subway system (Grinberg 2018). As controversial as it was, Article 4, paragraph 3 of the law was revoked less than a year later, on June 25, 2019 with the support of then Senator Flavio Bolsonaro, son of Brazil's authoritarian far-right 2019–22 President Jair Bolsonaro. This was the article that allowed presentations inside the subway cars and ferries. In 2020, the artists were heavily impacted by the COVID-19 pandemic[2] and until the publication of this book, they continued to use civil disobedience to perform in public transit in Rio. After being suspended to comply with sanitary restrictions, *"Palco Carioca"* returned in May 2022 (Ventura 2022).

We remain in the dark in terms of data about the real impacts of the pandemic on buskers, which prevents policymakers from being able to assess the best ways to design proper cultural policies that legitimize, fund and regulate the presence of street performances in the public spaces of the city.

Montreal: From disobedience to stardom

In Montreal, the subway was officially open to the public on October 14, 1966, in the context of Expo 67, and it is currently operated by the "*Société de Transport de Montréal*" (STM). It has four lines and 73 stations that connect the islands in the Saint Lawrence River. For over a decade, buskers were not allowed to perform underground—but they did it anyway. Grégoire Dunlevy (2015), a Montreal busker with many years of experience performing in the metro, shed light on the history behind the legitimation and institutionalization of busking in the underground network of the city, a process that involved not only the metro administration and the musicians but also the municipal government, media and passengers. In 2009, an association to congregate and represent the interests of the metro musicians emerged, called "*Regroupement des Musiciens du Métro de Montréal—MusiMétroMontréal*," and in 2012 they created, in partnership with STM, a program for street musicians named "*Étoiles do Métro*" ("Stars of the Metro").

The "*Étoiles du Métro*" program was designed to legitimize and institutionalize busking, on the one hand, and to increase control over their presentations and occupations of the subway space, on the other. Musicians were generally supportive of this type of regulation, but some of them have stated that the auditions and payment of annual fees can be a burden and exclude those who do not fit the criteria or cannot afford them. For Kim Bélanger (2016), an STM representative at the time, most complaints related to the "*Étoiles du Métro*" program about musicians come from excessive noise. Frequently, the employees of certain stations complain about musicians who play the same song over and over again, in a repetition of hits that pay well. Musicians usually complain about working conditions, such as security issues, especially at night or at empty hours—a situation that was noted as more prevalent for the few women playing in the subway and streets.

In the subway, the battle for the regularization of buskers' situation began in the 1970s, through disputes between the subway security agents and the musicians themselves, seen as offenders. A previous version of the background story for the association of metro musicians affirmed that:

> In the late 1970s, musicians from the metropolis had a great opportunity to be seen and heard on the platforms and in the corridors of the Montreal metro. The police and security agents at the time did not welcome newcomers with open arms, and the musicians were escorted out of the metro. While the latter played cat and mouse, some of them were less fortunate and received tickets for illegally playing music on the subway. Among them, a certain Grégoire Dunlevy, who, after having receiving three tickets of CAD $100, $500 and $1,000, decided to form the first association with Gérald Cabot and two other accomplices in order to have musicians accepted

into underground stages. Meanwhile, a TV personality, Guy Sanche (Bobino), spoke in favor of musicians at Place-des-Arts so that they could have a place to play there, because they are "part of the culture of Montreal," he said. From then on, Place-des-Arts became the first station where musicians could play without the intervention of security guards.

(MusiMétroMontréal n.d.: n.pag.)

Grégoire Dunlevy was indeed a key actor in the process of regulating, institutionalizing and legitimizing buskers in the Montréal metro in the early 1980s:

> I found a small station which is Square-Victoria. I found an alley at Square-Victoria where I was sure that I wouldn't have too many problems with the security and metro staff. And I was sure that I wouldn't meet anybody that I know (laughs). And after I played there one time and I counted my money, I couldn't believe it. [...] I started going back there regularly. Then, within the following years, the metro system started to really step-up security because they've gotten the word from higher ups that they had to clamp down on the metro musicians. [...] I got three tickets. And the first ticket was a possible maximum $100 dollars fine. The second ticket was a possible maximum $500 dollars and the third one was a possible maximum $1000 dollars. I was facing a possible $1600 dollars in fines. And I was a single father with two kids. I just really didn't know how I was going to be able to do this.

(Dunlevy 2015: n.pag.)

Dunlevy then wrote a petition in December 1982 for the right to play in the subway and against the fines that were being imposed, mobilizing other musicians who were in the same situation to act, as there were more than 30 musicians who received tickets for busking in the metro system. After photocopying the petition, the musicians managed to convince the public to sign in support of the buskers: "we came up with over a thousand signatures on our petition—then a month later we got in hold of a legal aid lawyer, and he took our case" (Dunlevy 2015). The artists won:

> Our lawyer—his name is Pierre Denoix—sent the case to the judge and said: "I believe that we are in the province of Quebec" [...] "So, the metro regulations that we should be following is the French translation of it." [...] Because in the English translation, it said: "It is not permitted to play a musical instrument or a radio in the metro." But in the French translation, it said: "c'est interdit de faire fonctionner un appareil de radio ou un instrument de musique dans le métro". And so, our lawyer argued that "faire fonctionner" means "operate". You can operate a car, you can operate a

washing machine, you can operate any kind of a machine or a vehicle or whatever have you. But you cannot operate a musical instrument, you play the musical instrument. So the judge went through these tutorials, encyclopaedias and everything else and finally he agreed with the lawyer and he said: "Ok, I agree with you." Then he turned to all the musicians and said: "Ok, you can go back to work now." The next day, there was a big splash in all the newspapers that the musicians had won and the transport commission had three weeks to go into appeal, and they never did. It was just taken for granted that you are allowed to play.

(Dunlevy 2015: n.pag.)

The musicians benefited from loopholes and the support from the public. After this first battle, different attempts to frame the musicians in a system of permits and auditions began. According to Dunlevy (2015), the attention from the media and the support of residents played an important role. In the face of adversity and divided opinions about the relevance of busking for the city and its residents, buskers decided to take negotiations with the public transit agency into their own hands to guarantee the minimum fair conditions for their work. Two years later, the use of amplifiers was banned, alleging the sound of musical performances was bothering passengers and employees. At a city council meeting, musicians argued that it was easier to use a decibel meter than to simply ban all amplifiers. Thanks to a recently elected director of the transport commission, Louise Roy, negotiations between musicians and STM were largely facilitated. Dunlevy (2015) recounts several disputes of interest and personal nit-picking between musicians and transportation system workers, who only cooperated when given orders from above. At some point, one STM employee helped organize the signage system for the musicians, such as the lyre sign on the walls (Figure 5.2) indicating specific locations where musicians are allowed to play in around 52 spots at the time.

Soon after the trial, the musicians also decided that it was necessary to create an association that could bargain with the government on their behalf. In 1983, the "*Association des Musiciens Indépendants du Métro de Montréal—AMIMM*" was created. Dunlevy was involved in these musician representation activities until around 2007, when he says he got tired of negotiating with and for the musicians—who, according to him, were not very cooperative. The Association began to lose bargaining power and space within the subway system, leading to the demobilization of the association in the 2000s.

Amanda Boetzkes (2010) analyzed the musical performances at Lionel Groulx station in Montreal before the creation and consolidation of specific programs to foster the talent of subway musicians, dealing with the ephemeral stage that was created on the platform between the waiting for the trains. At that time, the performance space at the station was not pre-established or evident at first glance,

FIGURE 5.2: Lyre sign in the Montreal subway system indicating buskers can play there upon reservation, 2022. Source: author's personal archive.

with the flow of passengers between the green and orange lines delimiting the stage. For Boetzkes:

> The performances by buskers in metro stations are particularly effective in nourishing such solidarities. Performers work to solidify bonds between strangers, and to use these bonds as ways of framing their performances. Confronted with disaffected, hurried crowds, buskers seek to produce events that will anchor the experience of passengers, cutting across the barriers of ethnicity and culture that otherwise divide them.
>
> (Boetzkes 2010: 138)

These relations of solidarity were solidified in 2009 when the "*Regroupement des Musiciens du Métro de Montréal*—MusiMétroMontréal" was created, a non-profit organization whose main objective was to represent all musicians in the Montreal metro system and advocate for their interests. In 2012, they created the program "*Étoiles du Métro*" ("Metro Stars") in partnership with STM—and although the musicians still had to deal with the hurried and disinterested crowds, they received an endorsement of the legitimacy of the public transit agency itself to carry out their work. Clément Courtois, street musician responsible for communications at MusiMétroMontréal at the time of fieldwork, took care of conversations with musicians, STM and clients. According to Courtois, the MusiMétroMontréal was established as an administrative body organized around an executive committee and an administrative council, and his role encompassed "relations between the members and the committee and the committee with the STM [...]. I also manage customers, since we receive calls to hire musicians for parties and events, so I manage the contracts, fees, and booking" (Courtois 2016: n.pag.). In 2016, MusiMétroMontréal had 115 musicians as members. The work of the musicians involved in the management of MusiMétroMontréal is mostly voluntary, or they receive an allowance from STM.

At the time of fieldwork (mid to late 2010s), MusiMétroMontréal only represented musicians who signed up for membership. However, musicians were not required to be a member in order to play in the public spots within the metro system. Buskers willing to perform at specific (more prestigious) spots reserved for the "*Étoiles du Métro*," as well as participate in events organized by STM and MusiMétroMontréal, and schedule their presentations online had to go through an audition. If they fulfilled the requirements to pass the audition, they would pay the fees and join MusiMétroMóntreal as a member. Alternatively, any musician could play at spots not reserved for the *Étoiles*, provided they chose a time of day and put their name on a paper list located at that spot. Some musicians have claimed that many of these "free" spots were often busy, which caused artists to wake up very early to get their names on paper—and that paper often disappeared, according to musicians who spoke to me. The situation has now changed with the implementation of a new, online platform.[3] In addition to these options, it is possible to be a member of MusiMétroMontréal upon payment of an annual fee without necessarily being a metro star.

Juliana and Jesse, two siblings who play together in the streets and underground, believe that MusiMétroMontréal helped them gain more visibility as members of the program via shared opportunities to get extra gigs beyond the subway stations. According to Juliana, MMM sent "lots of emails about opportunities […] they take care of all the membership cards and everything," and Jesse stated, "they are not corporate people, they are musicians" (Juliana and Jesse 2015: n.pag.).

For Courtois, MusiMétroMontréal's focus on guaranteeing the rights of all buskers (even itinerant musicians who are not Montreal residents) and the "*Étoiles du Métro*" program serves, primarily, to prove street musicians are not beggars: "The goal was to enhance the image of metro musicians, to make it clear that buskers are not beggars who play in the metro but musicians who are good and who really have talent" (Courtois 2016: n.pag.).

Metro musicians are expected to follow rules and regulations, as well as a code of conduct that promotes cohabitation with passengers and employees in the underground environment. In a version from 2017, "stating that each musician, whether or not a member of MusiMétroMontréal, represents the category of subway musicians" and therefore must be a model to follow (MusiMétroMontréal n.d.). The document shows how buskers are expected to behave in a way to project a good public image. The rules dictate, for example, that musicians must show up at their subway stations well-dressed and clean. Consumption of alcohol and drugs is prohibited, and the artist cannot, under any circumstances, sit on the floor or on a newspaper, but is allowed to sit on "interesting fabric," such as a chair or bench. Courtesy and respect must be exercised among musicians and subway users as well as public transport workers. Many of these concerns are to ensure the continuity of the legitimacy of artists from a formal and legal point of view, but they also serve to legitimize them professionally for society, distancing them from beggars and itinerants. An earlier version of the MusiMétroMontréal website also showcased a map of the subway stations that have lyre signs, presented according to the conditions that interfere with the shows: weather (very cold or very hot), movement of passengers, levels of noise, temporary closures, number of lyres per station and spots reserved for "*Étoiles*."

In general, the activity of buskers in the metro is highly regulated and surveilled by STM, based on the use of security cameras and staff to control the noise level, the occupation of space, and overall behaviors. Three recent studies are dedicated to understanding the role of regulation, economy, creativity and power in relation to busking in Montreal (Chatterjee 2022; Garnier 2015, 2016; Wees 2017).

Julien Garnier (2016) looks at the power dynamics of the metro system, based on Foucault's concept of power, with a chapter dedicated to the metro and its control mechanisms. The changes in the words and themes covered by the subway's internal regulations show changes in the focus of the institution's action since the subway as a physical structure remains practically the same, as well as its purpose. When the metro started operating in 1966, the regulation had thirteen articles and was called "L'ordre public dans le métro"; in 1975, it contained seventeen articles and was called "Règlement concernant le transport et la conduite des voyageurs"; in 1986, it had 82 articles and was called "*Règlement concernant le transport, la conduite des personnes, dans ou sur les véhicules et les immeubles de la STCUM ainsi que concernant les titres de transports utilisés dans le cadre du serve as transport in common organisé par la Société*"; and finally, the regulation of 2003, still in force, which is called "*Règlement concerning les normes de sécurité et de behavior des personnes dans le matériel roulant et les immeubles exploités par ou pour la Société de Transport of Montreal.*" According to Garnier (2016), in the beginning, the management of the subway was the responsibility of the municipality, and the regulation's main objective was to uphold public order. In 1970, the municipal administrative context had changed, having to dialogue with the metropolitan community of Montreal, while the institution responsible for the metro could create its own internal rules, and this is reflected in the change in the regulation of metro activities in 1975, which became more complex.

The need to intervene in something general (public order) gives way to a specific intervention in the space being occupied (passenger transportation). In 1986, the delimitation of the transport entity's intervention through the regulation is even more specific: "The object of the regulations no longer only groups of users and their behaviours but aims to address all goods" within the network (Garnier 2016: 50). The current regulation brings new elements, such as "safety rules" and "people's behaviour" throughout the space occupied by the subway—dealing with specific issues, such as musicians, and other occupations that may be opposed, somehow, to the expected behaviors in the subway system as a whole. These regulations reflect a specific device that institutionalizes the regularity of space, orchestrating the adaptation of a specific power (Garnier 2016).

Beyond control and resistance, improvisation and creativity are also part of the everyday life of a busker in Montreal's metro. Nick Wees spent 500 hours under the city trying to understand what it means and how it feels to perform below ground—including the experience of performing at three metro stations. The intersection of materiality and creativity contributes to the understanding of busking as a practice that "should be understood as an assemblage-act, involving multiple participants—human and material—that emerges through the practices and creative tactics of an individual performer, in an ongoing process of cobbling together, of bricolage" (Wees 2017: 15).

Piyusha Chatterjee contributes to the scholarship about buskers in the metro with a much-need approach to the ambivalence of surveillance and the idea that buskers have always been there. By looking at archives while bringing into light global perspectives on busking, Chatterjee (2022: 24) shows that "[t]he entanglement of creative city, cultural economy and busking extends beyond the commodification of street music and performance and involves a shift in the figure of the busker from that of an itinerant to an independent musician, performer and entrepreneur."

The "*Étoiles du Métro*" program is quite popular among buskers and is in high demand. On the one hand, it offers legitimization as a hassle-free opportunity to do their jobs in visible spots in the subway system; on the other hand, it works for the STM as a mechanism to have more control and predictability over buskers within its underground infrastructure. During interviews, musicians who belonged to the program were supportive of its rules and formats, even if, sometimes, employees were not as cooperative as they would wish. Another issue raised by a few buskers was that charging fees can become a burden and be exclusionary. For instance, one of the interviewees had stopped being an "*Étoile*"—and even stopped playing in the streets with a permit—because she could not pay all the fees that year, being a single mother with two young children (Caroline 2015).

The fees are part of a gatekeeping process that the STM created to select musicians, along with auditions. The auditions take place annually, and aspiring "Étoiles" apply online by filling out an application and paying the fees, which in 2016 were CAD 17.25 for MusiMétroMontréal members and CAD 34.50 for non-members. If successful in the auditions, musicians had to pay an annual fee of CAD 58 per person—in the case of groups consisting of three or more people, each paid CAD 46. If fees were paid annually, without interruption, musicians did not need to pass an audition every year; however, if they skipped a year, they had to go through the entire process again. In addition to these costs, there was also the cost of the personalized banner with their names (CAD 40) that each "*Étoile du Métro*" was entitled to carry with them and to hang on the wall while they performed (Figure 5.3).

In November 2015, the auditions took place at the Berri-UQÀM station during the day (see Figure 5.4). Contrary to the closed auditions held by the Ville-Marie administration, the auditions held by STM were open to the public and happened near the turnstiles, so anyone passing by could stop to watch if they wanted to. A panel of judges was installed in front of the stage. On that day, many musicians performed in front of the judges and the public, featuring a myriad of musical

FIGURE 5.3: Jocelyn plays at the Place des Arts station with her "Étoile du Métro 2015" banner, Montreal, November 2015. Source: author's personal archive.

FIGURE 5.4: Auditions to become one of the Les Étoiles du Métro, Berri-UQÀM station, Montreal, November 3, 2015. Source: author's personal archive.

genres and approaches to busking. All musicians had an appointment to participate in the audition; upon entering the stage, one of the judges would write the name of the artist(s) on a whiteboard and take a picture of them holding the board. Then, the busker(s) could choose the first song, but the others were chosen from a list with the repertoire that must be provided beforehand by the candidates, proving that the artists had at least ten songs to perform in order to avoid repetition and to prove that they have some level of professionalism. The judges thanked the participation of the candidate(s) at the end of the quick presentation and said that the result would be available soon.

Once a busker became a "Metro Star," they could enjoy opportunities, such as the possibility of playing at the Jean-Talon public market (one of the most famous in the city), following a specific regulation; getting invited to (and paid to perform at) events organized by STM and MusiMétroMontréal; and performing in *Saint-Jean-Baptiste* celebrations, one of the main holidays in the province of Quebec. An opportunity worth mentioning is the Nuit Blanche festival, which takes place during the winter months, normally in late February or early March. An all-night festival focused on arts and creativity, it includes many activities in public and private spaces, despite the intense cold, and the metro is open for 24 hours (a rare thing in Montreal). Some musicians, part of the "*Étoiles du Métro*" program, are invited to play on the stage set up at the Berri-UQÀM (Figure 5.5) station and also on some of the bus lines that run at night for the festival.

FIGURE 5.5: The band Eclectic Django performs at the Festival Nuit Blanche, Montreal, February 26, 2016. Source: author's personal archive.

In the 2016 edition, people sang along, clapped their hands at the end of the songs, and stopped to enjoy a few songs. The show was called "*Les Étoiles du métro en concert*" and was included in the official program, free of charge, from 7:00 p.m. to 12:30 a.m., with the presence of buskers Brass Plus One, Flash-Back 57/97, Eclectic Django and Gypsy Vadrouille. In the program, there was a small explanation about the "*Étoiles du Métro*" program, stating that it was "designed to make your trips more pleasant."

Overall, STM positioned itself as a "proud partner of culture" ("*fière partenaire de la culture*"), supporting various cultural events around the city, from operas to festivals such as Mutek, which had part of the programming taking place in the subway facilities. Kim Bélanger, STM's corporate advisor in 2016, provided a comprehensive institutional view of the relationship with street musicians. Officially, the "*Étoiles du Métro*" program had four main objectives: improving the experience with customers, valuing the musical talent of metro musicians, framing the musical performance within a transparent and equitable system, and offering a greater variety of talents. According to the information I received from her in February 2016, the program had 58 stars, with 37 stars remaining from past editions (2012–15). In November 2015, almost 100 groups participated in the auditions to be an "*Étoile*."

Kim Bélanger worked in the marketing department of STM and was responsible for cultural partnerships with associations and corporations, as well as working with the programming of the 375éme de Montreal and the "*Étoiles du Métro*" program since its inception in 2012. Bélanger talked about the process of legalization and institutionalization of music in the subway, highlighting the illegality of the performances before the regulation of these activities, such as persecution by the police, and how Montreal relied on models from abroad to create the legal framework for musicians. It took a lot of work to map the network to find the best spots for busking:

> They went around the network, to each station, to identify places where there would be enough space to install at least one musician with their case open, a space where the level of the sound reverberation would be adequate, with a space with enough room to circulate, and where no employees would be inconvenienced by the sound, [...]. From there, over the years, the association of metro musicians was created—it plays the role of a union or an agency.
>
> (Bélanger 2016: n.pag.)

A certain level of bargaining and negotiation between buskers and the STM, mediated by the association of metro musicians, plays out constantly. According to Bélanger, the choice of the lyre spots was initially made by STM only, but currently, it is done in a collaborative way among all interested parties. Nonetheless, as much as buskers propose changes in the lyre spots or the overall system within the subway network, the decision-making process takes time as it goes through several departments at STM, being "slow and not easy" (Bélanger 2016). Bélanger had an inventory of performance spots within the STM network, a document that was not available to the public; it contained the lyre number, station, location in the station, "*Étoile*"—only spots, and the timeframe in which performances could happen. STM then had 57 locations, of which seven were reserved for subway stars who passed the auditions. Another document unavailable to the public was a proposal for new lyre spots, written by Adam Shugar in 2014 and updated by Kim Bélanger in 2015. It contained the musicians' proposals for creating new spots at certain stations—with suggestions for specific locations with photos and detailed descriptions. Added to the buskers' suggestions, there was the evaluation of the engineering and infrastructure division, followed by the feedback from Bélanger and, finally, the positioning from the operation team. There were many layers of data, interests and power dynamics that needed to be disputed and balanced to decide whether or not any new spots would become available. The justification varies: on the one hand, musicians seek to expand their network of possibilities, while infrastructure departments seek to maintain the movement and safety of passengers, as well as the maintenance of order and proper operation of the subway.

At the time, the financial counterpart from STM toward the musicians was primarily focused on managing the Metro Stars program, promoting the program, updating the website, and engaging buskers in local events, from Nuit Blanche to the Fête National du Québec (Bélanger 2016). Additionally, STM always participated in the auditions, having a representative of the public transit agency as one of the judges.

When asked about the reception of the public, Bélanger (2016) said that the program has become increasingly known, receiving good feedback, mainly because the program recognizes musicians with great potential, standing out from the image of the musician as a "dirty street performer" who makes "one or two noises with a harmonica" and raising the bar for music on the subway. This stigmatized view of buskers is not new (Bieletto-Bueno 2019), as seen throughout this book, and draws from a problematic view on class, poverty and often, race and ethnicity. It also corroborates the discourse of professionalization versus amateurism of many musicians, loaded with judgments of what talent should look like in an orderly way. The closer a busker gets to the ideal of cleanliness, order and institutionalization, the more they legitimize themselves before the system that controls the space and the society that observes them.

For the STM representative, it would be necessary to increase the number of lyres that are exclusive for the musicians who have been validated (and monitored) by the program, making sure "the majority of musicians playing in the metro went through an audition" (Bélanger 2016). The desire to increase control over buskers does not necessarily come with more capacity-building for STM employees—there was no specific training for staff to learn how to deal with musicians appropriately and fairly or to properly address all the challenges that their presence imposes on the network.

After listening to both buskers and the STM representative, it was clear that one of the most common complaints is related to excessive noise. Employees often complain about musicians playing the same song over and over again because it appeals to people and makes more money. Artists often receive warnings for these behaviors, which requires the mediation of the busking association (Bélanger 2016). Artists have to learn to navigate what works and what does not in terms of engagement with the audience. Jocelyne, for example, prefers to play at lunchtime at the Place-des-Arts station:

> For me, this is an ideal time because people are going somewhere. They are going to lunch or they are going to school, but they are not stressed like at the end of the day. My kind of music is not for them at the end of the day. They need something soft or a band that's stimulating. I sometimes go with that hour because that's what I've won in the draw and I have to put six hours, but I really prefer quieter and daytime.
>
> (Jocelyne 2015: n.pag.)

The musicians can be a nuisance for the employees, just as the noise of the subway also interferes with the musicians' performance. Philippe Mius d'Entremont (2015) mentioned the constant announcements interrupt the performance, making the metro not the "ideal place to play; there are stations worse than the others." Both sides try to find a balance between nuisance and coexistence.

Complaints about safety issues usually come from the musicians themselves. In some of the main stations (such as Place-des-Arts, Bonaventure and Berri-UQÀM) unhoused people, normally addressed as itinerancy ("*l'itinerance*") by the city government, cohabit (and overlap) with passengers, buskers and STM employees. Sometimes, musicians have their lyre spots taken by people seeking shelter inside the metro system—and buskers told me that they have to deal with aggression and panhandlers near them. These problems are not easy to solve because they are intertwined with the right to the city, poverty, colonialism and a neoliberal model of urban planning that leaves many without proper housing (Gordilho Souza 2018; Rolnik 2019).

The STM focuses on maintaining order and a positive public image for the residents. For this, Bélanger stated that it is important to promote cultural activities—and in the case of the buskers' program, it offers people the opportunity to enjoy a little break and come together as a community: "We put a melody or an artistic experience on the path of your daily life, in a moment when you walk from A to B; we are focused on [...] helping you to see other things" (Bélanger 2016: n.pag.).

In general, busking has been receiving greater attention from the media and society at large, through comprehensive coverage, the emergence of conferences, and international research projects. These are signs that, after being neglected for so many years, artists who perform in the streets and in the subway are gaining spaces of legitimacy and greater visibility for their work—despite the fact that several of the historical problems that afflict them still persist. Recently, the MusiMétroMontréal changed its name and approach to encompass street musicians as well, now being known as "*Les Musiciens du Métro et de la Rue de Montréal.*"[4]

The personal is political

Listening to the buskers was a crucial part of the process of writing this book. While talking to the association of metro musicians and the STM helps us to understand the rules and circumstances in which street performance exists, asking the artists about their experiences opens a window into the meaning-making behind their practice. There is a myriad of motivations, perspectives, instruments, musical genres, backgrounds, ages, nationalities, mother tongues and professionalization. On a late afternoon stroll at Ville-Marie in Montreal or in downtown Rio, you can listen to bossa nova and choro, as well as rock and the latest pop hits. Instruments as ancient as the hurdy-gurdy or electric guitar, songs in Portuguese, English, Spanish, French, or instrumental. The common denominator for them is being a musician and, at times, using urban public spaces of the city to perform. Other than that, it is difficult to make any generalizations.

Some issues are more pervasive according to who the musicians are. Throughout fieldwork, it was noticeable that most musicians were men. Considering the diversity of gender identities and gender expressions—and how challenging it can be to categorize them—this is a brief attempt to understand specific issues faced by buskers who do not identify as men. Regardless of age and experience in the streets and underground, women said they have faced harassment and have felt insecure or threatened during their performances. These women mention different circumstances in which they felt unsafe, and Jamie (2015) affirms that belonging to a program that legitimizes their existence as buskers makes them feel safer.

Kim Bélanger (2016) stresses how most of the safety complaints come from musicians; many stations in the city are places where the unhoused community seeks shelter, and the vulnerability of these people can be exacerbated by mental health and addiction issues. By occupying the same spaces as musicians, without proper policies and staff trained to deal with them in a humane, fair and welcoming way, disputes arise between panhandlers and musicians. Bélanger mentions the difficulty that some women may have when disputing an unsafe space with other people. Women performing in the streets and metro have had at least one experience of feeling unsafe, being harassed or disrespected while busking in the city:

> It's hard to be a woman in the streets. Whether on the subway or on the streets, we can be confronted with people who are not always pleasant. Sometimes, people who come to talk to us and who are not in their normal state, people who come to take up our space. [...] Several times I have met people who wanted to beat me up, fight with me, so I had to call security. [...] And I'm scared, but I'm not afraid. I defend my right to make money. Once, I really almost got kicked and I still remember it.
>
> (Caroline 2015: n.pag.)

> It scares me a bit to play in the streets. [...] When I started [to play in metro] in Montreal, around 1983, I was almost the only woman, and now there are many women who play in the metro. [...] At some point I stopped, maybe for 7 years, because it was too dangerous in the metro. But since the "*Étoiles du Métro*" program exist we feel more protected, people respect me more, we are more valued, so they are all inclined to intervene. [...] When I was mostly singing like very late at night, around 11:30 in the evening, there was nobody and I had problems, yes. I still have problems. I really have to have a thick skin and then try to create an invisible wall of distance for them to leave.
>
> (Jamie 2015: n.pag.)

> I've read about young women who were being bothered and harassed; they don't harass me. [...] One young man, who was a little bit disturbed once came up to me, he was kind of a smarty-pants. And I said: "No, no!" And I had a big sweater on, and he grabbed my sweater and put money down on my front. I was really mad, an instinctive reaction, and I said: "That's enough, that's enough! I'll call the security!" I went, I got up, I put my instrument down and kind of chased him along.
>
> (Jocelyne 2015: n.pag.)

In terms of motivations and life stories on how they became musicians (and buskers), artists in Montreal told stories about learning trajectories and paths to urban public spaces. Some buskers started playing when they were young, like Philippe;

others, like Jocelyne, began their music careers as kids but only began performing in public after retirement. There are musicians trained from an early age in music theory and practice, as well as those who are self-taught and learn to play "by ear." Caroline (2015) started playing her guitar when she was 18 years old in France but fell in love with the accordion—an instrument that "makes people dance"—and decided to play regularly in the streets when she moved to Montreal. Jamie (2015) affirmed: "we are born artists, we don't choose to be an artist"; she started to sing and write poems as a kid, then later on decided to sing in the streets in Ottawa, her hometown, before moving to Montreal without a job—where "she found herself playing in the metro, by chance." Philippe Mius d'Entremont (2015) began his music journey as a kid, then in college, until music became his profession; the metro is his main platform to this day. FX Liagre (2015) was "more or less forced to play the piano" as a child but, after receiving a guitar as a Christmas gift, started to play it and fell in love with the instrument; then he started to play outside until he joined the busking association and the "*Étoiles du Métro*" program—which he really enjoys being a part of. Lucas (2015) is part of a trio, Street Meat, who played together for years and traveled to Brazil a couple of times to perform in festivals such as the Red Bull Sounderground; suddenly, the band became more professionalized, and they were able to make a living from music. Juliana and Jesse (2015) are two siblings who came from a musical family; Juliana started to play the guitar when she was 18 and, at 21, she decided to play in the metro "just to practice and gain confidence," while her brother Jesse started playing music much younger, around the age of 9 or 10, and by age 18 he was singing and playing the guitar with Juliana.

In Rio, Michel Moreaux, a musician from France, wears two hats: one as a busker (he is a member of the band Bagunço)[5] and the other as a researcher of street music. He started playing in the streets as a child, but he did not pass his hat at the time—he only started passing the hat in his presentations when he arrived in Rio, where he played in different bands and venues, combining his experience from circus performance and music. As part of Bagunço, he relies on "the idea of messing up the space, this street performance that invades; at the same time, musically, we like mixing sound influences [...], we are into rock'n'roll, but we also really like jazz and everything else" (Moreaux 2015: n.pag.). Wagner José, a musician from the West Zone of Rio who was involved with the Carioca Festival of Public Art in 2016, and leads the band Wagner José e seu Bando (Figure 5.6), also works as a licensed teacher in Arts Education. He was interested in music from a young age but started to play the guitar when he was 18 and knew that he would like to create his own songs, as for him it only makes sense to play what he produces himself: "I want to have a career and be a musician [...] to make music that reaches people" (Wagner José 2017: n.pag.). According to Wagner, what he

FIGURE 5.6: Wagner José e seu Bando performing in Praça Seca, May 23, 2015. Source: author's personal archive.

and his bandmates were playing around 2002 (blues and ballads) was not of big commercial appeal at the time, so they decided to try playing it to the people in the streets.

A transversal question was whether or not the musicians considered themselves to be buskers. In both cities, artists shared divergent opinions. There is a clear attempt to differentiate themselves from beggars and talentless musicians who play in the streets because they have no other option. Another relevant aspect of this equation is the fact that most of these musicians have other jobs and sources of income, meaning that the metro and the street are not their main professional spaces.

Philippe Mius d'Entremont (2015) performs as a metro and street musician but has other projects on a regular basis, and the metro helps him to "make some money" on a flexible schedule. Lucas says that despite having started in the streets and still playing in them, Street Meat bandmates consider themselves only musicians (instead of street musicians):

> Now we do everything, so we sort of consider ourselves musicians, and that means we'll still play on the streets, but we'll also play in bars and concert halls. But it's playing on the streets that allowed us to get to that point.
>
> (Lucas 2015: n.pag.)

For Grégoire Dunlevy (2015), one of the musicians who fought for buskers' rights in the 1980s, being a street performer means being "somebody who likes doing it, somebody who likes performing for the public." In addition, he mentions the gratitude the public expresses for brightening up their days with music, especially for those who cannot pay for pricey tickets to attend concerts in traditional music venues. On that note, Jamie (2015) also said that busking provides opportunities to interact with people from all over the world while receiving small acts of kindness through impromptu encounters. Grégoire talked about this affinity for bringing joy to everyday life as an intrinsic part of being in the streets, since the audience:

> listen to all kinds of different music. They can listen to jazz, folk, rock, and classical music. And always music performed, in a lot of cases, by fairly good musicians. It doesn't make me a lot of money, but when I don't have anything else happening, it helps to pay the bills. But what I get out of it, from these people, is so enriching for me. The energy, the smiles, the appreciation. All the good energy that a lot of people give is fantastic. And knowing that I can actually make people smile and brighten up their day makes a big difference to me.
>
> (Dunlevy 2015: n.pag.)

FX Liagre (2015) agrees with this experience, saying it is an "extremely good place to work, to practice. To learn the interactions with the audience because the people that are listening to your music in the metro are not your real audience, they are not here for you." Juliana and Jesse (2015) say that being a busker, for them, is deeply related to the connections and encounters catalyzed by the presentations, good or bad (such as being seen as starving artists).

Michel, with his international experience, believes that being a street performer is not for everyone. Many people try and give up because one must "see the street by what it really is to avoid delusions," since it is not always easy to make money—especially if you are part of a large group of performers (Moreaux 2015). When asked what busking means for him, Michel talked about the ancestry of the activity and new trends: "I consider myself as a street performer who belongs to a more recent trend of people who do not only do this out of necessity, but for experimentation," and it is necessary to have a constant negotiation with the streets and their occupants. Michel has a unique background as a busker and scholar and offers a perspective of busking beyond lived experiences, but also as an inherently political act, by trying "to shake people up, stop being passive, a mere spectator of their own life" (Moreaux 2015: n.pag.) through these urban encounters.

Wagner José, when asked about whether he considered himself a street busker, introduced an interesting separation between "a street performer who survives from the streets" (more authentic busker) and "the one who found in the streets the main platform to present their art"—and he belongs to the latter since he also performs in other venues (Wagner José 2017). For him, people talk a lot about informality and precarity among buskers, but the working conditions of Brazilian musicians outside the streets are also quite precarious, pushing them to the streets. Contrary to the experience of several musicians in Montreal who play cover songs above and below ground to attract more public attention and, consequently, more money— and this practice is also widespread in Brazil—both Bagunço and Wagner José and his Bando write and produce their songs. For Bagunço, that means playing a mix of "salsa, tango, several Brazilian rhythms like maracatu, frevo, forró and samba" (Moreaux 2015: n.pag.), while Wagner José e seu Bando announces during the show they will only play their own songs, allowing people "to turn their backs on them and leaving if they were expecting to hear famous hits" (Wagner José 2017: n.pag.).

Songwriting or covers, as well as the different perceptions of talent or professionalization, permeate the conversations with buskers. As a historically marginalized and criminalized activity, street performance questions our understanding of talent and worthiness. Precisely, because it takes place in the public space, in a way within reach for almost all aspiring artists, the differentiation that musicians make between "professionals," "amateurs," and "beggars" emerges. For most buskers, it is crucial to be recognized as a professional, talented musician— unlike people subject to an unhoused or itinerant condition who sometimes play an instrument and sing in exchange for money. All the musicians interviewed also play in concert halls, bars, restaurants, parties and formal events, and many of the contracts they sign come from the visibility they have in public spaces or through special programs such as the "*Étoiles*." Some buskers interviewed here are full-time musicians, but a significant number have other jobs to pay the bills, and music is an important financial and emotional complement in their lives.

This professionalization of street music is directly linked to the strict regulation of the activity in cities, as it allows the legitimation of the activity, as well as the acceptance of the population, the public authorities and the institutions involved—even though there are still several artists who defy rules and law enforcement, playing irregularly around the city. At the same time, regulatory frameworks targeting buskers aim to end their persecution and frame them as a slightly more formal activity, at least from a legal and administrative point of view. However, these frameworks still keep buskers as informal workers from a labor and economic point of view. Another outcome of poorly designed regulatory efforts is the further marginalization of those artists who fail to meet the expected criteria for auditions or are unable to cover the expenses related to regularizing their work (such as membership fees). The result might be a spectrum of professionalization and legality even among similar groups of buskers.

Within the discussion of professionalization, the ability to make a living in the streets also was a topic of conversation. In general, many musicians I interviewed said it was possible to make a living by busking and passing the hat—even though it was not a lot of money, many said they were able to pay their bills at the end of the month. All musicians claimed to also play in music venues and other places, such as concert halls, bars, restaurants, parties and commissioned shows, among others. As mentioned before, many of the musicians have other jobs to support themselves, most connected to teaching, crafts and music itself, in addition to the money that comes from passing their hats.

As much as the professionalization and legitimation of street and subway musicians has advanced and guaranteed some rights, while giving visibility and certain recognition to artists, other issues, such as informality, remain pending. Often, musicians perform without any type of labor protection; when they get sick, they have to stop playing in public spaces, thus not earning money for a while. The same happens while they are composing or creating their presentations. The weight of carrying their instruments around the city, up and down staircases, the investment in equipment and tools, the exposure to adverse weather conditions, and the challenging circumstances of being in public spaces performing for hours end up having a significant impact on their health and plans to keep passing the hat. Jamie (2015), for example, mentioned having back issues that pushed her to change her instrument for busking and the way she organizes her life around it—also shedding light on the lack of accessibility in the metro stations, plus the fact she is aging "makes life harder."

Even the donations received in the artists' hats can be surprising. Several artists reported receiving not just money, but all kinds of things: food (even half-eaten), objects and notes. Philippe Mius d'Entremont (2015) shared on his Instagram profile what he called "unusual gifts," which were all the unusual donations he received while busking. Money contributions will vary according to the location, time of the day, number of passengers, the public's attention and the musician's repertoire. Caroline, for example, tried not to repeat the same places at similar times while she was an "*Étoile*," so people would hopefully not get used to her presence and ignore her:

> There is a phenomenon of habit, especially with the "*Étoiles*". People are used to always seeing the same musicians, in the same spots at peak hours because, so I think it can get worse in such places. [...] There are places that work better too but there are places where it is very changeable, we cannot know in advance.
>
> (Caroline 2015: n.pag.)

Being in the streets performing is also shaped by nationalities and languages. The multiplicity of languages spoken by street and subway musicians is quite interesting, reflecting the varied origins and trajectories of these individuals. Just as in Brazil, many street artists are immigrants, in Montreal this is also remarkable. Coming from other provinces or countries and speaking several languages, they contribute to the cultural diversity of street music in cities. They see the streets as an opportunity to perform and earn a living. Musicians speak different languages, way beyond just English and French. Jocelyne, for example, is one of the musicians on the subway and is a native English speaker. She has lived in Montreal for many years and also speaks French but says that the language does not influence her songs, which are instrumental. Juliana and Jesse are two young brothers who were born in Brazil, grew up in Mexico and now live in Montreal, but prefer to communicate and compose their music in English. Lucas, who is part of the Street Meat group, is an anglophone from Toronto, has lived in Montreal for many years and prefers to give the interview in English; he and his group spent a few months in Brazil, playing in the streets, thanks to the invitation of a festival (Reb Bull Sounderground)—and they even learned a little Portuguese. Despite singing most songs in English, they try to include French songs in their repertoire. Musician Jamie has an interesting background: she is English-speaking but prefers to do the interview in French. She also speaks Portuguese because she plays and sings bossa nova, having learned to repeat the words of songs without knowing Portuguese initially; however, she has been taking language classes and has even traveled to Brazil recently. Lucia, who is Colombian, has Spanish as her mother tongue but prefers to communicate in French. FX Liagre is French but has lived in Quebec for many years and chooses to give the interview in English. Michel is from France but has been living in Brazil for many years, being fluent in Portuguese too. Buskers cover songs in languages that are appealing to their public, sometimes without being fluent in them. These are fascinating connections that showcase the plurality of experiences that street musicians bring to our cities and highlight the need for regulation that is inclusive and aware that buskers have various national origins or legal statuses.

Given the nature of the work they do, not all musicians are comfortable with being registered on camera by the public, just as not all of them make a point of publicizing their work on the internet, especially through social networks. The main social network they used during my fieldwork research was Facebook—where the musicians had group pages to share tips and build community—and some also had Instagram accounts. Mailing lists and personal websites were also common and used to promote their work. The use of the internet and social media is quite instrumental for most artists.

In addition to social media, artists also keep articles from newspapers and other media when they appear in them. When Jocelyne was interviewed, she showed a bound folder of newspaper articles, with an interview she had done a few years ago. Grégoire also mentioned that he appeared in several newspaper articles in the 1980s, as he and other musicians fought over the legality of music on the subway. For him, it is very important to have media outlets (and consequently, the public) as an ally: "[t]he media is a very powerful tool if you can use it properly. So, if you can get the media behind you—radio, television, newspapers—that can actually sway public opinion and force the politicians to recognize you" (Dunlevy 2015: n.pag.).

Beyond public opinion, buskers value the public recognition of what they do. When questioned about the importance of busking and how it can change urban life, artists mentioned preserving memory through songs and practices, helping people to go through their routines, making the public smile, bringing accessible culture to the streets and brightening the days. For Caroline (2015), buskers "help people to remember, to not forget, because we play music that is part of certain eras, certain moments of life, certain traditions, certain countries; we are memory too." Lucas (2015: n.pag.) says that busking is "an important creative outlet for a lot of people, [...] and every society needs outlets for art." The idea of interrupting everyday life in a positive way, bringing joy and smiles to people's lives—both for the audience and for the musicians themselves—is quite present in the artists' perspectives. Clément Courtois (2016: n.pag.) affirms that if he "hadn't seen people, [he] might never have done it himself. [...] Artists are there to shed some light on some people's life." For Grégoire Dunlevy (2015: n.pag.), buskers "have an effect on the public," and he often hears people saying, "Oh, it's so wonderful to hear your music because when I'm on my way to work, or coming home from work, I feel so stressed out, and your music helps make my whole day better." Jocelyne (2015: n.pag.) believes that connecting to people is one of the most important aspects of busking since "each small connection that is made amongst people is always to the good." If it's a smile or a chat or somebody donating or saying: "You made my day" or "I like this" or "Oh, you are here again" or whatever. And it's not about me, I just mean the music." Lucas shares a candid view of both sides of the same coin, stating that street performance:

> definitely changes the city for better or for worse. It changes some people's day. I'm sure some people walk by sometimes and they are like: "Oh God. It's the last thing I want to deal with." But then some people will walk by, and they give you a smile and they seem to be cheered up a bit. It definitely has an effect. I wouldn't say it has a huge effect [...]—sometimes a kid walks by and sees an accordion for the first time in his life and then goes home and says: "Mama, I want an accordion." It definitely can affect people's lives, but at the end of the day you are on a street corner or in the metro making something vibrate and hoping for a couple of bucks. So, I tend to not think it's too gigantic.
>
> (Lucas 2015: n.pag.)

Despite the difficulty in measuring how much impact busking has on city life—from numbers or qualitative data—the perceptions shared by street performers help us to understand how they see themselves, their practice, the public and the work conditions imposed on them. Be it navigating uncertainty and informality, disobeying rules, or fighting for their rights to occupy public spaces, buskers shape urban music governance.

NOTES

1. Available at: https://www.metrorio.com.br/PalcoCarioca. Accessed June 27, 2024.
2. See the afterword of this book for a brief account of the consequences of the pandemic for buskers.
3. In 2022, STM was using an online platform to book all presentations, getting rid of the paper. According to the website, musicians should keep proof of the reservation with them in case an employee of the metro system requests it. See: https://www.stm.info/fr/a-propos/espace-affaires/partenariats-et-autorisations/les-musiciens-dans-le-metro. Accessed June 27, 2024.
4. See: https://mmetrm.com/. Accessed June 27, 2024.
5. Playing with Bagunço for two years, Michel explains that the band's name came from the "masculinization" of the word "mess" in Portuguese, made by his colleague, also French, who before performing said, "Let's make a big mess today." They thought the term was funny and that it would make a great band name; found a guitarist and a bassist and four months later the band Bagunço appeared.

Afterword:
Pandemic, Digitalization and Evidence-Based Policy

As the management of the COVID-19 pandemic imposed a combination of sanitary measures to contain the severe health crisis, from social distancing to lockdowns and curfews, city life became quieter. People with access to proper housing, isolated in private, personal and domestic spaces saw their streets devoid of non-essential activities. Several sectors suffered greatly from the closedown, most notably those connected to the performance arts and night-time economies (Straw and Reia 2021).

The pandemic shed light on existing social justice and exacerbated inequalities. Given the often precarious, informal nature of busking and its work conditions, artists suddenly lost sources of income as they could no longer perform and, most likely, there would be no audience to perform for. Various musicians also worked in closed venues, taught classes and produced music; these activities were highly impacted, draining those sources of income as well.

In Montreal, the STM suspended busking for 19 months, starting in April 2020 (Brousseau-Pouliot 2020) and allowing the performances again in November 2021 (Radio-Canada 2021). In January 2021, Mathieu Paquette interviewed buskers for *La Presse*, collecting stories about hardships and the need to change professions. Many relied on financial aid from the government to cover their living expenses while the world waited to understand the tragedy unfolding in front of us. During the previous summer, the city government let musicians play at specific spots downtown, but that was a temporary solution. With the end of the financial relief provided by the Canadian Government, buskers had to seek other ways to make a living. At the recently rebranded MusiMétroMontréal, "the demand for hiring musicians dropped visibly during the pandemic. Its director of communications, Claire Dellar, confirmed that more than 75% of artists' contracts were cancelled in 2020" (Paquette 2021).

Even after reopening the lyre spots for musicians in late November 2021 (Caillou 2021), the STM had to shut them down again in January 2022 as the number of infections and deaths soared through the province of Québec (Nopieyie

2022). It was at this time that STM also implemented the new online platform for buskers to schedule their times of performance (Meunier 2021). Two months later, the public transit agency had a plan to gradually reopen the spots to the artists. By late 2022, STM affirmed that over 600 musicians were registered on their new online platform and ready to perform in the metro (Dussault 2022).

When I interviewed the artists during fieldwork, they had mixed feelings about social media and being recorded in public; some expressed enthusiasm for platforms that allowed them to promote their work, some used it in a pragmatic way, and others barely had any online presence. This shifted during the pandemic, when online everything became the norm, from telehealth to virtual concerts and drag shows (CBC Radio 2021). Recent studies (Elkins and Fry 2022; Elkins and Fry 2022a) analyzed the dataset about donations to buskers on the virtual platform The Busking Project during the pandemic, discovering "a lift both in street performers signing up to the platform and in individuals' donations to street performers after the announcement (of the pandemic)." Elkins and Fry (2022) also affirm that digital payment might become a requirement for busking in the future. Indeed, on October 13, The Busking Project announced its cashless payment feature that uses a QR code to facilitate tipping and donations to artists in the streets (Nick 2021).

In Rio, buskers had to look for sources of income online, too. In July 2020, a piece by Julia Amoêdo and Robert Oliveira (2020) investigated how street performers in the city of Rio de Janeiro were surviving those harsh months of social distancing and strict health measures. At the time, Law Aldir Blanc was waiting for the presidential approval to come into force and provide financial relief to informal workers in the cultural sector in Brazil in the amount of BRL 600 per month, in three installments. While waiting for the much-needed help, buskers were performing online—often without any tips or donations—or offering virtual courses on cultural production. However, as the authors rightfully affirm, "Migrating from street corners to digital media comes at a price. It requires technical and operational adaptations. It requires, among other things, a good internet connection and devices that most street performers don't usually have access to" (Amoêdo and Oliveira 2020). Some of the buskers interviewed were hoping to use the money allocated by Law Aldir Blanc to purchase equipment and have an online presence. The law was soon approved, and payments started in September 2020.

A country facing brutal historical inequalities, Brazil went through the pandemic led by an authoritarian, far-right president who was a science denier. Support for informal workers was scarce and non-continuous; over time, the country was submerged into an economic crisis, with a large percentage of the population not having access to basic services and facing food insecurity—in 2022, the UN added Brazil back to the Hunger Map. In this heart-wrenching context, informal workers and people without financial security are still dealing with the aftermath of the (ongoing) pandemic. The digital divide also became an international topic of conversation about the exacerbation of inequalities by the pandemic. It is no different in Brazil, where many regions still do not have proper access to broadband, and the access is shaped by race, gender, rural–urban residence and geographic location (Cetic.br and NIC.br 2022).

Amidst all these challenging circumstances, we still cannot properly understand the affected population of informal cultural workers. The almost complete absence of data, despite the data collected by communities via platforms led by buskers or the organizations regulating them, leaves us without much evidence to design proper public policies. Their stories are not yet being told by official numbers, and the needs and experiences probably overlap with other contemporary informal workers who make the streets their main platform and workplace. I hope this book sums up the efforts to tell these stories and incentivize a responsible approach to understanding and fostering busking in a society that is increasingly relying on digital infrastructure, data and official numbers.

References

Ahmed, S. (2017). *Living a feminist life*. Durham, NC: Duke University Press.

Alves, J. C. M., & Noe, M. (2006). *O palco e a rua: a trajetória do teatro do Grupo Galpão*. Belo Horizonte: Editora PUCMinas.

Amoêdo, J., & Oliveira, R. (2020, June 11). Os malabarismos dos artistas sem rua para sobreviver à pandemia. *Veja Rio*. https://vejario.abril.com.br/puc-rio/artistas-de-rua-trabalho-pandemia/. Accessed December 10, 2022.

Amster, R. (2004). *Street people and the contested realms of public space*. New York: LFB Scholarly Publishing.

Areias. (2015, May 23). Música embala viagens de metrô, apesar de proibição. *O Dia*. https://odia.ig.com.br/noticia/rio-de-janeiro/2015-05-23/musica-embala-viagens-de-metro-apesar-de-proibicao.html. Accessed July 14, 2023.

Arnauld, D. (1889). *Fakirs et jongleurs*. Paris: Librairie de Firmin-Didot.

Attali, J. (2009). *Noise: The political economy of music*. Minneapolis, MN: University of Minnesota Press.

Baibarac-Duignan, C., & Lange, M. (2021). Controversing the datafied smart city: Conceptualising a "making-controversial" approach to civic engagement. *Big Data & Society*, 8(2), 1–15. https://doi.org/10.1177/20539517211025557

Bain, A. L., & Podmore, J. A. (2023). Queer(ing) urban planning and municipal governance. *Urban Planning*, 8(2), 145–49. https://doi.org/10.17645/up.v8i2.7012

Barbot, J. (1899). *Jongleurs et troubadours du Gévaudan*. Mende: Imprimerie Typographique Auguste Privat.

Barroso, F. M., & Fernandes, C. S. (2018). Os limites da rua: uma discussãosobre regulação, tensão e dissidênciadas atividades culturais nos espaçospúblicos do Rio de Janeiro. *Políticas Culturais Em Revista*, 11(1), 100–21. https://doi.org/10.9771/pcr.v11i1.26706

Bass, M. (1864). *Street music in the metropolis: Correspondence and observations on the existing law, and proposed amendments*. London: John Murray, Albemarle Street.

Bedford, W. (2015). "Montreal might eat its young, but Montreal won't break us down": The co-production of place, space and independent music in Mile End, 1995–2015. *Journal of Urban Cultural Studies*, 2(3), 335–45. https://doi.org/10.1386/jucs.2.3.335_1

Bélanger, A. (2005). Montréal vernaculaire/Montréal spectaculaire: dialectique de l'imaginaire urbain. Sociologie et sociétés. *Sociologie et sociétés*, 37(1), 13–34. https://doi.org/10.7202/012274ar [Translations in text.]

Bélanger, K. (2016). In-person interview with Jess Reia, Montreal, February 25. Translation added.

Bélanger, A., Reia, J., & Straw, W. (2020). *Portrait diagnostic de la vie nocturne à Montréal*. Service du développement économique, Ville de Montréal.

Belart, V. (2021). *Cidade Pirata: Carnaval de rua, coletivos culturais e o Centro do Rio de Janeiro, 2010–2020*. Belo Horizonte: Editora Letramento.

Belina, B. (2011). Ending public space as we know it. *Social Justice*, Special issue: Policing the Crisis—Policing in Crisis, 8(1/2), (123–124), 13–27. http://www.jstor.org/stable/23345522. Accessed July 20, 2023.

Benjamin, R. (2019). *Race after technology: Abolitionist tools for the New Jim Code*. Oxford: Polity.

Bennett, E., & McKay, G. (2019). *From brass bands to buskers: Street music in the UK*. Norwich: Arts and Humanities Research Council/ University of East Anglia.

Bessa, P. (2013, January 17). Músicos driblam proibição e quebram monotonia dos vagões de metrô no Rio. *Mobiliza Brasil*. https://www.mobilize.org.br/noticias/3389/musicos-driblam-proibicao-e-quebram-a-monotonia-dos-vagoes-de-metro-no-rio.html. Accessed July 3, 2023.

Bieletto-Bueno, N. (2019). Construcción de la marginalidad de los músicos callejeros. El Caso de Rey oh beyve. *Cultura y Representaciones Sociales*, 309–47. https://doi.org/10.28965/2019-27-10.

Bieletto-Bueno, N. (2020). *Ciudades vibrantes: Sonido y experiencia aural urbana en América Latina*. Santiago de Chile: Ediciones de la Universidad Mayor.

Bild, E., Steele, D., & Guastavino, C. (2022). Festivals and events as everyday life in Montreal's entertainment district. *Sustainability*, 14(8), 4559. https://dx.doi.org/10.3390/su14084559.

Blum, A. (2007). *The imaginative structure of the city*. Montreal and Kingston: McGill-Queen's University Press.

Boetzkes, A. (2010). The ephemeral stage at Lionel Groulx Station. In A. Boutros & W. Straw (Eds.), *Circulation and the city: Essays on urban culture* (pp. 138–54). Montreal: McGill-Queen's University Press.

Bonneau, C. (2016, May 24). In-person interview with Jess Reia, Montreal. Translation added.

Bouk, D. (2022). *Democracy's data: The hidden stories in the U.S. census and how to read them*. New York: MCD.

Bouk, D., Ackermann, K., & boyd, d. (2022). A primer on powerful numbers: Selected readings in the social study of public data and official numbers. *Data & Society*. https://datasociety.net/library/a-primer-on-powerful-numbers-selected-readings-in-the-social-study-of-public-data-and-official-numbers/. Accessed July 20, 2023.

Boulanger, A. (2002). *Les Arts de La Rue, Demain—enjeux et perspectives d'un "novel art de ville"*. Lyon: Mémoire, Université Lumière Lyon II.

Brandusescu, A., & Reia, J. (Eds.). (2022). *Artificial intelligence in the city: Building civic engagement and public trust*. Centre for Interdisciplinary Research on Montreal, McGill University. https://doi.org/10.18130/9kar-xn17

REFERENCES

Breyley, G. J. (2016). Between the cracks: Street music in Iran. *Journal of Musicological Research*, 35(2), 72–81. https://doi.org/10.1080/01411896.2016.1165051

Brousseau-Pouliot, V. (2020, April 7). La STM interdit la distribution des imprimés et les musiciens dans le métro. *La Presse*. https://www.lapresse.ca/actualites/covid-19/2020-04-07/la-stm-interdit-la-distribution-des-imprimes-et-les-musiciens-dans-le-metro. Accessed December 10, 2022.

Browne, S. (2015). *Dark matters: On the surveillance of blackness*. Durham, NC: Duke University Press.

Busk in London. (n.d.). *Buskers' Code*. https://www.foundinmusic.com/_files/ugd/63966d_c93c506e6f8b49b6967800658a1bca0a.pdf. Accessed June 27, 2024.

Bywater, M. (2007). Perfoming spaces: Street music and public territory. *Twentieth-Century Music*, 3(1), 97–120.

Cahen, A. (2011). *Compasso urbano: A vida de quem transforma asfalto em palco e necessidade em arte*. Holambra: Editora Setembro.

Caiafa, J. (2013). *Trilhos da cidade: viajar no metrô do Rio de Janeiro*. Rio de Janeiro: 7Letras.

Caillou, A. (2021, November 30). Les musiciens de retour dans le métro. *Le Devoir*. https://www.ledevoir.com/culture/musique/650730/montreal-les-musiciens-de-retour-dans-le-metro. Accessed December 10, 2022.

Campbell, P. J. (1981). *Passing the hat: Street performers in America*. New York: Decolarte Press.

Cardoso, B. V. (2013). Megaeventos esportivos e modernização tecnológica: Planos e discursos sobre o legado em segurança pública. *Horizontes Antropológicos*, 19(40), 119–48.

Caroline (2015, November 27). In-person interview with Jess Reia, Montreal. Translation added.

Carr, S., Francis, M., Rivlin, L. G., & Stone, A. M. (1993). *Public space*. Cambridge: Cambridge University Press.

Carreira, A. (2007). *Teatro de Rua: Brasil e Argentina nos anos 1980, uma paixão no asfalto*. São Paulo: Editora Hucitec.

Caswell, M., Punzalan, R., & Sangwand, T.-K. (2017). Critical archival studies: An introduction. *Journal of Critical Library and Information Studies*, 1(2), 1–8. https://doi.org/10.24242/jclis.v1i2.50

Catterall, P., & Azzouz, A. (2021). *Queering public space: Exploring the relationship between queer communities and public spaces*. London: Arup. https://westminsterresearch.westminster.ac.uk/item/v4wzq/queering-public-space-exploring-the-relationship-between-queer-communities-and-public-spaces. Accessed July 10, 2023.

CBC Radio (2021, February 7). Heels optional: How performers are reimagining drag for a Zoom world. *CBC Radio*. https://www.cbc.ca/radio/checkup/has-zoom-made-your-life-better-or-worse-1.5901547/heels-optional-how-performers-are-reimagining-drag-for-a-zoom-world-1.5904398. Accessed May 29, 2023.

Celis, A. M., & González, E. H. (Eds.). (2020). *Noche urbana y economía nocturna en América del Norte*. México: Universidad Nacional Autónoma de México.

Cetic.br; NIC.br. (2022). Executive Summary—Survey on the Use of Information and Communication Technologies in Brazilian Households, ICT Households 2021. https://cetic.br/pt/publicacao/executive-summary-survey-on-the-use-of-information-and-communication-technologies-in-brazilian-households-ict-households-2021/. Accessed June 14, 2023.

Chatterjee, P. (2022). "We Have Always Been Here": Busking, urban space and economy of Montreal (Ph.D. thesis). Montreal: Concordia University.

Chaudoir, P. (1997). L'interpellation dans les Arts de la rue. *Espaces et sociétés, 90*, 167–94. https://doi.org/10.3917/esp.g1997.90.0167

Chaudoir, P. (2003). Le théâtre de rue: Nouvelles formes d'expression en espace public. *La pierre d'Angle, "en scène", 34*. https://sites.univ-lyon2.fr/iul/pierreangle.pdf. Accessed July 20, 2023. [Translations in text.]

Chaudoir, P. (2004). Arts de la rue et espace urbain. *L'Observatoire*, Special issue: Ce que les artistes font à la ville, 26.

Coding Rights. (n.d.). *Mega-events: A surveillance legacy*. https://legadovigilante.codingrights.org/indexEN.html. Accessed July 20, 2023.

Costantini, S. (2015). De la scène musicale aux réseaux musicalisés: Les inscriptions territoriales et socio-économiques de l'activité artistique. *Réseaux, 192*, 143–67.

Courtois, C. (2016, February). Telephone interview with Jess Reia, Montreal. [Translations in text.]

Cruciani, F., & Falletti, C. (1999). *Teatro de Rua*. São Paulo: Editora Hucitec.

Cruz, C. (2014, October 13). Projeto de música no metrô gera polêmica entre artistas. *Extra*. http://extra.globo.com/noticias/rio/projeto-de-musica-no-metro-gera-polemica-entre-artistas-14227796.html. Accessed June 20, 2023. [Translations in text.]

Cura, T. F. (2019). Manas de Batalha: Feminismo(s) em rodas de ritmo e poesia (PhD thesis). Rio de Janeiro: Universidade Federal do Rio de Janeiro.

Dagenais, M. (2002). Inscrire le pouvoir municipal dan l'espace urbain: la formation du réseau des parcs à Montréal et Toronto, 1880–1940. *The Canadian Geographer / Le Géographe Canadien, 46*(4), 347–64.

Daphy, E. (1997). La gloire et la rue: Les chanteurs ambulants et l'édition musicale dans l'entre-deux-guerres. *Musiciens des rues de Paris, Catalogue de l'exposition au Musée des arts et traditions populaires, sous la direction de Florence Gétreau*, 95–99. [Translations in text.]

Dapporto, E. (2000). Des pratiques economiques informelles des arts de la rue: Ressources et limites dans une perspective de développement. Appel d'offre—Formes contemporaines de l'economie informelle: activités, échanges et réseaux de relations.

Daston, L. (2022). *Rules: A short history of what we live by*. Princeton: Princeton University Press.

Davis, S. (2020). *The uncounted: Politics of data in global health*. Cambridge: Cambridge University Press.

Delorme, P. (Ed.). (2009). *Montréal aujourd'hui et demain: Politique, urbanisme, tourisme*. Montreal: Éditions Liber.

REFERENCES

Dias, H. (2014, May 19). Boletim Informativo Fórum De Arte Pública. *Teatro de Rua e a Cidade*. https://teatroderuaeacidade.blogspot.com/2014/06/boletim-informativo-forum-de-arte_1.html. Accessed July 20, 2023.

Dickinson, G., & Aiello, G. (2016). Being through there matters: Materiality, bodies, and movement in urban communication research. *International Journal of Communication*, *10*, 1294–308.

Digital Freedom Fund. (2020). *Digital rights are human rights*. https://digitalfreedomfund.org/digital-rights-are-human-rights/. Accessed May 25, 2023.

Do Rio, J. (2010), *A Alma Encantadora das Ruas: the Enchanting Soul of the Streets* (M. Carlyon, Trans.). Rio de Janeiro: Editora Cidade Viva.

Duarte, A., Octavio, C., & Lim, L. (2016, December 21). Na gestão de Crivella, um ex-guerrilheiro e seu captor. *O Globo*. https://oglobo.globo.com/rio/na-gestao-de-crivella-um-ex-guerrilheiro-seu-captor-20677614. Accessed June 15, 2013.

Dufresne, S. (1984). Fête et societé: le carnival d'hiver à Montréal (1883–1889). In *Bleau et al. (org.) Montréal: activités, habitants, quartiers* (pp. 139–188). Montreal: Société historique de Montréal and Fides.

Duneier, M. (1999). *Sidewalks*. New York: Farrar, Straus and Giroux.

Dunlevy, G. (2015, November 26). Telephone interview with Jess Reia, Montreal.

Dussault. (2022, December 26). Ce n'est pas le Klondike, mais on s'ajuste. *La Presse*. https://www.lapresse.ca/actualites/grand-montreal/2022-12-26/musiciens-dans-le-metro/ce-n-est-pas-le-klondike-mais-on-s-ajuste.php. Accessed July 20, 2023.

Ellickson, R. C. (1996). Controlling chronic misconduct in city spaces: Of panhandlers, skid rows, and public-space zoning. *The Yale Law Journal*, *105*, 1165–248.

Elkins, M., & Fry, T. R. L. (2022a). Street performers and donations in an online environment in the wake of COVID-19. *City, Culture and Society*, *28*, 1–8. https://doi.org/10.1016/j.ccs.2021.100438

Elkins, M., & Fry, T. R. L. (2022b). Beyond the realm of cash: Street performers and payments in the online world. *Journal of Cultural Economics*, *46*, 231–48. https://doi.org/10.1007/s10824-021-09421-8

Escudier, G. (1875). *Saltimbanques: Leur vie, leurs moeurs*. Paris: Librairie Nouvelle.

Essinger, S. (2015, June 6). Bandas ocupam praças, calçadas e trens do Rio, passam o chapéu e multiplicam vendas de discos. *O Globo*. https://oglobo.globo.com/cultura/musica/bandas-ocu-pam-pracas-calcadas-trens-do-rio-passam-chapeu-multiplicam-vendas-de-discos-16362472. Accessed July 20, 2023. [Translation in text.]

Faulhaber, L., & Azevedo, L. (2015). *Remoções no Rio de Janeiro*. Rio de Janeiro: Mórula Editorial.

Fernandes, C. S., & Herschmann, M. (2014). Ativismo musical nas ruas do Rio de Janeiro. In *Conference Proceedings XXIII Encontro da Compós, 2014*, Belém, pp. 1–15.

Ferrara, L. (2008). Cidade: meio, mídia e mediação. *MATRIZes*, *2*, 39–52.

Fischler, R., & Wolfe, J. M. (2012). Planning for sustainable development in Montreal: A qualified success. In Igor Vojnovic (Ed.), *Urban sustainability* (pp. 531–60). Ann Arbor, MI: Michigan State University Press.

Floch, Y. (Ed.). (2007). *Diversity of street arts in Europe—international colloquium in Tàrrega (Spain)*. Paris: Circostrada Network / HorsLesMurs.

Francisco, P. A. P. (2014). Fronteiras estratégicas: o contrabando de cigarros paraguaios no Brasil (Master's thesis). Rio de Janeiro: Federal University of Rio de Janeiro.

Frehse, F. (2016). Da desigualdade social nos espaços públicos centrais brasileiros. *Sociologia & Antropologia, 6*(1), 129–58.

Freitas, R. F., Lins, F., & Santos, M. H. C. (Eds.). (2016). *Megaeventos, comunicação e cidade*. Curitiba: Editora CRV.

Froment-Meurice, M., & Fleury, A. (2016). Orchestrer la présence des musiciens dans le metro parisien. *Géographie et cultures, 98*, 113–34. https://doi.org/10.4000/gc.4516

Foucault, M. (1997). *Vigiar e punir: História da violências nas prisões*. Petrópolis: Vozes.

Fournel, M. V. (1863). *Les spetacles populares et les artistes des rues*. Paris: E. Dentu Éditeur.

FX Liagre. (2015, December 4). In-person interview with Jess Reia, Montreal.

Fyfe, N. R. (1998). *Images of the street: Planning, identity and control in public space*. New York: Routledge.

Gaffney, C. (2010). Mega-events and socio-spatial dynamics in Rio de Janeiro, 1919–2016. *Journal of Latin American Geography, 9*(1), 7–29. http://www.jstor.org/stable/25765282. Accessed July 20, 2023.

Gandarilla Salgado, J. G., García-Bravo, M. H., & Benzi, D. (2021). Two decades of Aníbal Quijano's coloniality of power, eurocentrism and Latin America. *Contexto Internacional, 43*(1), 199–222. https://doi.org/10.1590/S0102-8529.2019430100009

Garnier, J. (2015). La constitution d'un cadre routinier au prisme du « pouvoir » : l'exemple du métro à Montréal. *Espace populations sociétés, 1–2*. https://doi.org/10.4000/eps.5970

Garnier, J. (2016). Métro, quartiers, ville: Étude de quelques dimensions de l'expérience quotidienne de Montréal au travers du concept foucaldien de pouvoir (Ph.D. thesis). Montreal: Université du Québec à Montréal.

Genest, S. (2001). Musiciens de rue et règlements municipaux à Montréal: La condemnation civile de la marginalité (1857–2001). *Les Cahiers de la Societé Québécoise de Recherche en Musique, 5*(1–2), 31–44. [Translations in text.]

Germain, A. (2013). The Montréal school: Urban social mix in a reflexive city. *Anthropologica, 55*(1), 29–39.

Germain, A. (2016). The fragmented of cosmopolitan metropolis? A neighbourhood story of immigration in Montreal. *British Journal of Canadian Studies, 29*(1), 1–23.

Gétreau, F. (1998). Street musicians of Paris: Evolution of an image. *Music in Art, 23*(1/2), 63–78. [Translations in text.]

Gétreau, F. (2001). La rue parisienne comme espace musical réglementé (XVIIe-Xxe siècles). *Les cahiers de la société québéquoise de recherche en musique* (pp. 11–24).

Gétreau, F. (2003). Le son dans l'exposition "Musiciens des rues de Paris". *Cahiers de musiques traditionnelles, 16*, 123–36. [Translations in text.]

REFERENCES

Gétreau, F., & Daphy, E. (1999). Musiciens des rues, musiques dans la rue. *Ethnologie Française*, *29*(1), 8–10. http://www.jstor.org/stable/40990095

Girard, G. (2016, June 13). In-person interview with Jess Reia, Montreal. Translation added.

Gomes, C. H. S. (1998). Formação e atuação de músicos das ruas de Porto Alegre: Um estudo a partir dos relatos de vida (Master's thesis). Porto Alegre: Federal University of Rio Grande do Sul.

Gomes, P. (2015, December 12). Músicos são agredidos por seguranças do metro. *O Dia*. https://odia.ig.com.br/noticia/rio-de-janeiro/2015-12-21/musicos-sao-agredidos-por-segurancas-do-metro.html. Accessed July 20, 2023.

Gordilho Souza, A. M. (2018). Urbanismo neoliberal, gestão corporativa e o direito à cidade: impactos e tensões recentes nas cidades brasileiras. *Cadernos Metrópole, 20*(41), 245–65. https://doi.org/10.1590/2236-9996.2018-4112

Graham, S. (2011). *Cities under siege: The new military urbanism*. London and New York: Verso.

Graham, S. (2016). *Vertical: The city from satellites to bunkers*. London and New York: Verso.

Gray, S. F., & Lin A. (2021). The design politics of space, race, and resistance in the United States. *Ardeth, 9*, 29–49. https://journals.openedition.org/ardeth/2613. Accessed July 20, 2023.

Green, R. A. (2016). *The Hurdy-Gurdy in eighteenth-century france* (2nd ed.). Bloomington, IN: Indiana University Press.

Grinberg, F. (2018, September 26). Apesar de lei que permite apresentações artísticas, músico é expulso de composição do metrô. *Extra*. https://extra.globo.com/noticias/rio/apesar-de-lei-que-permite-apresentacoes-artisticas-musico-expulso-de-composicao-do-metro-23104966.html. Accessed July 20, 2023.

Guyan, K. (2022). *Queer data: Using gender, sex and sexuality data for action*. London and New York: Bloomsbury.

Gwiazdzinski, L., Maggioli, M., & Straw, W. (Eds.). (2020). *Night studies: Regards Croisés Sur Les Nouveaux Visages de La Nuit*. Grenoble: Editions Elya.

Gwiazdzinski, L., & Straw, W. (Eds.). (2015). Habiter (la nuit)/Inhabiting (the night), Special Issue. *Intermédialités, 26*.

G1 Rio (2015, October 6). 06/10/2015 21h56—Atualizado em 06/10/2015 21h56 Projeto de lei que autoriza músicos em trens e metrô é discutido na Alerj. *G1 Rio*. https://g1.globo.com/rio-de-janeiro/noticia/2015/10/projeto-de-lei-que-autoriza-musicos-em-trens-e-metro-e-discutido-na-alerj.html. Accessed July 20, 2023.

G1 SC (2017, February 18). Malabaristas dos semáforos de Criciúma agora terão de usar crachás. *G1 SC*. https://g1.globo.com/sc/santa-catarina/noticia/2017/02/malabaristas-dos-semaforos-de-criciuma-agora-terao-de-usar-crachas.html. Accessed July 20, 2023.

Haddad, A. (2014, June 25). In-person interview with Jess Reia and Micael Herschmann, Rio de Janeiro. [Translation in text].

Haedicke, S. C. (2013). *Contemporary street arts in Europe: Aesthetics and politics*. Hampshire: Palgrave Macmillan.

Harel, S., Lussier, L., & Thibert, J. (2015). *Le Quartier des spectacles et le chantier de l'imaginaire montréalais*. Laval: Presses de l'Université de Laval.

Harrison-Pepper, S. (1990). *Drawing a circle in the square: Street performing in New York's Washington Square Park*. Jackson, MI: University Press of Mississippi.

Harvey, D. (2014). *Cidades rebeldes: do direito à cidade à revolução urbana*. São Paulo: Martins Fontes.

Herbert, S. (1997). *Policing the space: Territoriality and the Los Angeles police department*. Minneapolis, MN and London: University of Minnesota Press.

Herschmann, M., & Fernandes, C. S. (2011). Territorialidades sônicas e re-significação de espaços do Rio de Janeiro. *Logos: Comunicação e Universidade, 18*(2), 6–17.

Herschmann, M., & Fernandes, C. S. (2014). *Música nas ruas do Rio de Janeiro*. São Paulo: Intercom.

Hirsch, L. E. (2010). "Playing for change": Peace, universality, and the street performer. *American Music, 28*(3), 346–67.

Jacobs, J. (2011). *The death and life of great American cities. 50th Anniversary edition*. New York: Modern Library.

Jamie. (2015, November 30). In-person interview with Jess Reia, Montreal. Translation added.

Jassem, H., & Drucker, S. J. (Eds.). (2018). *Urban communication regulation: Communication freedoms and limits*. Lausanne: Peter Lang Publishing.

Jennings, A. et al. (2014). *Brasil em jogo: O que fica da Copa e das Olimpíadas?* São Paulo: Boitempo/Carta Maior.

Jocelyne. (2015, November 27). In-person interview with Jess Reia, Montreal.

Juliana, & Jesse. (2015, December 11). In-person interview with Jess Reia, Montreal.

Karaganis, J. (2011). Media piracy in emerging economies. Social Science Research Council. https://www.ssrc.org/publications/media-piracy-in-emerging-economies/. Accessed July 20, 2023.

Karniewicz, V. (2004). *Les arts de la rue: Étude comparative de la situation en France et en Italie*. Paris: Université Paris 8.

Keller, L. (2009). *Triumph of order: Democracy & public space in New York and London*. New York: Columbia University Press.

Klopfer, N. (2009). "Terra Incognita" in the heart of the city? Montreal and Mount Royal around 1900. *Architecture—Technology—Culture, 3*, 137.

Kwon, J., & Nguyen, M. T. (2023). Four decades of research on racial equity and justice in urban planning. *Journal of Planning Education and Research, 0*(0), 1–13. https://doi.org/10.1177/0739456X231156827

Kyba, C. C., Pritchard, S. B., Ekirch, A.R., Eldridge, A., Jechow, A., Preiser, C., Kunz, D., Henckel, D., Hölker, F., Barentine, J., Berge, J., Meier, J., Gwiazdzinski, L., Spitschan, M., Milan, M., Bach, S., Schroer, S., & Straw, W. (2020). Night matters—why the interdisciplinary field of "Night Studies" is needed. *Journal of Multidisciplinary Scientific Studies, 3*(1), 1–6. https://doi.org/10.3390/j3010001

REFERENCES

Laignier, P., & Fortes, R. (2010). A criminalização da pobreza sob o signo do "Choque de Ordem": uma análise dos primeiros cem dias do governo Eduardo Paes a partir das capas de O Globo. *Comunicação & Sociedade, 31*(53), 53–78. https://doi.org/10.15603/2175-7755/cs.v31n53p53-78

Lamoureux, L. (2016, June 23). In-person interview with Jess Reia, Montreal. Translation added.

Lefebvre, H. (1991). *The production of space*. Oxford: Blackwell Publishers.

Lefebvre, H. (2001). *O direito à cidade*. São Paulo: Centauro.

Leonelli, S. (2019, October 15). Data—from objects to assets, *Nature*, 317–20. https://www.nature.com/articles/d41586-019-03062-w. Accessed July 20, 2023.

Lichote, L. (2015, December 16). Batalha underground: veto a músicos no metrô e trens do Rio gera debate. *O Globo*. https://oglobo.globo.com/cultura/musica/batalha-underground-veto-musicos-nometro-trens-do-rio-gera-debate-18302179. Accessed July 20, 2023. [Translations in text.]

Lins, M. N. (2016, August 9). A cada dia, novos artistas de rua lotam o Boulevard Olímpico. *Extra*. http://extra.globo.com/noticias/rio/a-cada-dia-novos-artistas-de-rua-lotam-boulevard-olimpico-19889343.html. Accessed July 20, 2023.

Loison, L., & Fischler, R. (2016). The quartier des spectacles, Montreal. In R. Thomas (Ed.), *Planning Canada: A case study approach* (pp. 348–60). Oxford: Oxford University Press.

Loukaitou-Sideris, A., & Ehrenfeucht, R. (2009). *Sidewalks: Conflict and negotiation over public space*. Cambridge: MIT Press.

Low, S. (2000). *On the plaza: The politics of public space and culture*. Austin: University of Texas Press.

Low, S., & Smith, N. (2006). *The politics of public space*. New York: Routledge.

Lucas. (2015). In-person interview with Jess Reia, Montreal, December 15.

MACCNO. (n.d.). Guide to street performance. https://maccno.com/guide-to-street-performance-1. Accessed July 20, 2023.

Madanipour, A. (2003). *Public and private spaces of the city*. New York: Routledge.

Maricato, E. (1985). Direito à terra ou direito à cidade? *Revista de Cultura Vozes, 89*(6), 405–10.

Maricato, E. (2015). Para entender a crise urbana. *CaderNAU—Cadernos do Núcleo de Análises Urbanas, 8*(1), 11–22.

Maricato, E., Harvey, D., Davis, M., Braga, R., Žižek, S., Iasi, M. L., Brito, F., Vainer, C., de Lima, V. A., Maior, J. L. S., Peschanski, J. A., Secco, L., Sakamoto, L., & MPL São Paulo. (2013). *Cidades rebeldes: Passe Livre e as manifestações que tomaram as ruas do Brasil*. São Paulo: Boitempo/Carta Maior.

Martin, A., & Lynch, M. (2009). Counting things and counting people: The practices and politics of counting. *Social Problems, 56*(2), 243–66. https://doi.org/10.1525/sp.2009.56.2.243. Accessed July 20, 2023.

Mascarenhas, G., Bienenstein, G., & Sánchez, F. (Eds.) (2011). *O jogo continua: Megaeventos esportivos e cidades*. Rio de Janeiro: EdUERJ.

Meunier, H. (2021, November 29). Les musiciens et musiciennes du métro enfin de retour sur scène. *Urbania*. https://urbania.ca/article/les-musiciens-et-musiciennes-du-metro-enfin-de-retour-sur-scene. Accessed December 10, 2022.

Ministère de la Culture et de la Communication. (2000). L'economie des arts de la rue. *Développement culturel*, 127.

Mirza, M. (2014, April 23). Busking in London is dying, leaving a hole in the heart of the city. *The Guardian*. https://www.theguardian.com/local-government-network/2014/apr/23/support-londons-buskers. Accessed July 20, 2023.

Mitchell, D. (2003). *The right to the city: Social justice and the fight for public space*. New York: Guilford Press.

Mius d'Entremont, P. (2015). Telephone interview with Jess Reia, Montreal, December 14. [Translations in text.]

Moreaux, M. (2013). Expressões e impressões do corpo no espaço urbano: Estudo das práticas de artes de rua como rupturas dos ritmos do cotidiano da cidade (Master's thesis). Rio de Janeiro: Pontifícia Universidade Católica do Rio de Janeiro.

Moreaux, M. (2015). In-person interview with Jess Reia, Rio de Janeiro, April 15. Translation added.

Moroni, S., & Chiodelli, F. (2014). Municipal regulations and the use of public space: Local ordinances in Italy. *City, Territory and Architecture*, 1(11), 2–7.

Morozov, E., & Bria, F. (2018). *Rethink the smart city: Democratizing urban technology*. Rosa Luxemburg Stiftung. https://rosalux.nyc/wp-content/uploads/2021/02/RLS-NYC_smart_cities_EN.pdf. Accessed July 11, 2023.

Moyencourt, A. (2015). La grande histoire des musiciens-chanteurs de rues en France. https://ritournelles-et-manivelles.org/wp-content/uploads/2021/07/Grande-histoire-par-periodes-2015.pdf. Accessed July 20, 2023.

MusiMétroMontréal. (n.d.). Previously at: http://musimetromontreal.org/. Currently available at: https://web.archive.org/web/20170817102435/http://musimetromontreal.org/. Accessed June 27, 2023. [Translations in text.]

Myrdahl, T. M. (2023). At the intersection of equity and innovation: Trans inclusion in the city of Vancouver. *Urban Planning*, 8(2), 223–34. https://doi.org/10.17645/up.v8i2.6461

Navarrete-Hernandez, P., Vetro, A., & Concha, P. (2021). Building safer public spaces: Exploring gender difference in the perception of safety in public space through urban design interventions. *Landscape and Urban Planning*, 214. https://doi.org/10.1016/j.landurbplan.2021.104180

Nick. (2021, October 13). Everything you need to know about cashless payments on Busk.Co. *The Busking Project*. https://busk.co/blog/busking-tips-tricks/everything-you-need-to-know-about-cashless-payments-on-busk-co/. Accessed December 10, 2022.

Nopieyie, Y. (2022, January 7). STM: suspension des musiciens dans le métro. *Métro*. https://journalmetro.com/societe/mobilite/2754907/stm-suspension-musiciens-metro/. Accessed December 10, 2022.

REFERENCES

Nowak, R., & Bennett, A. (2014). Analysing everyday sound enviroments: The space, time and corporality of musical listening. *Cultural Sociology, 8*(4), 1–17.

O Globo. (2013). Verba municipal: Secretário responde a Amir Haddad. *O Globo*. December 26. https://oglobo.globo.com/cultura/verba-municipal-secretario-responde-amir-haddad-11152581. Accessed July 20, 2023.

Oliveira, N. G. (2015). *O poder dos jogos e os jogos de poder: interesses em campo na produção da cidade para o espetáculo esportivo*. Rio de Janeiro: Editora UFRJ.

Osborne, R., & Laing, D. (Eds.). (2021). *The use and abuse of statistics in the music industries*. Bristol: Intellect.

Paquette, M. (2021, January 3). Musique Où sont passés les musiciens du métro? *La Presse*. https://www.lapresse.ca/arts/musique/2021-01-03/ou-sont-passes-les-musiciens-du-metro.php. Accessed July 20, 2023.

Parreira, C. G. (2014). Imigração, Trabalho e Artistas de Rua Latino-Americanos na Cidade do Rio de Janeiro (Master's thesis). Rio de Janeiro: Universidade Federal do Rio de Janeiro.

Pennafort, R. (2014, August 6). Metrô do Rio terá músicos internacionais. Estadão. http://brasil.estadao.com.br/noticias/rio-de-janeiro,metro-do-rio-tera-musicos-internacionais,1539904. Accessed July 20, 2023.

Pereira de Sá, S. (2011). Ando meio (des)ligado? Mobilidade e mediação sonora no espaço urbano. *E-compós, 14*(2), 1–18. https://doi.org/10.30962/ec.666

Pereira de Sá, S. (2019). Cartographies of Brazilian popular and "peripheral" music on YouTube: The case of Passinho dance-off. In M. Iqani & F. Resende (Eds.), *Media and the Global South: Narrative, territorialities, cross-cultural currents* (pp. 200–20). New York: Routledge.

Petty, J. (2016). The London spikes controversy: Homelessness, urban securitisation and the question of "hostile architecture". *International Journal for Crime, Justice and Social Democracy, 5*(1), 67–81. https://search.informit.org/doi/10.3316/informit.241315629391400

Phillips, P. (1998). Maintenance activity: Creating a climate for change and peggy digs: Private acts in public life. In Nina Felshin (Ed.), *But is it art? The spirit of art as activism* (pp. 283–308). Seattle: Bay Press.

Picker, J. M. (2003). *Victorian soundscapes*. New York: Oxford Univesity Press.

Pinheiro-Machado, R., & Scalco, L. (2020). From hope to hate: The rise of conservative subjectivity in Brazil. *HAU: Journal of Ethnographic Theory, 10*(1), 21–31.

Porter, T. (2020). *Trust in numbers: The pursuit of objectivity in science and public life*. Princeton: Princeton University Press.

Prato, P. (1984). Music in the streets: The example of Washington Square Park in New York City. *Popular Music, 4*, 151–63.

Quijano, A. (2000). Coloniality of power, eurocentrism, and Latin America. *Nepantla: Views from South, 1*(3), 533–80.

Rabossi, F. (2011). Negociações, associações e monopólios: a política da rua em Ciudad del Este (Paraguai). *Etnográfica (Online), 15*(1), 83–107. https://doi.org/10.4000/etnografica.814

Radio-Canada. (2021, November 29). La musique de retour dans le métro de Montréal. *Radio-Canada*. https://ici.radio-canada.ca/nouvelle/1843641/musique-musiciens-retour-metro-montreal. Accessed December 10, 2023.

Rafael, P. (2017). Telephone interview with Jess Reia, Rio de Janeiro, March 27. [Translation in text.]

Reia, J. (2017). "We are not a protest": Street performance and/as public art in the city of Rio de Janeiro. In Laura Iannelli & Pierluigi Musarò (Eds.), *Performative citizenship: Public art, urban design and political participation* (pp. 133–50). Fano: Mimesis International.

Reia, J. (2018). A lei no bolso: Música de rua e a luta pelos espaços públicos no Rio de Janeiro. In C. Fernandes & M. Herschman (Eds.), *Cidades Musicais* (pp. 79–107). Porto Alegre, Brazil: Editora Sulina.

Reia, J. (2019). Can we play here? The regulation of street music, noise, and public spaces after dark. In G. Botta & G. Stahl (Eds.), *Nocturnes: Popular music and the night* (pp. 163–76). London: Palgrave Macmillan.

Reia, J. (2021). Coabitando a noite urbana: entre políticas públicas e (in)visibilidades de gênero. In C. Fernandes, J. Reia, & P. Gomes, *Arte, comunicação e (trans)política: A potência dos femininos nas cidades* (pp. 37–62). Belo Horizonte: Fafich/Selo PPGCOM/UFMG.

Reia, J. (2022a). Data for the night: Digital rights, trust, and responsible engagement with data in 24-hour cities. *Data for policy*, 1–4. https://doi.org/10.5281/zenodo.7272288

Reia, J. (2022b, October 3). Request for information (RFI) on the federal evidence agenda on LGBTQI+ Equity (87 FR 52083) submitted to the White House Office of Science and Technology Policy (OSTP). https://datascience.virginia.edu/news/responding-federal-evidence-agenda-lgbtqi-equity-request-information. Accessed March 31, 2023.

Reia, J., & Belli, L. (Eds.). (2021). *Smart cities no Brasil: regulação, tecnologia e direitos*. Belo Horizonte: Letramento.

Reia, J., & Cruz, L. (2021). Seeing through the smart city narrative: data governance, power relations, and regulatory challenges in Brazil. In B. Haggart, N. Tusikov, & J. A. Scholte, *Contested power and authority in internet governance: Return of the state?* (pp. 219–42). Abingdon and New York: Routledge.

Reia, J., & Cruz, L. (2023). Smart cities in Brazil: Connections between corporate power, rights, and civic engagement. *Cad. Metropole*, 25(57), May–Aug 2023, 467–90. https://doi.org/10.1590/2236-9996.2023-5705

Reia, J., & Rouleau, J. (2021). *Rapport sur les consultations citoyennes pour la nouvelle politique de la vie nocturne à Montréal*. MTL 24/24 et Service du développement économique, Ville de Montréal.

Reimont. (2017). In-person interview with Jess Reia, Rio de Janeiro, May 2. [Translation in text.]

Riguetti, R. (2015). In-person interview with Jess Reia and Micael Herschmann, Rio de Janeiro. [Translation in text.]

Rio De Janeiro (2012, June 5). Law N° 5.429. Rio de Janeiro, RJ. http://mail.camara.rj.gov.br/APL/Legislativos/contlei.nsf/50ad008247b8f030032579ea0073d588/67120c-4c1ae54a6603257a14006d2b1d?OpenDocument. Accessed July 20, 2023.

REFERENCES

RIO DE JANEIRO (State) (2018, September 25). Law N° 8.120, Rio de Janeiro, RJ. https://gov-rj.jusbrasil.com.br/legislacao/630601652/lei-8120-18-rio-de-janeiro-rj. Accessed July 20, 2023.

Rodrigues, C. (2016, August 6). Artistas de rua faturam até R$ 2 mil por dia no Boulevard Olímpico. *G1*. https://g1.globo.com/rio-de-janeiro/olimpiadas/rio2016/noticia/2016/08/artis-tas-de-ruas-faturam-ate-r-2-mil-por-dia-no-boulevard-olimpico.html. Accessed July 20, 2023. [Translation in text.]

Rolnik, R. (2019). *Urban warfare: housing under the empire of finance*. London and New York: Verso Books.

Rolnik, R. (2022). *São Paulo: o planejamento da desigualdade*. São Paulo: Editora Fósforo.

Rousselin, E. (2013). Les arts de la rue : mutations esthétiques et nouveaux enjeux politiques de territoire(s) (Master's thesis). Bordeaux: Université Michel de Montaigne. [Translations in text.]

Saar, S. S. (2012). Teatro de Rua: Arte democrática e subversiva (Bachelor's thesis). São Paulo: University of Sao Paulo.

Sadowski, J., & Bendor, R. (2019). Selling smartness: Corporate narratives and the smart city as a sociotechnical imaginary. *Science, Technology, & Human Values*, 44(3), 540–63. https://doi.org/10.1177/0162243918806061

Sadre-Orafai, S. (2020). Typologies, typifications, and types. *Annual Review of Anthropology*, 49, 193–208. https://doi.org/10.1146/annurev-anthro-102218-011235

Salmen, D. (2010, November 22). Prefeitura expulsa artistas de rua da av. Paulista; para jurista, proibição é "ato nazista". *UOL*. https://noticias.uol.com.br/cotidiano/ultimas-noticias/2010/11/22/prefeitura-expulsa-artistas-de-rua-da-av-paulista-para-jurista-proibic-ao-e-ato-nazista.htm. Accessed July 20, 2023.

Sánchez, F. (2010). *A reinvenção das cidades para um mercado mundial*. Chapecó: Argos.

Santos, F. A. (2014). Palhaços: Poética e política nas ruas, direito à cultura e à cidade (Master's thesis). Rio de Janeiro: FGV.

Santos, M. (1998). As exclusões da globalização: pobres e negros. *Thoth*, 4, 147–60, January/April. https://ipeafro.org.br/acervo-digital/leituras/obras-de-abdias/revista-thoth/. Accessed July 20, 2023.

Santos, M. (2021). *The nature of space*. Durham, NC: Duke University Press.

Santos, R. E. (Ed.). (2012). *Questões urbanas e racismo*. Petrópolis: DP et Alii; Brasília, DF : ABPN.

São Paulo. (2013). Law N° 15.776, 29 May 2013, São Paulo, SP. http://legislacao.prefeitura.sp.gov.br/leis/lei-15776-de-29-de-maio-de-2013/. Accessed July 20, 2023.

São Paulo. (2014). Decree N° 55.140, 23 May 2014, São Paulo, SP. http://legislacao.prefeitura.sp.gov.br/leis/decreto-55140-de-23-de-maio-de-2014/. Accessed July 20, 2023.

Savedra, P. (2015, August 22). Procon autua metrô por agressão a músico em estação. *O Dia*. https://odia.ig.com.br/noticia/rio-de-janeiro/2015-08-22/procon-autua-metro-por-agressao-a-musico-em-estacao.html. Accessed July 19, 2023.

Scheuerman, M. K., Pape, M., & Hanna, A. (2021). Auto-essentialization: Gender in automated facial analysis as extended colonial project. *Big Data & Society*, 8(2), 1–15. https://doi.org/10.1177/20539517211053712

Schiavo, E. C., & Gelfuso, A. G. (2018). Urbanismo de mercado: Las ciudades latinoamericanas y el neoliberalismo realmente existente. *Cadernos Metropole*, 20(42), 423–42. https://doi.org/10.1590/2236-9996.2018-4206

Sennett, R. (2002). *The fall of the public man*. London: Penguin Books.

Simon, S. (2006). *Translating Montreal: Episodes in the life of a divided city*. Montreal: McGill-Queen's University Press.

Simpson, P. (2015). The History of Street Performance: "Music by handle" and the Silencing of Street Musicians in the Metropolis. Lecture delivered at the 2015 City of London Festival, London, July 9, 2015. https://www.gresham.ac.uk/watch-now/history-street-performance. Accessed July 20, 2023.

Sloan, J. (Ed.). (2007). *Urban enigmas: Montreal, Toronto, and the problem of comparing cities*. Montreal & Kingston: McGill-Queen's University Press.

Smith, M. (1996). Traditions, stereotypes, and tactics: A history of musical buskers in Toronto. *Canadian Journal for Traditional Music*, 24(6), 6–22.

Spielmann, F. (2000). Mission d'étude sur les questions de formation, qualification, transmission dans le domaine des Arts de la Rue. Report submitted to the Ministry of Culture and Communication.

SRZD. (2013). Amir Haddad desmente secretario de cultura carioca. December 26. https://www.srzd.com/brasil/amir-haddad-desmente-secretario-de-cultura-carioca/. Accessed July 20, 2023. [Translation in text.]

Stafford, L., Vanik, L., & Bates, L. K. (2022). Disability Justice and Urban Planning. *Planning Theory & Practice*, 23(1), 101–42. https://doi.org/10.1080/14649357.2022.2035545

Stahl, G. (2001). Tracing out an Anglo-Bohemia: Musicmaking and myth in Montréal. *Public 22/23: Cities/Scenes*, 99–121.

Stevens, C. S. (2016). Irasshai! Sonic Practice as Commercial Enterprise in Urban Japan. *Journal of Musicological Research*, 35(2), 82–99. https://doi.org/10.1080/01411896.2016.1155924

Stoffel, L. (2011). Quand l'Art descend dans la rue.... *Analyse de l'IHOES, 91*.

Stoler, A. L. (2009). *Along the archival grain: Epistemic anxieties and colonial common sense*. Princeton, NJ: Princeton University Press.

Straw, W. (2002). Scenes and sensibilities. *In Public, 22/23*, 245–57.

Straw, W. (2010). Montreal and the captive city. *Quebec Studies*, 33(48, Fall 2009-Winter 2010), 13–24.

Straw, W. (2014a). "A City of Sin No More": Sanitizing Montreal in print culture, 1964–71. *International Journal of Canadian Studies*, 48, 137–52.

Straw, W. (2014b). Some things a scene might be. *Cultural Studies*, 29(3), 476–85.

REFERENCES

Straw, W. (2015). Above and below ground. In Paula Guerra & Tânia Moreira (Eds.), *Keep it simple, make it fast: An approach to underground music scenes* (vol. 1,pp. 403–10). Porto: Universidade do Porto—Faculdade de Letras.

Straw, W. (2017). Night. In Christie Pearson & Will Straw (Eds.), *Scapegoat: Architecture, landscape, political economy*. Toronto: Scapegoat Publications.

Straw, W. (2020). Night studies: Thinking across disciplines. *Voices of Mexico, 111*, 7–10.

Straw, W. (2021). Montreal Bohemia and the Mile End Apartment party scene. In Norbert Bachleitner & Juliane Werner (Eds.), *Popular Music and the Poetics of Self in Fiction* (pp. 121–37). Leiden: Brill Publishers.

Straw, W. (2022) Montreal, funkytown: Two decades of disco history. In Flora Pitrolo & Marko Zubak (Eds.), *Global dance cultures in the 1970s and 1980s: Disco heterotopias* (pp. 29–49). New York: Springer.

Straw, W., & Reia, J. (2021). Nightlife in a pandemic. In Denis, J. L., Régis, C., & D. Daniel Weinstock, *Pandemic societies* (pp. 9–29). Montreal: McGill-Queen's University Press.

Talbot, D. (2007). *Regulating the night: Race, culture and exclusion in the making of the night-time economy*. Hampshire: Ashgate Publishing.

Ta na Rua et al. (2014). *Arte Pública: Uma Política em Construção*. Report. [Translation in text.]

Tanenbaum, S. J. (1995). *Underground harmonies: Music and politics in the subways of New York*. Ithaca: Cornell University Press.

Tardáguila, Cristina, & Reis, Luiz Felipe Milen (2013, December 20). Secretaria de Cultura repassa R$ 13 milhões para cinco convênios. *O Globo*. https://oglobo.globo.com/cultura/ secretaria-de-cultura-repassa-13-milhoes-para-cinco-convenios-11116823. Accessed July 20, 2023. [Translation in text.]

Targino, R. (2015). Coletivo AME em defesa da arte no metrô do Rio. *Biblioo*. November 19. https://biblioo.info/coletivo-ame-em-defesa-da-arte-no-metro-do-rio/. Accessed July 20, 2023.

Tavolari, B. (2016). Direito à cidade: uma trajetória conceitual. *Novos estudos CEBRAP, 35*(1), 93–109.

Taylor, L. (2017). What is data justice? The case for connecting digital rights and freedoms globally. *Big Data & Society, 4*(2), 1–14. https://doi.org/10.1177/2053951717736335

Telles, N., & Carneiro, A. (Eds.). (2005). *Teatro de Rua: olhares e perspectivas*. Rio de Janeiro: E-papers.

Telles, V., & Hirata, D. (2007). Cidade e práticas urbanas: Nas fronteiras incertas entre o ilegal, o informal e o ilícito. *Revista de Estudos Avançados da USP, 21*(61), 171–91.

Telles, V., & Hirata, D. (2010). Ilegalismos e jogos de poder em São Paulo. *Tempo Social: Revista de sociologia da USP, 22*(2), 39–59.

Telles, V. S. (2009). Ilegalismos urbanos e a cidade. *Novos Estudos, 84*, 152–73.

Telles, V. S. (2010). Nas dobras do legal e do ilegal: Ilegalismos e jogos de poder nas tramas da cidade. *DILEMAS: Revista de Estudos de Conflito e Controle Social, 2*(5–6), 97–126.

The Economist. (2009, November 12). Brazil takes off. *The Economist*. https://www.economist. com/leaders/2009/11/12/brazil-takes-off. Accessed July 20, 2023.

Todd, A. L. (2010, November 19). Choque de ordem contra a cultura popular. *Brasil de Fato*. https://www.brasildefato.com.br/node/4585/. Accessed July 20, 2023.

Todd, J. (2016, July 6). The 40-year hangover: How the 1976 Olympics nearly broke Montreal. *The Guardian*. https://www.theguardian.com/cities/2016/jul/06/40-year-hangover-1976-olympic-games-broke-montreal-canada. Accessed July 20, 2023.

Trotta, F. (2020a). *Annoying music in everyday life*. New York and London: Bloomsbury Academic.

Trotta, F. (2020b). Música y violencia en el transporte colectivo: Conflictos cotidianos en las metrópolis de América Latina. In N. Bieletto-Bueno. *Ciudades vibrantes: Sonido y experiencia aural urbana en América Latina*. Santiago de Chile: Ediciones de la Universidad Mayor.

Tsing, A. L. (2015). *The mushroom at the end of the world: On the possibility of life in capitalist ruins*. Princeton: Princeton University Press.

Turle, L., & Trindade, J. (2008). *Tá na Rua: teatro sem arquitetura, dramaturgia sem literatura e ator sem papel*. Rio de Janeiro: Instituto Tá na Rua.

Turle, L., & Trindade, J. (2016). *Teatro(s) de Rua no Brasil: a luta pelo espaço público*. São Paulo: Editora Perspectiva.

UN Women. (n.d.). Creating safe and empowering public spaces with women and girls. *UN Women*. https://www.unwomen.org/en/what-we-do/ending-violence-against-women/creating-safe-public-spaces. Accessed July 20, 2023.

Valverde, M. (2009). Laws of the street. *City & Society*, 21(2), 163–81.

Vaz, Ana L. (2010, November 19). Choque de ordem contra a cultura popular. *Brasil de Fato*. https://www.brasildefato.com.br/node/4585/. Accessed July 20, 2023.

Ventura, Larissa (2022, May 27). Palco Carioca retoma as atividades com programação especial no MetrôRio. *Diário do Rio*. https://diariodorio.com/palco-carioca-retoma-as-atividades-com-programacao-especial-no-metrorio/. Accessed July 20, 2023.

VibeLab. (2023). *Creative footprint Montréal—report 2023*. Montreal: VibeLab. https://montrealresults.creative-footprint.org/#summary. Accessed July 20, 2023.

Ville de Montréal. (2012). CA-24-006, o. 38 – Ordonnance relative au code d'éthique des musiciens et amuseurs publics exerçant leurs activités sur le domaine public. https://ville.montreal.qc.ca/pls/portal/docs/1/89356866.PDF. Accessed October 7, 2024.

Ville de Montréal. (2015). *À Nous Montréal: pour vivre pleinement la ville*, 2(1), summer.

Ville de Montréal. (2018). CA-24-006 – Règlement relatif aux musiciens et aux amuseurs publics exerçant leurs exerçant leurs activités sur le domaine public (Codification administrative 2018-04-14). https://montreal.ca/reglements-municipaux/recherche/60d7caa6f-d653112af59b639. Accessed October 7, 2024.

Ville de Montréal. (2023). *2017–2022 Cultural Development Policy*.

Xavier de Oliveira, L. (2019). "Vem pro Baile, Vem pra Rua": Territorialidades, Estilos e Identidades em um Baile Black no Rio de Janeiro. *Logos: Comunicação e Universidade*, 26(1), 9–24. https://doi.org/10.12957/logos.2019.36183. Accessed July 20, 2023.

REFERENCES

Wagner, J. (2017). In-person interview with Jess Reia, Rio de Janeiro, April 7. Translation added.

Wallon, E. (2001). Les arts de la rue. *Encyclopaedia Universalis*, 223–225.

Wees, N. (2017). Improvised performances: Urban ethnography and the creative tactics of Montreal's metro buskers. *Humanities*, Special Issue: Spatial Bricolage: Methodological Eclecticism and the Poetics of "Making Do", 6(3), 67, 1–17. http://dx.doi.org/10.3390/h6030067

Wheeler, B. B. (2003). The institutionalization of an American avant-garde: Performance art as democratic culture, 1970–2000. *Sociological Perspectives*, 46(4), 491–512.

Wong, K. K. T. L. (2016). An ethnomusicological understanding of the street performance of Cantonese Opera 街檔 (*Jie Dang*) in Hong Kong. *Journal of Musicological Research*, 35(2), 100–12. https://doi.org/10.1080/01411896.2016.1154408

Wylie, C. D. (2020). Who should do data ethics? *Patterns*, 1(1), 1–3. https://doi.org/10.1016/j.patter.2020.100015

Index

ill refers to an illustration; *map* to a map; *n* to a note; *t* to a table

A

Ackermann, Kevin 16
Amêndola, Coronel 109
Amoêdo, Julia 160
Andrew W. Mellon Foundation Architecture, Urbanism and the Humanities Program xiv
Arcade Fire (band) 69
Arnauld, Daniel *Fakirs et Jongleurs* 23
artificial intelligence (AI) 18
Association des Musiciens Indépendants du Métro de Montréal (AMIMM) 138
Astro Venga (band) 105–6
Attali, Jacques 26–27
audiences 26–27
Azmon, Ezra 76

B

Babbage, Charles 36, 39–40
Bagunço (band) 105, 151, 154, 158*n*
Baird, Stephen 51–52
Bass, Michael Thomas *Street Music in the Metropolis* 36–41
Beach Combers (band) 105
beggars 44, 78, 84, 141, 152
Bélanger, Anouk 65
Bélanger, Kim 136, 146–49, 150
Benjamin, Ruha *Race After Technology* 30
Benjamin, Walter xi
Bennett, Andy 34
Beraldo, Marcelo 130

Berri-UQÀM station, Montreal 143, 144*ill*, 145
Bieletto-Bueno, Natalia 28
Blum, Alan 7, 9
Boetzkes, Amanda 138, 140
Bolsonaro, Flavio 135
Bonneau, Christiane 68
Boston 51–52
Bouk, Dan 16
Bourque, Pierre 62
boyd, danah 16
Brasília, Brazil 94–95, 98
Brazil 160–1
    Aldir Blanc Law 160
    coup (2016) 98
    see also Copacabana; Corcovado; Rio de Janeiro
Brazilian Street Theatre Network 102
Britain 18, 40–43
    see also England; London
Browne, Thales 132
buskers *see* street performers
Bywater, Michael 33, 41, 50

C

Cabaret du Mile End, Montreal 69
Cabot, Gérald 136
Calatrava, Santiago 106
Camelos, Os (band) 105
Campbell, Patricia J. *Passing the Hat: Street Performers in America* 49–53

Canada see Montreal; Ottowa; Toronto
Carioca Festival of Public Art 114–23, 118*ill*, 121*ill*, 122*ill*
Carioca Public Art Forum 3
Carioca Stage (*Palco Carioca*) 133–35, 134*ill*
Casa del Popolo, Montreal 69
Ceciliano, Andre 131
Chatterjee, Piyasha 143
Chatterton, J. Balsir 38–39
Chaudoir, P. 46–47
Chiodelli, Francesco 31
Cinelândia, Rio de Janeiro 22, 104
Cirque du Soleil xii
Coleltivo Artistas Metrovários (AME) 132–33
colonialism, impact on urban areas 9
Copacabana, Rio de Janeiro 6
Corcovado, Rio de Janeiro 94
Costa, Ricardo 105
court musicians 27, 40
Courtois, Clement 140–41, 157
COVID-19 pandemic 80, 109–10, 135, 159–61
Crespin, Michel 48
Crivella, Marcelo 109, 121, 123*n*
Cruz, Cíntia 129–30

D

Dagenais, Michèle 63
Dantas, Valdir 106–7
Daphy, Eliane *La Gloire et la Rue* 44
Daston, Lorraine *Rules* 30
data collection 16–19, 120, 132–33
    for policy-making 17–18, 133
De Crauzat, Paul 26
Dellar, Claire 159
Delorme, Pierre 63
Denoix, Pierre 137
Dias, Herculano 113
Dickens, Charles 36
Diversity of Street Arts in Europe (colloquium) 47

Dominga Petrona (band) 105
Drapeau, Jean 66–67
Drucker, Susan D. 32
Dunlevy, Grégoire 136–38, 153, 157
DuoPlex (band) 135

E

Eclectic Django (band) 145*ill*
Economist, The 94, 98
Eliot, T.S. 41
England 36–43
    Industrial Revolution 38, 41
    see also London
Escudier, Gaston 25
    Saltimbanques, Les 26
Étoiles du Metro (Metro Stars) 1–2, 91, 136, 140–41, 143–47, 144*ill*, 145*ill*, 150–51
Étoiles do Metro En Concert (show) 146
Expo 1967, Montreal 64, 136

F

facial recognition systems 18, 96
Faubourg Saint-Laurent, Montreal 65–67
Ferrara, Lucrécia 32, 84
Festival Internationale des Arts du Cirque 64
Fischler, Raphaël and Jeanne M. Wolfe 61–62, 65
Flamengo, Leila do 108–9, 124*n*
Foucault, Michel 142
Fournel, Victor *Spectacles populaires et les artistes des rues* 23–25, 43
France 23–26, 43–49
    1970s 46–47
    Economie des Arts de la Rue, L' 48–49
    HorsLesMurs (arts centre) 48–49
    Lieux Publics (arts centre) 48, 56*n*
    Middle Ages 2, 23–27, 43
    Ministry of Culture programs 46, 48–49
    policy-making in 48–49
    see also Paris

INDEX

Francos de Montréal, Les (music festival) 64

Frehse, Flaya 33

FX Liagre (musician) 87–88, 91, 151, 153, 156

G

Garnier, Julien 142

Genest, Sylvie 36, 76–77

Genuncio, Yuri 132

Germain, Annick 61

Gétreau, Florence 43–46

    Le Son dans l'Exposition Musiciens des
      Rues de Paris 43

    Street Musicians of Paris: Evolution of
      an Image 45

Girard, Guylaine 81–84

Globo, O 105, 116–17, 132

Godspeed You! Black Emperor (band) 69

Gomes, Celso 110

Gomma, Bernard 106

Graham, Stephen *Vertical* 127

Guardian 42

H

Haddad, Amir 15, 18–19, 103–4, 106,
  110–14, 116–20, 123, 132

Haedicke, Susan 115

Harrison-Pepper, Sally 2, 36, 53–54, 75

    Drawing a Circle in the Square
      49–50, 59

Herculano, João 120

Hirsch, Lily E. 50

Hogarth, Willliam *The Enraged Musician*
  (engraving) 41

hurdy-gurdy 2

I

International Festival of Subway Musicians
  (2014) 130

Itinéraire, L' xii

itinerant musicians 27–28, 44–45

J

Jacobs, Jane xii

Jason, Ray 53

Jassem, Harvey and Susan D. Drucker *Urban*
    Communication Regulation 32

José, Wagner 31, 135, 151–54, 152*ill*

jugglers (*jongleurs*) 23–27, 43

K

Karniewicz, Virginie 47

Koch, Edward 54

Kubitscheck, Juscelino 94

L

Lachine Street Festival (FTRL) 69–73, 70*ill*

Lamoureux, Lucie 70–72

Latin America 28

Leitão, Sergio Sá 116–17

Lemon, Mark 37–38

Leonelli, Sabina 16

Lily (singerl) 45

Loison, Laurie and Raphaël Fischler 65

London 41–42

    Busk in London project 42

    Street Music Act 37, 41

    Victorian era 2, 36–40

Longeuil, Montreal 62

Loto-Québec (government agency) 70–72, 92*n*

Lucas (musician) 78–79, 151–52, 156–57

M

Ma Non Troppo (band) 105–6

May, Andrew xi

media piracy 17

Mello, Thiago 132

MetrôRio, Rio de Janeiro 128–35

    Music Station Project (*Estãçion de*
      Música) 129–30, 133

    policy-making by 129–30

Mile End district, Montreal 69

minstrels *see* street musicians

Mirza, Munira 42

Mius d'Entremont, Pierre 87, 89, 148, 151–52, 155

Montreal xii, 35, 59–92, 60*map*
 administrative division of 61–63
 Conseil des Arts de Montréal 68
 Cultural Development Policy Project (2017–2022) 68
 homeless people in xii, 150
 immigration in 60–61
 languages in 60–61, 156
 regulations in 35, 73, 77–86, 80*t*, 90–92
 reputation of 66–67
 sponsorship of events 70–72
 winter carnival 64
 see also Olympic Games

Montreal First People's Festival 64

Montreal International Jazz Festival 64

Montreal Metro xiv 34
 see also Étoiles du Metro; Société de Transport de Montréal

Montreal Metropolitan Community 62

Moreaux, Michel 110, 151, 153, 158*n*, 156

Moroni, Stefano and Francesco Chiodelli 31

Mount Royal mountain, Montreal 63

Mural Festival, Montreal 64

Museum of Tomorrow, Rio de Janeiro 106

Musgrave, John 75–76

Music and Culture Coalition of New Orleans (MACCNO) 52

musical instruments 242–45
 see also specific instruments

Musiciens du Métro et de la Rue de Montréal 149

Mutek Festival, Montreal 64, 146

N

New Orleans 52

New York 51, 53–55

night 34–35

noise
 complaints of 34–41, 73, 81, 128, 148
 policies to control 39–42

Nowak, Raphaël and Andy Bennett 34

Nuit Blanche Festival 64, 145

O

Off-Sina (band) 102, 108, 117

Oliveira, Carlos Adriano 132

Oliveira, Robert 160

Olympic Boulevard, Rio de Janeiro 106–7, 107*ill*

Olympic Games
 (1976, Montreal) xiv, 64, 70
 (2016, Rio) xiv, 94, 106–7, 116, 121, 123*n*

Olympic Stadium, Montreal 64

one-man orchestras 25

Ontario 76

organ grinders 39, 45, 75

Osheaga Music Festival, Montreal 64

Ottowa 75

P

Paes, Eduardo 96–97, 102–3, 116, 120, 123, 123*n*

Paquette, Mathieu 159

Paris 44–46
 Ordonnance de la Préfecture de Police de Paris du 2 Septembre 1822: 45

Paris qui Brille (magazine) 44

Pernambuco, Brazil 105

Phillips, Patricia 113

Piaf, Edith 45

Picker, John M. 38, 41

Piknic Életronik music festival 64

Place des Arts, Montreal 67

Place Jacques Cartier, Montreal 80, 85, 85*ill*

Plateau Mont Royal borough 73, 78, 78*ill*

POP International Music Festival Montreal 64

INDEX

Porter, Theodore *Trust in Numbers* 15
Portes de la Nuit, Les (film) 44
Porto Maravilha, Rio de Janeiro 123*n*
poverty, criminalization of 97
Praça Seca, Rio de Janeiro 119
Prato, Paolo 50
Presse, La 159
Procon, Rio de Janeiro 132
public art 111–15
    policy-making for 120–21
Public Art Forum 4, 112–14, 132
public space 32–34

Q

Quartier des Spectacles, Montreal 65–67, 70

R

Rao, Vyjayanthi and Robles-Anderson, Erica xii
Red Bull Sounderground festival 130, 151, 156
Regroupement des Musiciens du Métro de Montréal (MusiMétroMontréal) 136–37, 140–41, 159–60
Reimont, Luis Otoni 99–100, 102–4, 108–9, 115–16
Riguetti, Richard 102, 108
Rio, João do 6
    The Enchanted Soul of the Streets 1, 28–29, 94
Rio de Janeiro 94–123, 95*map*
    Atlântica Avenue 6
    mega-events in 96
    Municipal Department for Public Order 96–97
    policy-making in 96–100, 109–10
    regulation PL.958 (Law 8.120/2018) 131–32, 135
    regulations in 98–115, 100*t*, 108*t*
    'shock of order' regulations 97, 103, 104, 123

Street Performer's Law 3, 22, 35, 98–103, 107–8, 115–16
subway system
    see MetrôRio *see also* Olympic Games; World Cup; World Fair
Ritournelle et Marivelles (association) 43
Robles-Anderson, Erica xii
Rolnik, Raquel 8–9
Rousselin, Elodie 48
Roy, Louise 138

S

Sá, Estácio de 95
Sá, Simone de Pereira 34
Sadre-Orafai, Jenny 19
Saint Jean Baptiste celebration 145
San Francisco 51
Sanche, Guy 137
Santos, Milton *The Nature of Space* 94
São Paulo 104–5
Science, Technology, Engineering, Mathematics (STEM) disciplines 17
Shugar, Adam 147
Simon, Sherry *Translating Montreal* 59, 61
Simonin, Stéphane 47
Simpson, Paul 31, 40
Sloan, Johanne *Urban Enigmas* 6–7
Smith, Murray 74–76
Société de Transport de Montréal (STM) 136, 141, 143–49, 158*n*, 159–60
    lyre spot locations in subway 138, 139*ill*, 141, 146–48, 159
Sous les Toits de Paris (film) 44
Spielman, Franceline 48–49
Stoler, Ann Laura 23
Straw, Will 34–35
Street Meat (band) 78, 130, 151
street music and musicians xii, 27, 34–43, 76–77, 78*ill*, 85*ill*, 149

185

auditions for 82–84, 83t, 143, 145
categories of 19–21, 44
earnings of 26, 155
and gender 25, 149–50
see also women
languages and nationalities of
155–56
original music by 88–89, 154
police brutality to 2–3, 104–5, 127–29,
131–32
professional levels of 21, 154–55
safety of 90, 148–50
stereotypes of 40–41, 45
see also court musicians; itinerant
musicians
Street Music Map project 18
Street Music Conference (2019, Norwich)
42–43
Street Musicians from Paris (exhibition 1997-
78) 43–44
street performance and performers xi–xiv, 32,
46, 53
and ancestrality 22–24
colonial attitudes to 23
criminalisation of 18
earnings of 26, 106
fieldwork in 8
fines and penalties for 79
involvement in policy-making by 21–22,
99, 112, 115
licensing of 51–52, 54
numbers of 4, 15–19
permits for 77–86, 86t, 90, 92
regulation of 3–5, 31–33
and "right to the city" 3, 8, 10, 31,
97–98, 102–3, 105
romanticizing of xi–xii, 55
street theatre 110–12
street vendors xii, 6, 31, 52
surveillance 4, 18, 96, 141–42, 63–64

*Syndicat des Chanteurs et Musiciens March-
ands de Chansons* 44

T
Tá na Rua (theatre group) 15, 102–3, 106,
110–13, 116–23
Tanenbaum, Susie J. 27–28, 54–55
*Underground Harmonies: Music and
Politics in the Subways of New York*
50, 127
Toronto 75
traveling musicians *see* itinerant musicians
Tremblay, Gérald 62
Troubadour Day, Toronto 76
Tsing, Anna L. *Mushrooms at the End of the
World* 8

U
Union of Professional Musicians in the State
of Rio de Janeiro 129
United States 49–56
Prohibition era 59
see also Boston; New Orleans;
New York; San Francisco
University of Toronto. School of Cities xiv
urban areas, policing of 31–32
urbanism xii–xiii

V
Valverde, Mariana *Laws of the Street*
30–31
Ville-Marie, Montreal 63, 73, 74*map*, 78–79,
81–84
CA-24-006 regulation 79, 81, 84–85
Viola, Paulinho da 104

W
Washington Square Park, New York 54
weather, impact on street performers of
87–89

Wees, Nick 142
Wheeler, Britta B. 47
Wolfe, Jeanne M. 61–62
women performers 25, 149–50
Workers' Party, Brazil 99–100

World Cup (2014, Rio de Janeiro) 94, 116
World Fair (1922, Rio de Janeiro) 96

Z

Zukin, Sharon xii

www.ingramcontent.com/pod-product-compliance
Lightning Source LLC
LaVergne TN
LVHW060352040425
807275LV00002B/2